FAMILY FIRST

FAMILY FIRST

FAMILY FIRST

*Tracing Relationships
in the Past*

Ruth A. Symes

PEN & SWORD
HISTORY

First published in Great Britain in 2015 by
PEN AND SWORD HISTORY
an imprint of
Pen and Sword Books Ltd
47 Church Street
Barnsley
South Yorkshire S70 2AS

ISBN 978 1 47383 388 3

Printed and bound in England
by CPI Group (UK) Ltd, Croydon, CR0 4YY

Typeset in Times New Roman by
CHIC GRAPHICS

Pen & Sword Books Ltd incorporates the imprints of Pen & Sword
Archaeology, Atlas, Aviation, Battleground, Discovery,
Family History, History, Maritime, Military, Naval, Politics, Railways,
Select, Social History, Transport, True Crime, Claymore Press,
Frontline Books, Leo Cooper, Praetorian Press, Remember When,
Seaforth Publishing and Wharncliffe.

For a complete list of Pen and Sword titles please contact
Pen and Sword Books Limited
47 Church Street, Barnsley, South Yorkshire, S70 2AS, England
E-mail: enquiries@pen-and-sword.co.uk
Website: www.pen-and-sword.co.uk

Contents

Dedication

To my mother, Olive Symes,
who has always put her family first.

ACKNOWLEDGEMENTS

For general encouragement and recent interest in my writing thanks to Andrew Chapman, Mairead Mahon, Naomi Symes, Helen Tovey, Philip Watts and Sarah Williams. Thanks to the staff of Manchester City Archives; and Emma Marigliano of the Portico Library, Manchester, for specific information relating to that city. For information on club records, thanks to Stuart Halsall and Jim Spence of the Manchester Geological Society, Nick Bryam, Dartford Working's Men's Club; Mary Sharp, Assistant Secretary, Administration and Membership, The Carlton Club; and Colin R. Merton, Hon. Librarian, The Savile Club. Thanks also to Pat Morant for the story and images relating to Ellen Clementina Higley.

Finally, thanks to Zainul and Ruby Sachak for their unfailing love and support.

INTRODUCTION

A Sense of Family
1800–1950

For our ancestors, family came first. Whether rich or poor, from the North or the South of Britain, Protestant or Catholic, indigenous or immigrant, the relationships between spouses, parents, children, siblings, aunts, uncles, cousins and the older generation were the chief structural ties of everyday life in the period 1800–1950.

Between the censuses of 1831 and 1901, the population of England and Wales rose rapidly from around 15 million to 32.5 million. Those millions of individuals were significantly grouped into small clusters – the families and extended families of our ancestors. A particular forebear might fascinate us because of the exceptional life he led, the aspects of individual personality and character that made him stand out from the crowd, but crucial to his identity will have been the fact that he was a relational being – at one time or another, a son, a grandson, a brother, a husband, a son-in-law, a father, a cousin, an uncle or a grandfather. In large families with many branches living close by, your nineteenth- or early twentieth-century ancestor might have exercised all these roles and interdependencies simultaneously – in a life very different from the highly individuated existences of today.

It is the task of establishing the genealogical ties between people that keeps all family historians busy, but such ties were, of course, never just lines on a diagram. The bonds between family were biological, legal, moral and emotional, in various combinations, and as we come to learn more about them through our research, they almost vibrate off the page with emotion – the passion, sorrow, animosity and even tedium that characterised those relationships in real life. As we all know, the branches and twigs of our family trees were often supportive and nurturing, sprouting forth new foliage in every generation, but they could also be desiccated and rotten, cracking and splitting or producing nothing worth harvesting.

Genealogical records, of course, everywhere back up the strength and subtlety of these ties of blood and marriage. Wills are one written source where the intricate and endlessly fascinating matter of relationships are made most apparent, not least in the bizarre wordings of the bequests left to different relations. Witness, for example, the will of Elizabeth Brew of Lezayre on the Isle of Man in 1808 who bequeathed to her daughter Jane Brew, 'the sum of one hundred and fifty pounds British, a feather bed, bedding, the cow and the desk above the parlour . . . to [her] son Thomas, the feather bed with the blue and white check [and] the desk in the factory, and . . . to [her] daughter Elizabeth, one of the feather beds in the room above the kitchen.' (see: http://brew.clients.ch/willslezayre.htm). Were Jane, Thomas and Elizabeth to inherit beds of different quality (not to mention other assets) because of their respective ages, their marital status or the good deeds that they had done for their mother? We shall never know, but the will points us fascinatingly towards the shadows of the family connections and the possible tensions and rivalries between the three siblings.

And the same is true, to one degree or another, of many genealogical records. The most personal (including cards, letters and diaries) might spell out these relationships painfully clearly. Other official records ask us to read the hidden qualities of the relationships between the lines: Bastardy Examinations, for example, in which unmarried mothers are coerced into naming the fathers of their children; letters of application for widows' pensions in which the good reputation of the woman in question is paraded in front of the authorities in a bid to secure her entitlement to funds; or court records in which brothers or neighbours denounce each other for supposed transgressions. And finally, there are the many other records which seem, at first glance, to be simply statements of fact but which hint at the quality of the life and the relationships between those documented: the census returns which evidence how a mother must have given birth every couple of years from her late teens into her early forties; the workhouse registers which show a family of three young children admitted together and then separated the same day; and the school attendance logs, which consistently show a boy present whilst his sister is absent, kept at home perhaps to look after the youngest members of the family.

Family Size
It is a fascinating thought that most of our nineteenth-century ancestors will have had experience either of being a child in a large family, or of being the parents of numerous children, or both. Until the third quarter of the nineteenth century, unrestricted childbirth was the regime for the majority of married women. For many generations in the distant past, indeed, your family tree probably resembled a pyramid with couples tending to have more children than their parents. Broadly speaking, for most of the nineteenth century creating a family was seen as the only proper end of marriage and constant child-bearing was considered the only natural role for women of all classes. Family numbers reached a peak in the 1860s as medical knowledge, developing public health facilities and a better diet improved fertility and reduced infant and maternal mortality.

At the same time, there was an intensity of connection between what we now call the nuclear family and its other branches. Aunts, uncles and cousins may have been almost as much a part of your nineteenth-century ancestor's life as parents and siblings. Grandparents, great-grandparents and other elderly relatives might have lived nearby or within the family home. The social circles of these people (their friends, neighbours and the people they associated with in clubs and organisations), which are also investigated in the last chapter of this book, were generally localised, and interconnected with family life.

Even in the latter part of the nineteenth century, there was an average of 6.7 inhabitants in middle-class households headed by a married man (Davidoff, *Thicker than Water*, p. 76). If you are able to compare the size of your ancestor's home with the number of people living in it at certain times in the past, you will probably see that domestic life was crowded. Various different kinds of historical records can indicate the size of your family's dwelling place in the past. These include the decennial censuses, which from 1851 asked how many rooms in a dwelling were occupied (after 1891 the number of rooms was recorded only if it were fewer than five), and Property Field Books (kept in County Record Offices) used by the Valuation Office between 1910 and 1915 to carry out a survey of land for tax purposes, which regularly show the number of rooms in a house and the purposes for which these rooms were used. Whilst it was easier to achieve domestic peace in a larger house as a member of the upper or middle classes than in the terraces, tenements and cottages of the lower classes, even those at the top end of society were used to sharing space in a way which we might find uncomfortable today. As the historian Leonore Davidoff has so graphically put it, 'physical bodies jostled in rooms, hallways, landings and on staircases'.

Family size is a matter that requires a good deal of thought and understanding as we research our family trees from the late nineteenth and early twentieth centuries. This period is fascinating because it covers a time when the numbers of children in a family – in very general terms – actually began to dwindle. Already by the end of the eighteenth century, in fact, whilst the extended family model was the dominant one, there are indications that family structure was beginning to move towards smaller units, conjugal (centred around a marriage and children), rather than consanguineal (including extended blood ties).

By comparing information from the ten-yearly census returns of the nineteenth century, historians have proved that – in general terms and with various exceptions dependent on a number of factors which are discussed below – British families really did shrink after 1870. The statistics bear out this broad decline in family size. In the decades immediately following 1837 (the start of Civil Registration), the crude birth rate was roughly thirty-two to thirty-seven babies per thousand people per year. However, in the 1870s, this figure started to fall dramatically. By 1911, there were just over twenty-five babies born per thousand people per year and by 1930, the number was just fifteen per thousand. Another set of statistics produced by a group of historians studying demographic change puts the decline in family size more graphically, 'among those married women born between 1851 and 1855, over one third experienced at least seven live births and as many as 15 per cent had ten or more confinements during the course of their lives. But, of those women born half a century later, between 1901 and 1905, less than 5 per cent of those who married had seven or more children and only 1 per cent had ten or more.' (Garrett et al, *Changing Family Size in England and Wales*, pp. 1–2).

This pattern of decline in family size is common to the story of many of our ancestors. Typically, families who boasted twelve or even fifteen children in the mid-nineteenth century, often went on themselves to have as few as five or even just three children by the end of that century. A typical case in point is the family of Benjamin Wilkinson (a Lancashire miner) and his wife Anne who in the 1840s, 1850s and 1860s worked their way through the Old Testament in search of names for their brood of twelve children: Rachel (b. 1845), Aaron (b. 1847), Moses (b. 1850), Rueben (b. 1853), Sarah (b. 1854), Simeon (b. 1856), Sarah Ann (b. 1858), Levi (b. 1860), Eli (b. 1862), George (b. 1866), Joseph (b. 1868) and John (b. 1870). By contrast, Benjamin and Anne's son George, who started his family in the last decade of the nineteenth century, had only five children – Janette (1893), Wilfred (1896), Elsie (1898), Alfred (1898) and George (1904). In his turn, this young George (who became a father in the 1930s), had just two children, Olive (b. 1934) and Wilfred (b. 1939). It's likely that, as with the Wilkinsons, fewer children were born into your family in the early twentieth century than had been customary in earlier decades and fewer again were born around the time of the Second World War.

A combination of marriage and birth certificates (or parish records of marriage and baptism) will give you the ages at which your ancestors married and started a family. The censuses will chart the growth of their families. Once you have discovered your family in an online census, scroll up and down to view other families of the same occupational background in the same area. Compare the size of their families with the size of your own. Look at a more recent generation of your family and its neighbours and do the same analysis. You are likely – though not certain – to find a reduction in family size and a similarity between the sizes of families of the same general occupational type living in the same area.

The next step is to consider what the reasons for these family shapes and sizes might have been. In an age when contraception was not properly understood, not widely available, largely ineffective and very much frowned upon, family size, for most people, until the 1930s, could be limited only by abstinence from sexual activity or other natural methods of birth control, such as prolonged lactation (breastfeeding). We must then look for other, less obvious factors at play in the determination of family size. Historians have postulated that the number of children in a family was a statistic influenced by a combination of the regional background, employment patterns, class status, religious affiliations, ethnic heritage and more nebulous community norms (a local idea of what a morally-acceptable size for a family actually was). When researching your own family history, you should try to get to grip with what these factors actually might have been in the lives of your ancestors.

A first step towards doing this is to find out something about the location in which your family lived. Books on the local history of an area will give you an understanding of the kinds of industries or rural activities practised there and the proportion of people employed in them. Families from the mining or heavy industry backgrounds of Lancashire, for example, tended to be large in every generation right up to the end of the nineteenth century. For them, it was useful to have many children who could ultimately bring in a wage. But there are always subtle exceptions. In Lancashire mill towns, such as Bolton, for example (where there were many women in the labour force), fertility rates among the working classes were generally low.

The social class to which your ancestor belonged will also have played a part in determining the size of his or her family. Working-class families who had fewer of the time-saving household amenities (not to mention servants) of middle-class families, welcomed extra children as helpers in the many domestic tasks including lighting fires, fetching water, cooking and cleaning as well as potential supporters for their old age. On the whole, poorer families did tend to be larger than middle- and upper-class families by the end of the nineteenth century. Although even middle-class families in the nineteenth century were large by today's standards, there was a tendency for higher-income couples to wait longer before marrying – a fact which inevitably limited the number of children that they had. In general, it would seem that those higher up the social scale were sometimes more willing to limit the size of their families in order to be able to afford a better lifestyle and to provide those children that they did have with a better (often private) education.

Ask yourself also about the religious and ethnic background of your ancestors. There is no record of religion on the censuses but you may well be aware of an ancestor's faith from a number of other clues, their names, the places in which they are buried, as well as other records linking them to particular churches, chapels or other places of worship. It's worth reminding yourself of some of the salient features of these faith groups; Methodists, for example, tended to advocate self-restraint in many areas of life and this was sometimes interpreted as sexual abstinence which, of course, led to smaller families. Quakers were a group who tended to marry at older ages and consequently had noticeably lower fertility than other groups. Catholic families, on the other hand, tended to be large because birth control of any kind was strictly forbidden by the Catholic Church.

As the historian Sian Pooley has put it, the shift to smaller families from around 1870 was not 'a national narrative' – in other words, it was by no means universal, but rather it was inflected by all the factors mentioned above (Pooley, 'Parenthood, child-rearing and fertility in England'). Nevertheless, as we have said, the *average* size of families across Britain did decrease towards the start of the Edwardian period. In very general terms it seems that as our ancestors moved into the new century, there was a new national mood which saw children no longer purely as economic assets but also as emotional burdens. By the start of the twentieth century, a degree of domestic comfort was within the grasp of many people within the population provided they didn't have reams of children draining their resources. The smaller family, seen as modern, educated and beneficial to personal success, increasingly came to be seen as the norm.

The Idea of Family

Alongside this shrinking of numbers, the very concept of family shifted in meaning (as did the meanings of the roles within it) as the nineteenth century moved into the twentieth.

In Victorian culture from Queen Victoria down, the idea of home and family was idealised. Quasi-sacred, protective and nurturing, the household took precedence over the world outside in the popular imagination. Whatever else they faced, the families of our ancestors had a sense of internal cohesion that helped to protect them against the outside forces of history: economic pressure, wars, diseases, changes in the law, national and local politics and other public currents too numerous to mention. Intimate relationships dominated life within the home environment, but were also crucial in helping family members to navigate the dangerous waters outside of it. These were the ties which came first, which mattered most. All in all, our ancestors in the nineteenth and early twentieth centuries probably experienced family life far more continuously and far more intensely than we do now.

By 1900, however, subtle shifts in the idea of the family were afoot. Developments in technology, improvements in contraception, a decline in religious practice, more geographical mobility, improvements in public health and longevity, and female emancipation (to name but a few factors) each helped to put what had been the central and unchallenged position of the family in culture at risk. And by the 1950s, the end of the period covered by this book, further influences, most particularly the effects of the two World Wars, meant that understandings about relationships moved on again – the dense interaction within families that had characterised the past 150 years was (in very general terms) coming to an end. Aunts, uncles and cousins, even if they lived nearby, became more tangential to the nuclear family; friendship and other social networks started to supersede connections of blood and marriage, at least at certain times within a life history. Increasingly, there was less of an onus on caring for the elderly within the family unit. Even communities themselves, made up of many different family groups, started to split and decline.

In your own family history, you will probably discover that, with the gradual shift to smaller and looser family units, the expectations on relationships within your ancestor's family altered. To be a father, a mother or a grandparent in the middle of the nineteenth century was rather different from being a father, mother or a grandparent after the First or again after the Second World War. Fatherhood, motherhood, childhood and all the other relationships covered in this book would also, of course, have been experienced differently by your ancestors depending on the region of the country from which your family came, the types of employment they were in, and the social class, religious or ethnic group to which they belonged. Yet, there were some overarching historically-contingent shifts in the meanings of family relationships that would have affected (to a degree) all members of a generation, making them products of their times and therefore, to some extent archetypal.

The Structure of this Book
Social and women's historians have long examined the history of the family and the roles of those within it. One of the aims of this book is to make some of that research accessible to the ordinary reader by focusing on those resources and those issues which will most interest and engage the family historian, from family photographs to censuses, certificates and other written records.

The seven chapters are organised around particular roles within the family: husbands and fathers; wives and mothers; infants; sons and daughters; adult siblings, aunts, uncles and cousins; and grandparents and great-grandparents. A final chapter looks at the ways in which families interacted with social circles through friendships, neighbourliness and club associations. In each case, a chapter opens with a brief consideration of the way in which Victorian and Edwardian photographers set about portraying particular roles. The characters in our family photographs were, of course, individuals, but they were also conforming to a particular idea of what it meant to take on certain family positions at particular historical moments; fathers play the role of Father, mothers the role of Mother, girls of fifteen take on the role of eldest female sibling, whilst great-grandparents assume the majesty of sensible old age (see Image 1).

Up and down the country, photographers, and the sitters themselves, were to some degree complicit in putting across these ideal stereotypes of family relationships, and among them was one of the most articulate photographers of the nineteenth century, Henry Peach Robinson (1830–1901), an ardent exponent of photography as an art form. At various points in his career Robinson ran photographic studios in Ludlow and Tunbridge Wells, and he was also a founding member of the Birmingham Photographic Society (1856), Vice President of the Royal Photographic Society (1870–91) and (from 1891) a member of Linked Ring – another prominent photographic society. His book *The Studio and What To Do In It* (1891) was an exceptionally useful practical guide for photographers, conveniently published right in the middle of the period covered by this book. Here, Robinson pontificated on the best way to photograph various sorts of people from babies to the very old. His advice on taking photographs of all different kinds of sitters, though it might not have been shared by all photographers, is included at the start of each chapter of this book and may be considered conventional thinking for the times.

Moving on from photographs, each chapter examines the meanings – and the broad changes in meaning – of particular family roles in the period 1800–1950. Perhaps there is an ancestor in your family whose role as a wife and mother especially interests you. Let's say she was a middle-class mother of the Victorian period with a brood of twelve children. You might have speculated on why she became a wife and mother at the time she did, why her family was as large as it was, what other life choices she might have had, what her experience of childbirth and of bringing up a family were like. You might also want to ask what rights women had over their own children at this time, what it meant to have a child out of wedlock, and whether women actually had any control over the size of their families. The questions you might ask of a mother from a different point in history, perhaps a working-class mother of two from the inter-war period, for example, will probably be the same, but the answers will be different. The potential of each of these areas for investigation is enormous and, unfortunately, only the main outline of each can be given within the parameters of this book, but the bibliography will point you to books and websites which might help you to find out more about any topic of particular interest.

INTRODUCTION

Of course, families in the past did not always consist simply of parents and their biological children. Complicated families with step-parents, step-children and half siblings are an on-going fact of human life, common to all periods of the past. Indeed, except perhaps for a brief period in the middle years of the twentieth century (when most people married only once and nearly everyone had children from that one partnership), our ancestors in the nineteenth and early twentieth centuries enjoyed the full range of marital scenarios often indulging in remarriage or re-partnership, starting second, third and even fourth families and frequently facing the challenge of bringing up children other than their own.

Whilst today's family trees are often tangled because of divorce and remarriage, this was not the case in the past. Divorce was not generally available before the Matrimonial Causes Act of 1857 except by Act of Parliament and subsequently continued to remain very difficult to obtain for most members of the population (and especially poor women) for many years thereafter. In the past, 'reconstituted' families appeared far more commonly because of the death of the first spouse and the remarriage of the widowed partner. 'Non-legalised' second unions – rather than remarriage – were also pretty common and bigamy was also far from unusual. Many second partnerships, as well as bringing emotional and (potentially) financial security for the partners, also brought more children. These complicated 'blended' domestic arrangements, fascinating though they undoubtedly are, must unfortunately fall outside the remit of this book.

The final section of each chapter will attempt to answer some of the many genealogical questions that have commonly puzzled family historians in respect of family relationships. Chapter 1, on husbands and fathers, will ask how fathers might potentially be traced when no record exists on a birth certificate, and what the repercussions were for a child that was born after its father died. Chapter 2 on wives and mothers will ask whether women were able to limit the size of their families in the past, and how we might find out more about their probable experiences of conception, pregnancy and childbirth. Chapter 3, on infants, will ask what strategies a family historian might use to work out why an ancestor was named in a particular way, and how we might discover our ancestor's godparents. Chapter 4, on sons and daughters, asks whether a child's position in the family mattered, and what we can learn about the special situation of twins in our family history. Chapter 5 on adult siblings, aunts, uncles and cousins asks why father couldn't marry aunty (and thus investigates the Deceased Wife's Sister's Legislation of the nineteenth and early twentieth centuries), and whether or not cousins could marry. Chapter 6 on grandparents and great-grandparents asks whether our aged relations were in fact as old as they said they were, and how, in particular, elderly widows fared in the years before the Welfare State. Chapter 7, on friends, neighbours and club associates, asks what we might learn from personal records about our ancestors' social circles and what the records of clubs and other organisations might tell us about our ancestors themselves.

The recent move towards very small families of just one or two children has meant that the modern end of our family trees are often tall and thin – a phenomenon which sociologists sometimes describe as 'the beanpole' or 'verticalised' family. And there are other very significant recent changes in the shape of families. The 2011 census records a 9.5 per cent increase in lone-parent families since 2001 and single parents now constitute 17 per cent of all families. The demographics of age are changing too, with almost 20 per cent of the population in the South West of Britain, for example, now estimated to be over the age of 65.

Despite the changing lived experience of family these days – indeed perhaps because of it – the ins and outs of intimate family relationships continue to fascinate, whether in the plots of soap operas, the strange waters of social media, or in popular televised political debate (e.g. the vexed questions of same-sex couples, adoption by homosexual couples, surrogate mothers, the acceptability of older mothers and so on). Historians of the future will undoubtedly have different kinds of records to search and slightly different questions to ask, but a sense of 'family' – in all the new stretched definitions of that word – will still essentially be what matters.

CHAPTER 1

'Protectors and Providers': Husbands and Fathers

The nineteenth-century husbands and fathers in our families were, of course, individuals with different personalities and personal histories but they also complied with well-recognised archetypes. Art, literature and the press all conspired to put forward a view of the way husbands and fathers (of all social classes) should behave and think; popular opinion embraced many of the same ideals. Whether they chose to reject, modify or exceed these 'role models', our male ancestors would have been aware, at some level, of the norms of behaviour to which they were expected to adhere.

How were Victorian and early twentieth-century photographers involved in putting across acceptable ideas of manliness? What roles and responsibilities did husbands and fathers have? What records do we have of those men who failed to live up to them? How did fatherly roles change over the course of time? How were husbands and fathers affected by the two World Wars, for example? Is there any way of finding out who the father of a child was if no name is recorded on its birth certificate? And what happened when a child was born after its father had died?

Husbands and Fathers in Photographs
If you have an old photograph of your family in the Victorian period or early twentieth century, the chances are that it will include the head of the household – most often, the father. Family photographs tended to be taken on special occasions – graduations, anniversaries, special birthdays, baptisms and weddings – those events in which the father's

financial input was pivotal. And, even if fathers worked long hours or were away from home for extended periods, their presence was expected on these occasions and gave a kind of validation to the proceedings.

Fathers in old photographs are usually identifiable from their position and pose, the clothes they are wearing and other props. More often than not, unless very elderly (or very short!), they will be standing. From the mid-Victorian era, adult males in your family may have worn a beard, moustache and/or whiskers to denote their age and position or more specifically their military or administrative service overseas. They might cross their legs, set them apart, or stand with one foot higher than another on a stool or chair. They might flourish an umbrella, cane or walking stick into the space around themselves – to suggest action, confidence and engagement with the world – or carry a tall hat and sport an impressive timepiece to distinguish themselves from elder sons or other younger male relatives. Typically in photographs of fathers with children, the sitters will be positioned slightly apart, not touching, and all will be looking at the photographer rather than at each other. For a wonderful gallery of photographs of Victorian fathers and their children see www.flickr.com/groups/thevictorianfather.

Your ancestor will also, more often than not, be looking straight out of the photograph in the noble and dignified manner encouraged of adult males regardless of social class by studio photographers. Victorian photographer Henry Peach Robinson lamented those photographs taken where a man's head was in profile, suggesting that the strain to turn the head sufficiently made it lean towards the camera and gave the impression that the man had been hanged! 'You have only to add a rope to make the thing complete,' he complained, adding that many photographs were ruined by the sitter being dazzled by over-bright lighting which forced them to look aside giving 'a shy, half-frightened wholly-deceitful glance of the eye' (Robinson, *The Studio and What to Do In It*, pp. 45–6).

To avoid these faults, Robinson suggested that adult male sitters, in particular, were better positioned looking straight ahead and recommended avoiding profile photographs and raising the lighting in a studio to aid this process. The result was, of course, photographs in which husbands and fathers look straight out at the camera in a manner that might seem unsmiling and distant from a 21st-century viewpoint but which was meant to convey qualities of candour, honesty and vigour. All of these factors contributed by the second half of the nineteenth century to the construction, by photographers and male sitters alike, of a familiar and definite ideal of manliness – religious, mannerly and business-like (as well as athletic, patriotic and, to some degree, scientific). It was an ideal that was simultaneously being developed in advice books and the press. Whether or not your ancestor actually exhibited all or any of these 'worthy' characteristics in real life may be debatable, but he certainly lived in a society where to succeed, he needed to look as though he did.

The clothing of men in the second half of the century very much reflected these ideal standards with straight-cut suits in dark colours and stiff materials being very much par for the course. In photographs of working-class families, husbands and fathers (often smaller and somewhat shabbier than their middle and upper-class counterparts), adopted similar poses and changed out of their work clothes into their best suits – outfits which were usually cut along the same lines as those worn by the middle classes but made from cheaper materials.

There were, of course, exceptions to all these conventions but the trends nevertheless persisted. Where differences do occur in your family photographs, you should ask yourself why. Aristocrats, for example, might still have been wearing 'old-fashioned' frock coats and cravats in the late nineteenth century; and vagrants – captured for documentary reasons rather than on family portraits – might be wearing rags. Both of these kinds of men were outside the normal world of work and hence not bound by the increasingly standardised dress code of the respectable middle- and working-class husband and father.

Husbands and Fathers in the Family
By any estimation, our male ancestors of the Victorian and Edwardian periods were in a very much better situation – in terms of education, work and political status – than their womenfolk. Regardless of which

class they came from, they were more likely to have received a schooling of some sort and be more literate than their prospective wives. They were also far more likely to be financially secure since they were favoured in wills and trusts, far more assured (in the middle classes) of having a professional career than women of equal class status and (in the working classes) guaranteed to be paid better wages than the opposite sex for similar work. Additionally, men (or at least those owning property to the value of £10), gained access to political representation in 1867, a good half century before women did.

Meanings of Marriage (for Husbands)
It was on marriage, however, that men really achieved their superior status and presence in society. And, for good or ill, marriage was, in fact, the desired state for most people in the mid-nineteenth century. In the previous hundred years, common-law marriage, spousal desertion and illegitimacy rates had been pretty high. But by 1850s, conventional marriage among the new rising middle classes and the so-called 'respectable' working classes was much more the order of the day. And indeed, there was much to recommend the marital state as far as our male ancestors were concerned. On tying the knot, a husband acquired rights not only to his wife's body and any property, capital or other assets that she held, but also to her legal identity in general.

Our ancestors' nineteenth-century marriages were far more likely to end in the death of one partner than in divorce. In fact, divorce was very rare until the Matrimonial Causes Acts of 1857 wrested the power to end a marriage away from the Church and placed it firmly in the hands of the courts. Even after this, though, cases of divorce tended to be limited to the very wealthy, and the terms of the dissolution of a marriage favoured a husband who could divorce his wife simply on the grounds of her adultery, whereas (until the Matrimonial Causes Act of 1923) the wife had to prove incest or cruelty in addition to adultery to get rid of her husband. It was only after the Matrimonial Causes Act of 1937 that either party in a marriage could divorce simply on the grounds of 'cruelty', 'desertion' or 'incurable insanity' (provided they had been married for at least three years). Additionally, until 1870 and the First Married Women's Property Act, a husband could claim all his wife's property and assets in the event of a divorce, thus leaving her destitute.

Marriage (and what made a good one) was discussed at length in books and periodicals in the nineteenth and early twentieth centuries, but descriptions of the expected role of a husband took up far less print space than did those for a wife. Good prospective male marriage partners were defined not so much by the tasks they undertook (it was, after all difficult to generalise about the infinitely various public world of men's work) as by habits of mind. The general consensus was that husbands should be God-fearing, hardworking, honest, punctual, sober, sensible and protective. Marriage was seen as both a physical and a spiritual union. For husbands, the more 'animal' of the two parties, the acquisition of a wedding ring would, it was suggested, rein in the otherwise dangerous passions, channel desire towards one woman only and hence ultimately keep property and assets within the family.

Male Age at Marriage

When looking at family marriage certificates, consider carefully the age at which your male ancestor became a husband. Sometimes marriage certificates can be disappointing for the family historian in that they do not give the exact age of a bride and groom at marriage, but simply record whether or not they were of 'full' age (i.e. over 21) or a minor. It is worth knowing, however, that males could marry from the age of just 14 until the Age of Marriage Act of 1929 raised the marriageable age to 16 (with parental consent required if the man was under 21). It was only with the Family Law Reform Act of 1969 that the legal age of majority was reduced to 18, and with it the legal age at which a person of either sex could marry without consent. In fact, despite the stipulations of the law, marriages at very young ages in the nineteenth century were very rare with only thirty-five males marrying under the age of 16 during the period 1846–1929. The average age for first time marriage for men in the Victorian period was actually 27 or 28 (two or three years older than the average age for women).

The gap between the ages of a bride and groom in your family might be worth investigating. The older the groom, the higher up the social scale he is likely to have been. He may have been away in the army or on foreign service overseas before feeling the time was right (and the money sufficient) for him to acquire a wife. It was also common for middle-class men of maturing years to become engaged to much younger women in the nineteenth century since the ideal of the wife as an innocent girl, very much less worldly than her husband, held great sway in art, literature and the press.

Alternatively, an older age of marriage for a man might also indicate that a previous marriage had occurred which had ended in widowhood. When William Symes, a townsman or carter, married Elizabeth Terrell in Manchester in 1884 at the age of 28, he neglected to tell the registrar that he was a widower (stating instead that he was a bachelor). In fact he had been previously married in 1876, at the age of just 21 to Emma Talbot (in Martock, Somerset).

Finding a Wife
If you are trying better to understand the circumstances in which your ancestor became a husband, consider the fact that men, on the whole, married women with whom their social standing, political affiliations (where applicable) and religion matched. Though in many marriages in the past, the husband would have been the dominant partner in terms of his public presence, in others (and increasingly so as the nineteenth century progressed), there were partnerships of men and women who were pretty much equals in terms of their social backgrounds. It is a useful task to try to work out whether or not this was the case in your family. Would the engagement have been pretty straightforward or might it have caused upset or concern to one or both families because of a difference in social, political or religious values?

You may go on to wonder how your male ancestor set about meeting his future spouse. For young people of the upper classes, who would probably have been educated away from home in single-sex establishments, even associating with members of the opposite sex to whom they were not related by blood might have been difficult. Middle-class boys too might have attended single-sex grammar schools and most probably found themselves working in kinds of employment that were overwhelmingly male-dominated. It is worth speculating, therefore, on in which private homes or public spaces your upper- and middle-class ancestors might have met or been introduced to each other. There was less segregation amongst the working classes, who might have been at co-educational schools and then might have worked alongside each other in workplaces such as factories and mills, with much courting taking place in particular streets or parts of town renowned for such practices.

The Role of a Husband

The expectations of a new husband depended very much on his social class. Your upper-class ancestor may have held a government office, a role in the army or a clerical position. As a married man, he would not have been expected to devote himself entirely to earning money but, when not overseas, would probably have spent more time at home than his middle- or lower-class counterparts. In the early part of the nineteenth century, a husband's time in the domestic environment would have been taken up mainly with entertainment, perhaps hunting, gambling and drinking. As the century wore on, however, it was increasingly seen as the duty of an upper-class husband to bring a moral and a religious tone to the household. He was expected to preside protectively over family and staff with a dignity arising out of his social position.

Your ancestor who was a middle-class husband would not have relied upon inherited wealth but would have earned his own living from one of a large variety of professions and trades. He might have been a member of the upper echelons of the middle class, an industrialist or banker, a clergyman, military officer, lawyer, doctor, civil servant, academic, civil engineer or architect, or a member of one of its lower ranks, a merchant or manufacturer, small shopkeeper or white-collar clerical worker. Society judged the success of these men almost entirely on their ability to provide for their wives and future children. A middle-class father-in-law would hence look at his daughter's prospective husband with an eye to his character, background and career prospects.

Many middle-class husbands were away from home for long periods of the day or week, commuting to factories or offices in city centre districts whilst their wives and children resided in the suburbs. The middle-class husband in your family would have been expected to pay rent, taxes and other expenses before passing over a housekeeping allowance to his wife. In the time when he was not working, he would have been considered free to enjoy – consume – the fruit of his labours. He was not expected to undertake a role in the day-to-day running of the house or control of the household budget, simply to take pleasure in the domestic comforts and the stability of the well-run home, for which he had financially provided. Each evening was seen as a mini-vacation from work during which a middle-class man was expected to develop his intellectual interests and to relax.

In the working classes, Victorian husbands were increasingly considered to be the main breadwinners and providers for the family. Working-class men were kept entertained outside the home in the evenings and at weekends by theatre, music halls, dancing and the like, but too much jollification was frowned upon by those higher up the social scale and considerable efforts were made to turn working-class husbands towards less reckless pursuits geared around self-improvement of one type or another – such as reading the newspaper, education, sport or a hobby.

Working-class men were often stereotyped in press reports (written, of course, by the middle classes and thus necessarily skewed) as abusive drunks. Those radicals (and later Labour politicians) who campaigned on their behalf tried to change this popular perception, however, and cast the working-class father, wherever they could, as a figure of respectability – a responsible breadwinner and sober householder. In general, there was powerful optimism in the nineteenth century that respectable working-class husbands should, and indeed would, emulate the middle classes in both character and behaviour. It was partly by describing working-class men as bourgeois-fathers-in-the-making that politicians were able to convince Parliament to extend the vote to many of them after the Second Reform Act of 1867.

Becoming a Father
Marriage and birth certificates from the nineteenth and early twentieth

centuries will confirm that our male ancestors usually became fathers within a year or two of their marriage (see Image 2). There were, of course, married men who remained childless. Two of the most well-known of these were the artists and cultural critic John Ruskin (1819–1900) and the Conservative Prime Minister Benjamin Disraeli (1804–81). In both cases, the childlessness it is not likely to have been through choice. Ruskin's marriage to the artist's model Effie Gray remained unconsummated – it is rumoured that he was startled by the sight of her pubic hair on his wedding night! Disraeli had travelled widely in Europe and the Near East as a young man and had caught venereal diseases which were treated with mercury, a known cause of sterility. His wife, Mary Anne Wyndham Lewis, was also some twelve years his senior and aged 47 when they married in 1839.

However, these childless married men were the exception rather than the rule and for many men, fatherhood tended to be a frequently repeated experience. Because the marriage age of men was commonly later than that of their wives, and because men who were widowed very often remarried, nineteenth- and early twentieth-century men commonly found themselves the father of very young children from their late twenties right through to their fifties and sixties. On 15 May 1874, *The Edinburgh Evening News* reported from London that when Matthew Canon, a wretched-looking boy of nine years of age, was found wandering around Spitalfields picking rotten fruit and refuse for his food, his father had been called to answer by the local School Board. The fellow, who was seventy years of age and apparently 'in full possession of his faculties and still strong' volunteered the information that he had had five wives and twenty-seven children!

The obscure Mr Canon's prodigious fatherhood may have been a newsworthy sensation, but in the mid-nineteenth century, the father of your Victorian family would have had plenty of better-known male role models with large families. William IV, who preceded Queen Victoria as British monarch, had fathered ten children, for example, but, as all were born out of wedlock to his mistress, the actress Dorothea Bland (stage name Mrs Jordon), none could inherit the throne. Some of the most powerful and well-known men of the nineteenth and early twentieth centuries also presided over extensive families. One of these was Thomas Jex-Blake (1832–1915), the educationalist and Anglican clergyman who was Dean of Wells Cathedral from 1891 to 1911; he was father to two sons and nine daughters. Charles Darwin, the evolutionist, had ten children (six boys and four girls); Charles Dickens, the writer, also had ten children (seven boys and three girls). Four times Prime Minster William Ewart Gladstone was father to eight children (four boys and four girls), David Lloyd George, Liberal Prime Minister, to five (one boy and four girls). It has been rumoured that some of these men (including Charles Dickens and David Lloyd George) fathered children outside wedlock as well. And even larger families were by no means unusual. Lord Lyttleton (1817–76), British aristocrat and Conservative MP, had eight sons and four daughters by his first marriage. When his wife Mary (Glynne) died in childbirth in 1857, he went on to marry Sybella Harriet Clive and had three more daughters.

The Role of a Father
Historians have suggested that until the mid-eighteenth century, fathers had actually been expected to be very much involved in the nurturing and training of their children. It was the Industrial Revolution (roughly the period 1780–1850) that changed everything. Working and domestic life for all classes would never be quite the same again. Significantly, in the Victorian period, for the first time in history, many fathers no longer had direct and continuous contact with their children. For those men who went away from home to work, empathy across the generations might have suffered. Additionally, it has been suggested that in working-class families, the wages brought home by children and young people might have weakened the family's dependence upon the father (see Image 3).

This looser relationship with children would have been played out in various ways in the lives of the nineteenth-century fathers in your family depending on their social circumstances. Though royals and aristocrats (including Prince Albert), were occasionally present at the births of their children, the vast majority of fathers were not. Additionally, infant feeding in the nineteenth and early twentieth centuries was most commonly undertaken at the breast – a state of affairs which inevitably meant that fathers played less of a role in bringing up their very young children than they might have done later after the introduction of formula milk (the first manufactured baby milk product was developed in 1867, but it was not widely available until the 1910s). Moreover, since many families (even within the lower middle classes) had the help of a nursemaid or general servant to change the nappies and dress the children (check on the censuses to see if your family had one), fathers in the middling ranks of society again had less chance for intimate contact with their young children than they might have had a hundred years earlier (see Image 4).

There was little published advice about what might constitute good fatherhood in the nineteenth century. The word 'fatherhood' itself turned up only thirty-two times in the millions of scanned pages of newspapers that can now be viewed online between 1800 and 1849. And although there were far more references to 'fatherhood' between 1850 and 1900, these usually concerned the term in its religious sense. Actual tips on how to be a good father or what constituted the male role in the home were notably absent, being absolutely dwarfed in the press by the huge amounts of advice given on how to be a good mother.

When husbands became fathers, they had economic control of their children as well as their wives. Though your ancestor might have acquired income or property from several different sources (including his wife's family), it was understood that he alone had responsibility for providing for all those under his authority. And it is highly likely that the husband and father of your family did just that. Census data from the last third of the nineteenth century confirms that most fathers were indeed the main financial providers for families (with only 20 to 25 per cent of mothers with children under the age of five working for pay if they had a husband present at home).

And fathers who failed to provide for their families could be severely punished. In 1866 (reported in *Lloyd's Weekly Newspaper* of 29 April), Walter Marsh, 'a foreman at Mr Byrne's in Leadenhall Market' was convicted of manslaughter against his seven-year-old son, Walter Robert Marsh. The motherless child, one of five, had died from 'privations, want of food and debility'. In court, Marsh's daughter,

Matilda, 'reluctantly described the miserable life of the family. Her father gave her five shillings every Saturday night and some 6lbs of mutton, and generally every morning, except Monday, he left her either sixpence or a shilling to support the family with. But, he never saw his children except on Sundays all week round. He sometimes never came home at night at all, and never before eleven o clock.' There was simply not enough money for Matilda to buy her younger brother enough food to keep him alive. The guilt, in this case, lay clearly with the improvident father.

In the working classes, fathers, in addition to providing for their children, were expected to help their sons to find useful work, often within the same manual occupation as themselves, and to protect their daughters. Where they visibly failed in upholding these unspoken but widely-held ideals, they were resoundingly vilified in the press in deliberately inflammatory language as 'unnatural' or 'inhuman' fathers. Newspaper readers were titillated with barely-disguised tales of fatherly incest, cases where fathers had murdered their offspring and other un-fatherly behaviour, often involving drink, and physical violence far in excess of what might be considered reasonable. These included the case of a father who reacted to his daughter's apparent suicide by calmly snatching the earrings from her corpse just after her body was recovered from the canal (*South Oxfordshire Gazette*, 4 January 1862), and the case reported in the *Lincolnshire Echo* of 21 May 1894, where James McGrath a labourer from Greenock (an 'inhuman father') was charged with the murder of his eight-year-old stepson, 'because he took too long delivering a message'. The Bench in the case of one abused child, Elizabeth Bainbridge (a young girl found sleeping in an outhouse with a broken arm and wounds to her head, both apparently imparted by Mr Bainbridge) declined to hear her father due to the 'disrespectful way in which he conducted himself in court' (*Sunderland Daily Echo and Shipping Gazette*, 22 July 1889). Whilst the norms of fatherhood may not have been written down in black and white, it was all too clear when they had been breached.

In the upper and middle classes, it was the unspoken task of fathers to develop understanding relationships with their children in order that they might smoothly transfer business interests to the next generation when the time was right. It was common for fathers to have the main responsibility over elder children and particularly sons. They were expected to play a crucial role in the transition of their male children from boyhood to manhood, introducing their sons to the male worlds of land ownership, the army, the professions and business.

Many Victorian and Edwardian fathers of the middle classes have gained a reputation for having been strict and censorious disciplinarians who ruled their homes with an iron will and an absolute power, men who firmly inhabited the public world of business and who left the care of the home and children entirely to their wives and/or a team of domestic staff. These were men who expected their sons to obey and their wives to serve. Examples of this kind of father in the middle classes certainly abound; Edward Barrett (1785–1857), father of twelve children including the poet Elizabeth Barrett Browning, famously kept his invalid daughter in the house and tried to prevent her forming romantic attachments. He went on to disown Elizabeth and all of his other children who had the audacity to marry. Patrick Bronte (1777–1861), father of the writers the Bronte sisters, is deemed to have been another stern father figure who when enraged supposedly threw the hearth rug on the fire, tore his daughter's silk gown and broke the back of a chair.

But whilst tales of strict men predominate, there are many other stories depicting indulgent Victorian fathers. On Christmas Day 1868, Charles Dickens wrote to his youngest son Edward Bulwer Lytton Dickens saying, 'I hope you will always be able to say in after life, that you had a kind father.' Bear in mind how many of our male ancestors might have been widowed as young or middle-aged men and left to bring up one, or several, young children. The wife of the Liberal statesman Sir William Harcourt (1827–1904) died a day after the birth of their son Lewis in 1863. From then on Harcourt's relationship with 'Loulou' was one of affection and indulgence to the extent that when the boy started at Eton, his father visited him every night for the first week, so upset were they both. It is a pity for us that we have so few examples of these emotional highs and lows written down or otherwise recorded – the need for fathers to maintain a stiff upper lip usually held sway in most representations.

There might not have been many books about the whys and wherefores of fatherhood in the Victorian period and the early twentieth century, but to imagine that your male ancestor, therefore, played no useful part in the family domestic set-up would be wrong. The distance between father and children for large portions of the week meant that 'daddy time' became more concentrated; the nightly or weekly reunion of the family in the 'back room' or 'parlour', for example, took on a greater importance. In fact, the time that a father actually spent at home was probably more precious and important than it ever had been. And, if they did little in the way of domestic work, nineteenth- and early twentieth-century fathers were often described (in novels, autobiographies, letters and diaries) as the source of entertainment and fun within a family.

Playing with daddy, an activity that required men taking time away from the business of making money (and also away from the vices of places of entertainment) curiously became part of what it meant to be middle-class or respectable. Victorian parlour games such as 'Blind Man's Buff 'and 'Hunt the Slipper' invariably involved the commandeering of items of daddy's property and required his participation. In 1850, Charles Dickens invented a game for his three-year-old son Sydney (the seventh of his ten children). He would repeatedly ask him to go to the station to meet a friend and then send another child to rush after him to bring him back. Sometimes he would send his five-year-old son Albert along on the fictitious errand too and then would encourage the rest of the family to hide in the garden to see what the little ones did on realising they were alone. In the last decades of the nineteenth century, there came a new twist in the ideal of masculinity fostered by tales of Empire emphasised bravery and derring-do, bold, decisive action and heroic behaviour. But this was tempered by the increased leisure time and professional security that many fathers now enjoyed. Suburban men may have read about and dreamed of adventure in far-flung places, but most confined their attentions to home.

Another important role for the father in the Victorian period was as gift-giver. Since most of our female ancestors of the middle and upper classes did not work away from home and did not have their own income, gift-giving was almost entirely the provenance of the father of the family. Look out for examples of fatherly gifts amongst your inherited family possessions. Brides often wore jewellery given by their fathers as in the case of Lady Agneta Harriet Yorke who at her wedding in November 1867 wore round her neck 'a magnificently rich ornament, and a wreath of pearls, the gift of her father' (*Cambridge Chronicle and Journal*, 30 November 1867). In tandem with the penchant for gift-giving amongst real fathers. the most popular Victorian father of all – Father Christmas – was transformed during the 1870s from a character who simply brought festive cheer to one who brought gifts.

All in all, the Victorian and early twentieth-century fathers in our families were seen as crucially important to the healthy life of the home. Conversely, home life was important to fathers. It was the one place where a man's deepest emotional and physical needs were met. In theory, at least, when at home with his family, a father could be periodically rejuvenated before going back into a public world that could sometimes be problematical and harsh.

The Status of Fathers

Whatever religious denomination your ancestor belonged to, faith would have underlined the absolute authority of his position in the family; the father was, after all, God's representative in the home. As well as providing for his wife and children, and protecting family and property, a father was expected to lead family prayers within the home, or, in families of religions other than Christian, to otherwise lead his family in acts of worship. The religious factor was increasingly important as the nineteenth century went on. The father stood between the public world and his family, simultaneously providing moral guidance and censoring the darker side of life. Characteristically, decent families didn't talk about sexuality, money, violence or death.

As well as the legal control he had over his wife mentioned earlier, the father of a family had virtually limitless rights in common law over his legitimate children in cases of separation or divorce. Even if he deserted his wife or became impoverished, he still had unchallenged rights to the custody of all of his children at the beginning of the nineteenth century. This changed somewhat in 1839 (with the passing of the Custody of Infants Act). At this point, a father no longer automatically had custody rights of his children under the age of seven. In 1873, the father's position was further weakened when a subsequent Custody of Infants Act gave custody of the children all the way up to the age of 16 (with caveats) to the mother. Even if your male ancestor was adulterous the law did not forbid him contact with his children (it was thought that such men posed no moral risk to children since the children were unlikely to be placed in direct contact with the lovers). The Guardianship of Infants Act 1925 gave more rights to mothers over their children in cases of separation and divorce but it was actually not until 1973 that mothers were given equal authority to fathers in such cases.

The legal position of fathers with regard to their children modified as the nineteenth century progressed and the result was a diminishing of some of their rights over their wives and children. Be aware that these changes may have affected the way some of your male ancestors conducted their affairs. From being in an unchallengeable position at the beginning of the nineteenth century, it is fair to say that the role of men in the family was unsettled at the start of the twentieth century.

The Changing Role of Fathers in the Twentieth Century
From the start of the twentieth century, fathers were encouraged in the press to take on a more active role in the day-to-day management of their children, to forge strong relationships with them and to watch their developmental progress more carefully. Mothers and fathers were seen to have complementary roles with fathers providing nurture and friendship for their children alongside discipline. On 13 March 1914, the Rector of Adel, Leeds, at a Conference of the Parents' National Education Union commented (as reported in *The Yorkshire Post* the following day):

> The full meaning of matrimony does not dawn upon a man until he looks into the eyes of his first-born child. It is gazing into a new world into which it has just entered; and he is responsible for its being. How will that young life fare? Will the sins of the fathers be visited upon the child? Will it inherit his weaknesses?

Such words augured well for a new public interest in the duties and responsibilities of fatherhood. But change was rather put on hold (if not actively held back) by the onset of the First World War (1914–18) which saw many fathers away from home for years at a time and many children subsequently left with fathers who were injured or worse still dead (see Images 5 and 6). With the resumption of peace in the 1920s, there was a new interest in fatherhood as a role which could be learned – something which had been sorely lacking from advice literature up to this point (as the following article makes clear).

> Innumerable books have been written about the subject of motherhood, and birth control, but as far as we are aware no work has appeared on fatherhood. This need is supplied by E. M. and K. M. Walker, in 'On Being a Father' (Cape, 5s) an interesting book which should help hitherto neglected fathers to take their place in their own nurseries and give them a greater understanding of the problems that arise before and after the birth of their children (*Aberdeen Journal*, 14 December 1928).

In the inter-war period, there were many fears in the press that the absence of a father figure might engender a dangerous rebelliousness in young people, and these fears were exacerbated with the onset of the Second World War. After 1945, indeed, many returning fathers found their marriages in disrepair, their jobs gone and their children out of control. The war with its removal of fathers was blamed for the worrying levels of delinquency amongst teenagers that characterised society in the next couple of decades.

Nevertheless, some of our ancestors who were fathers and who had survived the conflict seemed to be more determined to create a less distant relationship with their children than those that they had experienced with their own fathers. This state of affairs was easier to bring about since in the mid-twentieth century men in many kinds of employment had reduced working hours and more holiday time. Moreover, the lack of servants in most families after the War meant that the help of the husband and father with domestic tasks became increasingly important. After the 1950s more men were present at the births of their children and by 1960, this was up to 1 in 10 with the numbers increasing ever since. Smaller families with just one or two children led to a situation in which fathers more easily found their place within the heart of the family.

Issue 1: How might I identify my ancestor's missing father?
We have probably all experienced that sense of frustration when a birth certificate arrives from the General Register Office and no father's name is recorded upon it. The only fact that we can be reasonably sure about in these cases is that the parents of the child were not married at the time of the child's birth (see Image 7).

Sadly, the absence of a father's name on a birth certificate cannot tell us anything with certainty about the feelings of the father for that child, or whether or not he later took on any responsibility for it. Bear in mind that between 1837 (the start of Civil Registration) and 1850, there was actually some confusion over whether an unmarried father could register his name at the birth of his child. Some registrars allowed it and some did not. From 1850 to 1874, it became clearer that an unmarried father should not register his name. After the Births and Deaths Registration Act of 1874, however, an unmarried father could be recorded (though he was not required to be so) provided both parents were present and signed as informants of the birth.

Legal confusion aside, there a number of other reasons why a father's name might not appear on a birth certificate:

1. The mother might not have been sure who the father was (if there were two or more candidates);
2. The mother might have known who the father was but the father might have been unaware of the fact that he had fathered a child;
3. The father might have denied paternity of the child (wrongly or rightly);
4. After 1875, the (unmarried) father might simply have been absent at the time of registration.

Whatever the case, don't give up on finding out who your ancestor's father actually was. There are number of conventional and unconventional methods and sources that might help:

• *Baptism Records*
Sometimes unwed mothers were willing to confess the name of their baby's father to the vicar of the parish at the time when the child was baptised. This might have been days, weeks, months or even years after the child was born and the birth registered. On other occasions, the vicar might himself have added the name of the suspected father to the record of baptism if it was known to him. Search for parish records of baptism at any of the main commercial genealogy sites (www.ancestry.co.uk; www.findmypast.co.uk, or www.thegenealogist.co.uk). New records are being added all the time.

• *Parental Marriage Records*
Sometimes, the father went on to marry the mother of the child soon after the birth. This might have occurred because of pressure being applied by the local Church authorities. It is worth looking in the marriage indexes on one of the main commercial genealogical sites to see if the mother did indeed marry at around this time.

• *Other Records Relating to the Child*
Often, as they grew up, illegitimate children became aware of the identity of their fathers. Occasionally, the family might have decided spontaneously or consistently to use the father's surname in a record relating to the child (for example, on a census, or in a school admissions register). More often probably, illegitimate children were willing to name their fathers when they themselves got married. But be careful, at this point they might either have invented a father (for the sake of propriety) or recorded the name of someone whom they believed to be their father (erroneously). It was also common practice to record a grandfather's name and occupation in the

place reserved in the register for the father's details. This might have been because the bride or groom really believed that their grandfather was actually their father, or because it was the first set of plausible details to come to mind at the time.

• *Bastardy Records*
A child whose parents were unmarried and whose mother had no obvious financial support was likely to become a financial drain on the local parish. Before the Poor Law Amendment Act (1834), the local Churchwarden or Overseer of the Poor (or in some cases Justices of the Peace at the Petty or Quarter Sessions) would conduct a verbal 'examination' of the mother to establish the identity of the father who would then be tracked down and put under pressure to maintain the child financially by entering into a Bastardy Bond.

Maintenance was expected to continue until the child was old enough to be apprenticed out or otherwise employed. Those fathers who resisted this could be forced to pay by way of an Affiliation Order delivered by the Justices of the Peace at the Petty Sessions or Quarter Sessions. Punishment in the worst cases could involve a prison sentence. After 1834 parish officials became less active in bastardy cases and single mothers were largely expected to sort out the upkeep of their children themselves. Further bastardy legislation in 1844, 1868 and 1920 tweaked the law in favour sometimes of the mother and sometimes of the father, and kept the issue of child maintenance as high on the government's list of priorities as it still is.

The relevant records held in local archives and County Record Offices (and located via the website of the National Archives www.nationalarchives.org) include: The Bastardy Examination, Bastardy Warrants And Summons, Bastardy Orders, Affiliation Orders, Maintenance Orders and Bastardy Bonds. Take a look also at the Overseer of the Poor Accounts and Churchwarden's Accounts for the local area at the time in question which are particularly interesting in cases of disputed paternity. Such cases might be reported in local newspapers many of which can now be searched by date and keyword at wwwbritishnewspaperarchives.co.uk and at www.findmy past.co.uk. Here is an example, from Exeter in 1849.

> James Thomas, of Christow, miner was summoned by Anna Maria Luscombe, a single woman, to answer for the charge of her illegitimate child, of which, she said, he was the father; he had sent her 10s a fortnight after the birth; and her father proved an interview with the defendant at the Artichoke public house in Nov. last., when defendant did not deny the fatherhood, and promised to marry her in a month. The man now frankly admitted all this, and said he had offered to marry her, only last Tuesday, but she had refused. An order was made for 1s 6d a week (*The Exeter Times*, 17 February 1849).

• *Private Papers*
Private arrangements might have been made by the father for the child's upkeep. These would not have been recorded in any official records, but may be alluded to in diaries, letters or personal account books.

• *Wills*
Fathers often acknowledged illegitimate children in a will (if only to deny them any rights to assets), so it might be worth checking the will of anyone whom you might suspect to have been the father of your ancestor. In the will, bastard children might appear as 'reputed son' or 'reputed daughter'. To find details of your ancestors' wills made between 1858 and 1966, view the National Calendar of Wills available at www. ancestry.co.uk and order a copy of the actual will via the website www.justice. gov.uk/courts/probate/copies-ofgrants-wills.

• *Medical Records*
In the past, of course, there was no scientific certainty of paternity. If, however, you have access to medical records which give the blood group of your ancestor and his putative

father, you may at least be able to rule out a connection between them. (For example, two parents with O type blood groups can only produce a child with an O blood group, see: http://www.canadiancrc.com/paternity_determination_blood_t ype.aspx)

Our ancestors themselves sometimes sought certainty about the paternity of children for a variety of reasons, not least of which was inheritance. From the 1920s, 'blood typing' (the matching of blood types between a child and its alleged father) could be carried out. But such tests were not very accurate and were only able to exclude 30 per cent of the male population from being the possible parent. In the 1930s, blood typing was joined by the testing of serological bodily fluid and the exclusion rate went up to 40 per cent.

• *Middle Names*
A researcher recently described (in a genealogy chat group forum) how nine illegitimate children in his family (none of whom had a father recorded on its birth certificate) were all given the middle name 'Lee'. Further research showed that when a local man with the surname 'Lee' died, he named these children (evidently his own offspring) in his will and left money to them.

• *Local Names*
Even more ingenious family historians have searched the censuses, trade directories, newspapers and even telephone directories of local areas for young men with similar first names (and surnames) to the first names of their illegitimate ancestors. Could the illegitimate Rueben Simms have been the child of his mother's neighbour Harry Rueben, for example? This is probably only a viable field of enquiry if your ancestor has a reasonably unusual name.

• *Oral History*
Family history researchers have claimed to be able to

substantiate family rumours about an ancestor's paternity with reference to physical characteristics such as the shape of a head or chin. But before you are persuaded about a connection between two characters in old photographs, do bear in mind that a lot of speculation about apparent biological similarities between a father and a child, such as inherited eye-colour, have been blown out of the water by modern research into genetics. Just as today, of course, a child's paternity in the past was sometimes questioned when it was noted that it did not look very much like its father, or when dates of conception and dates of birth did not seem to match. And in a situation where the true paternity of a child could never be categorically proved, Victorian men went to great lengths to try to ensure that they had faithful wives who produced legitimate offspring.

The strategies detailed above may or may not help to enlighten you about the identity of your ancestor's real father. But it is worth remembering that even where the name of a father does appear on a birth certificate or parish record of baptism (or even a Bastardy Order), this may not necessarily be a true record of a child's biological paternity. As genealogists all we have to deal at the end of the day is the documentary record, and fascinating though the search is, there is always room for doubt.

The only absolute way of discovering the true identity of an ancestor's father would be through DNA testing. Scientists can now – in very particular circumstances and with a large number of caveats – use bones, teeth, fingernails and hair to extract DNA and help confirm parentage. See http://www.forensicmag.com/JJ14_Paternity for more fascinating information about this. To undertake such a test in respect of an ancestor, however, it would be necessary to exhume the remains of both the child and the putative father. It's very unlikely that a British court would ever grant such an exhumation simply for reasons of genealogical curiosity!

Issue 2: What were the implications of posthumous fatherhood?
It's surprising just how often family history research throws up

individuals who were born after the death of their fathers. A careful perusal of dates, comparing the father's decease with the child's birth may show that your ancestor was sadly born (as Charles Dickens's character David Copperfield put it) 'after [his] father's eyes were closed' (see Image 8).

With the high mortality rates for adults in the nineteenth century, it was more likely that a father's final child might be born after his death than it is today and examples among rich and famous families abound. The economist Adam Smith (b. 1823), for example, was the posthumous child of Adam Smith, Comptoller of Customs at Kirkaldy. Queen Victoria's grandson Charles Edward Duke of Saxe-Coburg and Gotha was born in July 1884, four months after the death of his father Prince Leopold, Duke of Albany. The phenomenon of posthumously-born children was also more common at times in history when large numbers of men died in military action or in sudden disasters. Many children were born posthumously after their fathers were killed in the First and Second World Wars.

The posthumous child in your family tree may have had a life shaped by that very fact. Sometimes the fact that a child was born posthumously could throw its paternity into doubt. In particular, a child born just about nine months after the death of a father may have raised a few eyebrows and caused more than a few problems for the grieving widow. An intriguing case which illustrates the uncertainties that could arise when a child was born posthumously was the case of John Dickens (father of author Charles), who was born to his mother Elizabeth, housekeeper to the Crewe family at Crewe Hall, shortly after the death of *his* putative father, another John Dickens in October 1785. Claire Tomalin, Dickens's recent biographer, speculates that 'John Dickens may have been the son of the elderly butler, but it is also possible that he had a different father' (Tomalin, *Charles Dickens: A Life*, p. 5). Was John, for instance, actually the son of John Crewe, the lord of the manor, or another gentleman guest at the Crewe residence? In a flight of fancy Tomalin even suggests that John's father might have been the dramatist Sheridan, another erstwhile guest at the hall (an idea which, if true, would give Charles Dickens a true literary pedigree).

Perhaps it is not important who the real father of the posthumous John Dickens was. What counts is the fact that he might have *believed* his father was one of the educated, well-travelled, impecunious gentlemen visitors to the Percy home. In any event, John Dickens grew up with a degree of flamboyance that belied his origins and consistently lived beyond his means, much to the sorrow of his son Charles.

The birth certificate of an ancestor born posthumously should include the father's name followed by the word 'deceased'. This information will of course only be present if the mother imparted the information that the father was dead to the registrar. Bear in mind that a birth certificate upon which no father is mentioned means only that the couple were not married at the time of the child's birth. The father might or might not have already been dead in this case.

Look out for a change of surname in the case of a posthumous child. If the mother of such a child married again, the child is likely to have taken on the surname of the stepfather. (This is of course possible in all cases where children acquire stepfathers – but is perhaps, more likely, in the case of children born posthumously.) American President Bill Clinton's father William Jefferson Blythe died just a few weeks before his birth on 19 August 1946 after a car crash in Missouri. Clinton's original name was William Jefferson Blythe III. He took on the surname of his mother's second husband, Roger Clinton, after she married again in 1950.

The birth of a posthumous child in your family might have been shrouded in pathos and mystery. According to the *Encyclopedia of Superstitions* (1949), posthumously-born children were traditionally seen as having great (and even magical) powers of healing. A belief that seems to have existed across Britain suggested that if a posthumous child breathed into the mouth of an infant suffering from thrush, the sick child would be healed instantly! Fantasy aside, the posthumous child in your family might have struggled to survive without a normal parental set-up or might have achieved great success in defiance of their fatherlessness.

Think carefully about the effect that a posthumous birth might have had on the way a father's estate was divided. Wills often name the children who will inherit but usually do not account for children born posthumously. This might have brought about complications when a son entered the world after his father had died and changed the line of succession. A case in point is that of Sir Ranulph Fiennes, the explorer, who was born on 7 March 1944. His father Lieutenant-Colonel Sir Ranulph Twisleton-Wykeham-Fiennes, commander of the Royal Scots Greys, had been killed in action five months before at the Battle of Monte Cassino on 24 November 1943. Ranulph Fiennes had three older sisters and no older brothers. This meant that at his birth he inherited his father's baronetcy (becoming the 3rd baronet of Banbury). Had Ranulph been another girl, the title would have skipped his sisters and passed to a different branch of the family entirely.

CHAPTER 2

'Hearts and Helpmeets':
Wives and Mothers

Many of our female ancestors will have spent pretty much all of their adult lives as wives, and much of their time from marriage to menopause dealing with issues of contraception, pregnancy, miscarriage, abortion, childbirth, the nursing and weaning of babies and the welfare and education of older children. It is perhaps therefore surprising that, until fairly recently, most of these experiences were not deemed worthy of serious historical investigation. As family historian Margaret Ward has shown, looking at the lives of the women in our families in the past, involves looking at different sources in different ways (Ward, *The Female Line*).

What images of wifeliness and motherhood were Victorian photographers trying to achieve? At what age was it recommended appropriate for our female ancestors to marry and become mothers? What rights did they have over those children as they grew up? How did women experience childbearing as they grew older? Were they able to limit the size of their families? How did they experience pregnancy and childbirth?

Wives and Mothers in Photographs
Our female ancestors presented photographers with a different proposition to the males. Photographer Henry Peach Robinson suggested that there were a number of reasons why a 'more effective picture' might be made when a woman was the subject than a man. The first of these was her 'costume' which 'offers greater facilities to the artist who desires variety in his poses than ugly masculine

garments will admit of'. Secondly, photographs of women allowed for a greater range of facial expression, than those of men – they did not always need to be serious and unsmiling. Thirdly, according to Robinson, the occupations and amusements of women (such as needlework, reading, the playing of musical instruments and so on), all of which were fairly sedate, offered 'much help to the photographer'. Finally 'the occasional beauty and grace' of some women might compel the photographer to make a really fine picture 'in spite of himself'.

Despite these apparent advantages, wives and mothers in nineteenth-century photographs were often asked to pose by photographers in ways calculated to emphasise their supposedly passive role in society. Their posture usually suggested the cast of mind deemed suitable for women at the time: purity, devotion to family and selflessness. There was rarely any indication of physical strength or athleticism in early studio photographs of women, and the suggestion of movement was tolerated only if it created a sensation of grace and elegance. The use of props which suggested gentle action from a seated position such as gloves (which could be buttoned), books, fans, cups of tea or writing implements could be instrumental in consolidating this ideal. Robinson suggested that 'when all other devices fail, a passable portrait can be got by making the sitter look down, as in reading a book, arranging flowers, knitting or sewing, thus evading the difficulties of staring eyes and open mouths'.

The result is that most female sitters in photographs of the Victorian and Edwardian periods are made to look calm, quiescent, their arms (when not holding props) held close to their bodies, their heads tilted at an angle suggestive of feminine modesty and even vulnerability (even if the lives they actually led were anything but delicate). Photographers struggled where women overplayed their role. Robinson complained that some women 'overstepp[ed] the modesty of nature [and] put too much "gush" into their poses, whilst others from 'what might be called 'the invertebrate school, [. . .] contort [ed] their figures into ridiculously strained attitudes, in their endeavour to make them graceful' (Robinson, *The Studio and What to Do In It*, pp. 64–5).

The general subject of women's fashions in old photographs is a fascinating one and ably dealt with by family historian Jayne Shrimpton (see the bibliography for a list of her books). Newly-engaged or married women often announced their new position in society in old photographs by posing with their engagement or wedding rings very prominently displayed, their left hand resting on a book, a table or the back of a chair (see Image 9). Don't be put off by early photographs of young women alone – these may well be wedding photographs which were following an earlier tradition from portrait-painting where companion marriage paintings rather than paintings of the bride and groom together were produced.

Marital state might be paraded in front of the camera, but there was no such overt advertisement of pregnancy. In the absence of clothing made specifically for expectant mothers, baby bumps could easily be disguised by the wide skirts, crinolines and bustles that dominated much of the mid-Victorian era. Mothers-to-be would also have adapted (or had adapted) their existing clothing (including corsets) to their new shape, by letting out seams and adding extra panels of material. In the last three months of pregnancy, upper and middle-class women would have gone into 'confinement' and would have been less likely to appear in a photograph at all. During this time, their clothing would have included wrapper-like garments which could easily be donned and taken off and which were suitable for informal gatherings with family and friends at home, but which would not have been worn in public. (See www.emblah13.wordpress.com/2014/06/08/victorians-in-the-family-way-photographs-of-pregnant-ladies/ for some interesting photographs of pregnant women in the Victorian era.)

In many photographs of mothers, young children sit on the lap, or have some physical contact and both parties often gaze adoringly at each other (see Image 10). These poses contrast with many of the rather less intimate photographs that depict Victorian fathers with their children mentioned in Chapter 1. In other photographs of very young children, mothers shroud themselves with curtains, or hide behind furniture whilst surreptitiously holding their offspring in position. (See http://www.theguardian.com/artanddesign/gallery/2013/dec/02/hidden-mothers-victorian-photography-in-pictures for a fascinating gallery of photographs of hidden mothers.) Henry Peach Robinson showed his ambivalence towards mothers in the photographic studio when he said, 'mothers are a very useful institution, but they are terribly in the way when children are to be photographed' (Robinson, *The Studio and What to Do In It*, p. 90).

Whether they are doing something, doing nothing, or holding a child, take particular note of your female ancestor's hands in old photographs. According to Robinson the biggest source of customer complaint at the photographic studio was women moaning that their hands had been made to look too big or inelegant. This was no idle worry since hands were one sure-fire way of identifying a person's class in the nineteenth century – something that many sitters were anxious to hide. Working-class women had rough hands, coarsened by labour, cold weather, boiling water and industrial grime. Ladies, or those who aspired to be ladies, had soft, white, delicate hands which looked unaccustomed to doing household tasks.

Whilst portrait painters had always been able to doctor the size of hands in paintings, photographers faced far more difficulties in their attempts to position hands 'on the same plane' as heads in order to minimise their size. Various ploys helped. Gloves might be worn, for example. In the nineteenth century these were usually made of leather, suede or kidskin. The middle-classes (of both sexes) would have had more than one pair: black for funerals, white for social gatherings and yellow for hunting and bloodsports. Women often wore long gloves to make up for any shortfall in the lengths of their sleeves and respectable women certainly did not offer up the skin on their arms for inspection. Where the hands went ungloved in photographs, they were carefully positioned, not usually joined together or with the fingers interlaced, for example. Views of the full backs of hands were avoided, care was taken that light did not fall too flatly or strongly upon them, bracelets were worn to avoid the sensation of an overlong wrist, and tight sleeves were avoided since these could make the hands look broad.

The mothers in your family who posed for photographs might have gone to great lengths to improve the appearance of their hands. Contemporary advice books such as *The Lady's Dressing Room* by Baroness Staffe (1893) describe how women combatted perspiring, chapped or chilblained hands. It was suggested that they use 'Marseille' soap, rinse their hands in oatmeal or bran dissolved in tepid water, or, if the hands were very much stained, in 'a little borax, ammonia, or fine white sand'. Brown hands, which in this mainly white society were occasioned by sunburn acquired through the new turn-of-the-century outdoor pleasures such as croquet, lawn-tennis, sailing or rowing, could be improved by lemon-juice and glycerine (or better still, buttermilk), rubbed into the hands at night and then covered with gloves. Hands that were stained with ink could be rubbed with the juice of 'ripe tomatoes, strawberries, a sorrel-leaf, or milk'. Fingernails were massaged with tinted powders and creams and then buffed to look polished rather than painted. It was not until 1917 that the first commercial nail polishes were manufactured by Cutex, and probably much later before our ancestors were commonly wearing them.

When Robinson reminded photographers that 'a well-formed hand is a beautiful object', he knew that it was the job of his profession to make women's hands – the prized soothers and comforters, makers and menders of their domestic lives – look aesthetically perfect, to fox the viewers into believing that his female sitters were idle ladies rather than hardworking wives and mothers.

Wives and Mothers in the Family
At the beginning of the nineteenth century, our female ancestors' position in society was very much inferior to that of their male counterparts. Whilst many men were enfranchised in 1867, women had to wait until 1928 (the Representation of the People Act – Equal Franchise) before they gained absolutely equal voting rights with men. The issue of suffrage aside, there were many other aspects of female lives which made them – regardless of their class background – very much second-class citizens. Limited by an education that was neither as lengthy nor as thorough as that of boys (and which was often conducted in the home rather than in schools), girls from the upper and middle classes rarely got the chance to exploit their true academic potential. The education of working-class girls (generally available for children up to the age of 10 after the Education Act of 1870), meanwhile, was perfunctory and domestic rather than academic, and seen, by many, as less important than that of working-class boys.

Moreover, there was an unspoken bar on paid employment for women of the middle classes throughout the Victorian period, with the professions opening up to them only very slowly from the end of the nineteenth-century onwards. Those unsupported middle-class women who needed to make a living really had only the option of teaching, in a school or as a governess in the homes of the wealthy. Working-class women invariably worked in jobs – domestic service, factories, mills and sewing sweatshops, for example – that were less well-paid than their male counterparts and which were not unionised, dangerous, part-time and temporary.

Meanings of Marriage (for Wives)

In addition to these political, educational and economic disadvantages, our female ancestors who married suffered further indignities under the law for much of the nineteenth century. From 1815, as the historian Paula Bartley has put it, 'the law stipulated that husband and wife were one, and that that "one" was the husband' (Bartley, *The Changing Role of Women, 1815-1914*, p. 11). As married persons, our female ancestors, under common law, lost their independent legal status and were considered to be the possessions of their husbands.

There was a way of avoiding such inequalities and that was by setting up a marriage settlement under equity law, which protected money and property held by wives. But only 10 per cent of the population could afford the costs of setting up such settlements or trusts. For the rest of the women in the population – including the majority of our middle- and working-class female ancestors, marriage involved a total surrender of any inherited property or even earned income. In addition, under the dictates of common law, most wives could not sue, sign contracts, run a business or make a will without the permission of their husbands (widows were considered differently – see Chapter 6). Husbands might beat their wives and even lock them up, all within the law, and, until the Custody of Infants Act of 1839 at least, if a marriage ended, the husband automatically got custody of the children. For our female ancestors then, getting hitched could be seen as a very serious act of self-sacrifice, certainly not something to be entered into lightly. Despite these drawbacks, a woman who married a good man would, in theory, be acquiring somebody who would protect her and provide for her for life and, for most women, the marital state was the only attractive prospect in life.

But, in fact, our female ancestors from the middle of the nineteenth century might actually have considered themselves lucky to have been married at all. In the 1850s, there was a perceived imbalance between adult females and males in the population (104 females to every 100 males), partly due to high male mortality rates (sometimes caused by disease and sometimes by death in foreign conflicts), and partly due to high emigration rates of men to the British colonies. The 1851 census shows a concerning number of unmarried adult women (1.7 million spinsters and nearly 800,000 widows). There was much public concern about what would become of all these women, so much so, in fact, that over the next few decades, many schemes to ship unmarried women out to the colonies were brought into play in an effort to find them partners.

Age at Marriage (Females)

As far as the law was concerned girls needed to be only 12 years old to tie the knot until the Age of Marriage Act of 1929. After this Act, it became legal to marry at 16 providing you had your parents' consent and at 21 if you did not have that consent. In practice barely any of our female ancestors in the nineteenth century married at very young ages. Part of the reason for this was probably the late age of puberty for girls: it is thought that 15 was the average age at which menstruation started in the Victorian period. Between 1846 and 1929, only 1,844 females married at an age lower than 14, according to the records. In fact, the average age at which our female ancestors married in the nineteenth century was 25. Perhaps surprisingly, it was upper-class women who most consistently married at somewhat younger ages than this, in their late teens and very early twenties.

The Role of a Wife

Marriage would certainly have brought about the biggest change in your female ancestor's life in the nineteenth century and it is therefore worth giving the details of her betrothal some deep thought. Whilst romance would have been high on the agenda, in many marriages there were also other underlying concerns (see Image 11).

An upper- or middle-class female ancestor of the nineteenth century was likely to marry within her class. Wives – in theory at least – were valued for their moral qualities more even than their physical ones. Ideally, they would bring to a marriage, love, companionship and mutual respect. They might also bring a settlement – sum of money, property or other assets – which, as we have said, immediately upon marriage passed into the husband's management and control.

The prime roles of upper-class wives were to bear children and attend social functions, certainly not to engage in paid work of any kind. Likewise, a woman could only claim to be truly middle-class if she did not work. If she needed employment it was an indication that her husband did not have the means to support her. Physical employment was entirely out of the question. Additionally, many kinds of intellectual work – academic, scientific, medical and the like – were deemed unsuitable for women in that such work might jeopardise their ability to be successful wives and mothers.

The chief obligation of the middle-class wife was to make the home pleasant and a place of peace, comfort and tranquillity for her busy husband. The actual household tasks themselves were delegated to servants, but the mistress of the house usually had control of the family budget and the overall management of the domestic arrangements (see Image 11). Acceptable reasons for failing to meet these wifely requirements could include extreme youth and inexperience, or too many philanthropic engagements – all of which could be corrected. But if a wife was considered to be lazy or careless in her household management, social censure would be absolute.

By contrast, our working-class ancestors who were wives were often prized on their ability to generate income, something which would have been dependent on their physical strength. Poor families looked for daughters-in-law who could work hard, save well and who would not drain a husband through unruly behaviour, alcohol or drug addiction. But not all working-class wives worked. Many relied solely on their husbands' wages. Look out for erstwhile working-class female ancestors who might have worked in menial occupations as single girls but who then moved up into the lower strata of the middle class by marrying male blue-collar workers and who no longer continued to work after marriage. In the twentieth century many upper working-class female workers (teachers, employees of the Post Office and the like, for example) were also automatically barred from working once they married.

The Role of a Mother

Very many of our female Victorian and early twentieth-century ancestors became mothers within a year or so of getting married and the change in their circumstances would have felt momentous. Queen Victoria was undoubtedly voicing the feelings of many new mothers of the period when she recorded in her journals on Christmas Day 1840, 'This *day*, last year, I was an unmarried girl, & *this* year I have an angelic husband, & a dear little girl 5 weeks old!'

Whilst in the late eighteenth century and early Victorian period, fathers – in books at least – had been revered as 'the originators' of the family with mothers relegated to the role of passive 'carrier' of children, as the nineteenth century progressed, the vital force of women as mothers, particularly in the middle classes, was recognised. The role of mother took on an importance in society and popular culture that it had never fully enjoyed before. Motherhood was no longer seen simply a reproductive function but became imbued with symbolic meaning.

To understand just how transformative this new focus on the mother was, it is helpful to take a look at some comments from the end of the century which charted this transformation and which attributed it largely to the marvellous example of motherhood set by Queen Victoria. Quoting an article by the Hon. Mrs H. Chetwynd in the *Lady's Realm*, *The Leeds Mercury* of 15 July 1899 commented on 'how much the Queen's example has altered relations between mothers and their children!' The article continued:

Fifty years ago, what did a fashionable mother know of her children, either when they were infants in the nursery, or later, when they were in the schoolroom? Nurses and governesses had it all in their own way. Sometimes they were good, sometimes they were bad – and too often engaged on the recommendation of some fashionable friend who wanted to get rid of them. The mother saw her babies once a day, sometimes not even that, and accepted as gospel whatever she was told – was perfectly satisfied if the children had pretty manners, were tolerably graceful, could play a little, dance a little, and speak a little French. The Queen's view of motherhood altered all this. When it became known that all the details of her nursery were her especial care; that every spare moment was spent with her children; that sanitary regulations were insisted upon; that a high character and high standard was expected of the nurses and governesses; that time was not to be wasted, every honest effort being instantly recognised: and that no public or other duties neutralised the Queen's sense of true motherhood; she at once set an example, which was largely followed. Other mothers felt ashamed of neglected duties, and good wives and careful mothers became the fashion: something higher and better came into vogue.

The Victorian, middle-class mother, then (and by extension her respectable working-class counterpart), was popularly represented as a paragon of virtue, and our ancestors cannot have failed to be affected by this. Look at any advert for soap, cough medicine or foodstuffs from the Victorian era and you are likely to see a mother gazing adoringly into the eyes of her child or children, arms encircling them comfortingly and totally absorbed in their welfare. Home and family were thought to be all that a woman needed for personal fulfilment. As the importance of the mother's role increased in the popular imagination, so too did the number of books devoted to advising or instructing women on how to become better mothers and good domestic managers.

The Child-bearing Years
Childbearing for many women would continue at regular intervals from marriage, right through what remained of their twenties, their

thirties and even their early forties. For some of our female ancestors then, childbearing lasted literally from marriage to menopause, though high levels of miscarriage, stillbirth and infant mortality meant that many instances of pregnancy did not inevitably lead to large families.

One late Victorian physician, A. L. Galabin, actually estimated that 20 per cent of all pregnancies ended in miscarriage (Nelson, *Family Ties in Victorian England*, p. 47), a very high proportion, explained perhaps by the high levels of malnutrition amongst the poor, inadequate provisions for public health and the trials of hard physical labour for women of the lower classes. The average number of births experienced by British women in the mid-nineteenth century was six, with 35 per cent of women having eight or more children. For most married women, who had no access to contraception, the pregnancies tended to come thick and fast and married life up to middle age could be measured in pregnancies.

Large Families and Older Mothers

Incidences of large numbers of children born to one mother were pretty commonplace. How many family historians have flicked over from one page of the census to the next in growing surprise at the number of entries referring to children apparently born to one mother? Newspapers reported excessively prodigious mothers with a combination of admiration and horror, with the *Sussex Agricultural Express* stating on 15 June 1894 that 'mothers of twenty children and upwards, are not so rare in these days of advanced civilisation as many would suppose', and remarking with grim resignation that such families all too frequently entailed 'anxiety, expense, and, only too frequently, the complete breakdown of the mother's health'.

Elizabeth Dorling, the mother of the cookery writer Mrs Beeton, had seventeen children, giving birth to her last at the age of 47 (she was also stepmother to four more!). Dorling is one example among many that gives the lie to the idea that women had babies only at younger ages in the past. In fact, as you may well discover in your own family, many of our female ancestors had babies at late stages in their reproductive life. Whilst in overall terms family size went down over the course of the nineteenth and early twentieth centuries, a considerable number of our female ancestors bore children into their fourth decade. Rather than being seen as toying dangerously with the laws of nature, giving birth over the age of forty in the nineteenth century was perceived as a relatively common experience (if not necessarily a welcome one).

Some rare women were first-time mothers in their forties. Elizabeth Barrett (1806–51) married fellow poet Robert Barrett Browning (six years her junior) against the wishes of her father when she was 40. The pair eloped to Italy in September 1846 and were promptly disinherited by Elizabeth's father. Barrett had been an invalid for years but in the warm climate of Italy she grew stronger and, just a few days after her 43rd birthday in 1849, gave birth to a son, Robert Wiedemann Barrett Browning (see Image 12). Elizabeth had suffered three miscarriages before he was born and attributed her successful pregnancy to the fact that she had given up laudanum (prescribed for her long-term condition of painful menstruation). She described her baby, known fondly as 'Pen' as 'so fat and rosy and strong that I am almost sceptical of his being my child'. A later pregnancy ended in miscarriage and Elizabeth herself died in 1861 at the age of 55.

But the majority of older mothers had had several – and often many – other children earlier in life. Former artist's model Effie Gray (1828–97), had eight children in twelve years and the last one, Sophie, was born when she was forty. This fertile boon in middle age was widely seen as testimony to the happiness of her second marriage (to the artist John Millais – father of all her children) and as a stark contrast to her first unhappy, unconsummated and childless marriage to the cultural critic John Ruskin.

There were some environmental factors which may have led to the lengthening of the childbearing years in the Victorian period. In general, the diet of most people got better and there were enormous improvements in public health from the 1860s onwards. There were also some special circumstances in which fertility in later life may well have been attributable to a better standard of living. Many female convicts sent to Australia and Tasmania, for instance, reportedly got pregnant more readily in their forties as a result of better food and a better climate!

Clutches of children born at the end of the mother's childbearing years could be a source of significant pride – suggesting, amongst other things, the continued health, attractiveness and fertility of the mother. In fact, late motherhood was somehow seen as testimony of the continuing success of the Victorian era itself. Look out in your family tree for the many cases of older women having the last additions to their family at the same time as their eldest daughters were starting families. In August 1887, newspapers reported the calamitous situation of a mother and daughter in Vienna, 'both highly respectable ladies', who had been expecting babies at the same time, 'the mother expecting her last and the daughter her first baby'. When the two boys were delivered at almost exactly the same moment, there was great rejoicing. The babies were passed about for general admiration but then confusion set in. Both children were fine boys and very much alike. It was impossible to work out which one belonged to which mother. In the days long before DNA testing, a newspaper could only lament that 'when these children grow up their lives will be embittered by the unanswerable problem – is my uncle my nephew or my nephew my uncle?' (*Aberdeen Evening Express*, 1 August 1887).

This was an exceptional case but, where mothers were still giving birth when their own daughters were starting families of their own, complicated domestic situations often ensued with children and grandchildren of approximately the same age housed under the same roof. Take care when reading censuses to ensure that you don't mistake youngsters as siblings of each other, when they are, in fact, of different generations. In poor families, babies born late in their mothers' reproductive life were often cared for in practical terms by their elder siblings.

For many women, multiple pregnancies well into middle age were probably a source of dread rather than of pleasure. As well as the usual fears about childbirth, with generally reduced life expectancy, late pregnancy for our female ancestors brought with it the possibility that children might be left motherless whilst still very young. Look out for women who died in their late forties and early fifties leaving behind youngsters who might then have subsequently been brought up by elder siblings or stepmothers. The lives of many women were often foreshortened precisely because they were worn out with childbirth and its attendant hazards. Mary Glynne (Lady Lyttleton) (1813–57), for example, gave birth to four of her twelve children after she turned 40 and died shortly after the birth of her twelfth child at the age of 44.

Some older mothers in the past inevitably gave birth to children with health problems – look out for correlations in the censuses between older mothers and children described as 'imbeciles'. Emma Darwin (1808–96), wife of the naturalist Charles Darwin, gave birth to four of her sons (out of ten children) after the age of 40: Francis at 40, Leonard at 42 and Horace at 43. Her last child Charles Waring Darwin was born when she was 48 in 1856. He unfortunately lived only eighteen months and passed away after succumbing to scarlet fever in the summer of 1858. His sister Henrietta had noticed that he did not have 'the full share of intelligence' and his father commented that he was backward in walking and talking though 'intelligent and observant'. It is now thought that he was probably suffering from Down's syndrome.

The Improving Position of Women

The position of women *vis-à-vis* men was somewhat better at the end of the nineteenth century than it had been at its beginning. Educational provision for middle-class girls now included a fair number of independent boarding and public schools. Working-class girls benefitted from the fact that education for all children up to the age of 10 was made compulsory in England and Wales by the Elementary Education Acts of 1870 and 1880, though females remained at a disadvantage in terms of subjects taught. Some white-collar jobs (such as shop assistants, clerical workers and civil servants) were beginning to open up to our female ancestors by the end of the nineteenth and beginning of the twentieth century and these opportunities swelled with the advent of the First and then the Second World Wars. Unions gave a voice to some of the concerns over the pay and conditions of working-class women as well as men by the end of the nineteenth century.

But it was perhaps in terms of the law that the position of women changed most radically. Through the Married Women's Property Acts of 1870, 1882 and 1893, women gradually gained control of their earnings, property and inheritance after marriage. Their rights to their children in the cases of divorce were secured first by the Custody of Infants Acts 1839 (which allowed them custody of their children under the age of seven in certain circumstances) and then by the Custody of Infants Act of 1873 which gave them access to or custody of children up to the age of 16 (again with certain caveats). The Guardianship of Infants Act of 1886 further stipulated that the welfare of a child had to be taken into account when the custody of a child was being determined – a factor which strengthened the position of mothers over fathers. But it was only in 1925 that married women gained the right to apply for the custody of their children of all ages and only after 1973 that they gained equal, unconditional guardianship rights. The numerous Matrimonial Causes Acts between 1857 and 1937 slowly gave women better access to divorce. To find out more about how any of these Acts might have affected the situation of your female ancestors see them described more fully at www.historyofwomen.org/timeline/html.

As the nineteenth century progressed, motherhood came to be seen more and more as a social responsibility – a duty to the state – as much as a domestic one. More and more, it was deemed that good mothers should devote themselves entirely to their children and not indulge even in part-time work. Many of our middle- and upper-class ancestors combined their domestic role with unpaid philanthropic activities outside the home. Do a keyword search for the names of your female ancestors and discover their associations with local organisations in local newspapers at www.britishnewspaperarchive.co.uk or at www.findmy past.co.uk. In many charitable endeavours, the skills of motherhood – domestic, educational and spiritual – were usefully employed in the public world, but not usually for pay. You may find that your otherwise rather uninteresting great-grandmother sponsored a local mother and baby home or kindergarten, assisted with temperance campaigns, or health and hygiene reform in the local area and carried out District Visiting to poor mothers in the local community. Some middle-class mothers even taught their household management and childcare skills to poorer women, and many others ran Sunday Schools.

Of course, this ideal of the non-working wife and mother was not attainable by many families. Our working-class ancestors who were mothers, even if they are not recorded in the censuses as being in employment, frequently took on part-time or even full-time jobs in mills and factories as well as undertaking other money-making endeavours from home – taking in washing or lodgers, making and selling food, caring for children, laying out the dead, needlework and the like.

So strong was the popular perception of mothers being utterly absorbed in their children, that those of our ancestors who did not fit the usual model were commonly derided and feared in literature and the press. As the nineteenth century drew to an end, for example, the so-called 'New Woman' came on the scene. Freed from the constraints of mid-nineteenth century feminine clothing, she might have worn trousers, ridden a bicycle, smoked cigarettes and was not afraid to voice her opinions in public; such creatures were castigated as putting their fertility at risk and short-changing any children they did have.

Mothers in the Twentieth Century
The mothers in our families had to wait until 1913 (following a successful campaign by the Cooperative Women's Guild and an amendment to the National Insurance Act of 1911) to receive maternity benefits directly from the State, rather than relying on hand-outs from their husbands. Only in 1914, were the first government grants for maternal and child health centres made and not until the First World War in 1918 (with the Maternity and Child Welfare Act) were grants extended to local authorities for maternal health services including ante-natal care. Most of the work in this field was undertaken by volunteers who were able to claim support for the resources they used. As a result, there was an astonishing decline in both maternal and infant mortality in the first three decades of the twentieth century.

The powerful cultural icon of the mother was used both as a means of arguing that women should not have political rights and as a means of proving just how necessary it was for them to have them. After a long struggle, our female ancestors finally gained the vote via the Representation of the People Act of 1918 (though there was still the caveat that they had to be over the age of 30 and to occupy premises to the value of no less than £5 a year). It was not until 1928 with the Representation of the People Act (Equal Franchise) that women over 21 (and with no particular property qualification) could vote on the same terms as men.

Improvements in maternal care continued. By 1938, there were nearly 1,400 prenatal clinics (a rise from just 120 at the end of the First World War). These clinics and services paved the way for the foundation of the National Health Service's maternal and child health division in 1946. Also in the 1940s came the first State-run nurseries which allowed many mothers to be employed in the War Effort. From just 14 of these existing in 1940, there were 1,345 in 1943.

After the Second World War, a combination of improved education, better job opportunities, improved childcare, smaller families, a developing respect for fathers as the carers of children and a completely redefined notion of what it meant to be female and middle class, amongst other factors, meant that more and more women were able to combine motherhood with work, through choice as much as through necessity.

Issue 1: Was my ancestor able to limit the size of her family?
In the nineteenth century, up until the Offences Against the Person Act of 1875, the legal age of consent – that is the age at which a girl might indulge in sexual intercourse without her partner falling foul of the law – was 12 in England. After this it was briefly raised to 13 for just one year. In 1885, the Criminal Law Amendment Act raised the age of consent to 16. The laws were changed in order to tackle the evil of child prostitution. For most of our nineteenth-century female ancestors, however, it is probable that sexual experience first occurred either within marriage or very shortly before it.

Unsurprisingly, with no foolproof method of contraception on offer, our nineteenth-century female ancestors who indulged in sex before marriage were often caught out. Don't be too surprised if there are children in your family born outside wedlock, or within nine months of the marriage. The poor were far more tolerant of illegitimacy than either the middle or upper classes, particularly at the beginning of the century, but an increasing social stigma came to attach itself to illegitimacy. In 1845, 7 per cent of all newborns were illegitimate, but by 1880 these had reduced to fewer than 5 per cent of newborns (figures from Nelson, *Family Ties in Victorian England*, p. 69).

You may have asked yourself why your female ancestor did not take measures to ensure against having an illegitimate child, why the birth spacing between the children in your family was the way it was, or why your family had fewer or more children than those families around them in the census. The question inevitably arises as to whether your ancestors practised any form of family limitation (birth control). As the introduction has made clear, the size of families was dependent to a large extent on a number of factors other than contraception: the age at which your ancestors married, the kinds of employment patterns they had (whether or not women were active in the workplace, for example), their religious background and the general culture of the area in which they lived. In general, fertility and family planning were considered taboo subjects in the nineteenth and early twentieth centuries and men and women hardly ever wrote down their feelings and decisions about these matters in letters, diaries or journals. It is, therefore, very difficult to know exactly what motivated particular families to have fewer children. In the case of your own family however – by knowing something of their circumstances – you may be able to make an educated guess as to why this came about.

Women who wished to limit their family size in the early nineteenth century actually had few methods available to them and those that did exist were notoriously unreliable. In the absence of technical advice, some superstitions about contraception had widespread acceptance right up to the Second World War. One old wives' tale that advised women on how to avoid conception, for example, suggested eating parsley or placing a spring of parsley in the vagina! *Coitus interruptus* (the withdrawal method) was probably widely practised as was prolonged lactation (breastfeeding). Commercial contraceptives included condoms made from vulcanised rubber (after 1843), rubber cervical caps, syringes and soluble pessaries, but none of these appear to have been much used before the start of the First World War. Additionally, in the Victorian period, a vocal moral majority, believed that, if contraception were more readily available, it would encourage sexual immorality and even prostitution. Moreover, it was sometimes suggested that the use of contraceptives might adversely affect women's health, causing illnesses as varied as cancer, sterility and madness.

Some women would have been put off having sex before marriage or even within it by the statistics about women dying in or shortly after childbirth. Giving birth to large numbers of children could, in itself, of course, hasten an early death. But each instance of childbirth was also dangerous because there was always the possibility of mothers catching puerperal fever or other infections and dying. Some early advocators of women's rights advocated barrier methods as a means of freeing women from the burden of yearly childbirth. But feminism is unlikely to have been the main reason for limitation in your family size. Indeed, some late Victorian women with feminist leanings were actually against birth control because they thought it would give free licence to men to indulge their sexual desires.

Towards the end of the Victorian period, spacing between births brought about (probably) by sexual abstinence seems to have been much more intensively practised, and the 1911 census shows that during the Edwardian period, active birth spacing from the start of a marriage was much more common. It became usual for those couples at the top of the social scale (members of the gentry and the professions), followed by those in the middle classes, to have between two and four children rather than the ten or more of previous generations. The decline in fertility took several generations longer to affect the working class, with Catholic families always remaining the exception.

If all else failed and an unwanted pregnancy occurred, abortion was a possibility, albeit an illegal one, for some women both inside and outside marriage. From 1837, the law expressly forbad abortion at any stage (as opposed to only after quickening – or when foetal movement could be felt). This law was only revoked by the Abortion Act of 1967 (operative in England, Scotland and Wales) which allowed abortion up until 28 weeks gestation (the current limit is 24 weeks). However, there is no doubt that many Victorian and early twentieth century pregnancies were deliberately brought to an end. Herbal 'remedies' containing abortifacients such as rat poison, gin and gunpowder were widely advertised in nineteenth-century newspapers as a means of procuring a miscarriage. The language of these adverts remained veiled – tablets claimed, for example, to remove 'the most obstinate obstructions and irregularities of the female system in a few doses' – but it was obvious what they were about.

The pressures to be the perfect mother in the Victorian period were huge and it is common to find in our family history records that many mothers fell through the net. Women's problems were of course exacerbated by the lack of a Welfare State (which started as a series of Liberal Reforms only as late as 1906–1914), and the frequent impossibility of bringing fathers to account. Unmarried mothers could be vilified and ostracised by society. The law, economic and social pressures of the Victorian periods and early nineteenth centuries did not make it easy for women (especially unmarried ones) to support their children and sometimes mothers took the only way out that they knew and committed infanticide.

If an ancestor was arrested for such an offence, the case will appear in court records (located through the records of The National Archives www.nationalarchives.org) and will probably also be reported in local, and possibly, national newspapers, as in the case of a 'girl mother', Harriet Ann Pascoe, aged 14, who was charged at the Cornwall Assizes in March 1878 with the murder of her newly-born illegitimate child. Papers reported that:

> The body of the child, with its skull fractured, was found in a lumber room; but, although there were very suspicious circumstances in the case, a verdict of concealment of birth was returned, and Mr Justice Grove sentenced the girl to two years' imprisonment (*Staffordshire Sentinel*, Stoke on Trent, 28 March 1878).

Harriet Pascoe was lucky: if infanticide had been proved, she would have suffered the consequences as if she had committed a murder – the death penalty. The kind of psychological explanations for infanticide which are sometimes attached to cases today, such as postnatal depression, were simply not known about in the Victorian and Edwardian periods. It was not until 1922 that an Infanticide Act covering England and Wales reduced the sentences of mothers convicted of killing their babies to the same as those given out for manslaughter. A further Infanticide Act of 1938 extended the defence to cases where 'at the time of the act or omission the balance of [the mother's] mind was disturbed by reason of her not having fully recovered from the effect of giving birth to the child or by reason of the effect of lactation consequent upon the birth of the child'.

It was not only the poor amongst our ancestors who fell foul of the perfect ideals of motherhood. Some wealthier women went to enormous lengths to conceal babies born out of wedlock, and others risked prosecution and their own deaths by procuring illegal abortions. Many women suffered postnatal depression and were committed to asylums, and illegitimate babies were sometimes passed over to other women with a fee for their upkeep. In many cases these so-called 'baby-farmers' are unlikely to have treated the infants well. As with all the narratives of family life in the Victorian and Edwardian era, the genteel façade of picture-perfect motherhood hid undercurrents of cruelty and heartache for many of our ancestors.

Whilst the kinds of contraceptives available to women changed relatively slowly over the course of the nineteenth and early twentieth centuries, books and pamphlets about birth control became much more widely available. People knew far more about possible methods of family limitation at the end of the period than they did at the beginning. This was, in part due to the efforts of social reformers such as Annie Besant (1847–1933) and brave members of the publishing world such as editor Charles Bradlaugh (1833–91) (see Image 13). In 1877, the two were prosecuted and charged with publishing material (a book titled *The Fruits of Philosophy* by Charles Knowlton) which advocated birth control and which was thus considered to be depraved and corrupt. In court, Besant and Bradlaugh argued that it was more moral to prevent the conception of children than 'after they are born, to murder them by want of food, air and clothing'.

The case of Annie Besant was widely publicised and even if your ancestors did not read the books, it is reasonably likely that they would have heard about the scandal. After Besant, the issue of birth control became a public one, discussed by all manner of people. The decline in family size from this point onwards may have had something to do with the fact that there was more information on the subject around and more debate about it.

After 1930 latex condoms, caps and diaphragms were used as contraceptives and in the inter-war period large families (even families where a third child arrived a long time after the first two) were even considered embarrassing among many middle-class people. But, it was not until the 1960s and the advent of the contraceptive pill that our female ancestors were really able to control their reproductive life effectively. In most cases, as well as enabling them to postpone their reproductive years, this also meant that they were able to ensure that they did not get pregnant later in life. The result of all this is that a new era was ushered in which the most acceptable years for women's reproduction came to be seen as the late twenties and early thirties.

Issue 2: How did my ancestor experience pregnancy and childbirth?

We have medical textbooks from the past on how to deliver babies and advice books – rather like the self-help books of today – on how to rear children. Neither of these types of historical source can be trusted as accurate accounts of what women actually went through in pregnancy and childbirth; the voices of real mothers, or those about to be mothers are strikingly absent in personal records. On the whole, in the Victorian and Edwardian periods, the bearing of children was considered an illness or a plight, pregnancy was not discussed but rather kept hidden – disguised even in family photographs. Even literature is virtually silent on the subject of childbirth, and diarists and letter writers, even female ones, skip over the painful facts of childbirth. Even in families where diaries were kept, birth was a moment of privacy and silence.

Whilst the joys of motherhood – after delivery – were vividly portrayed in paintings and other media, women's real feelings about childbirth were, of course, more complex. After Queen Victoria's child, Princess Beatrice, was born (the last of nine children born within seventeen years), when Victoria herself was almost 38, she wrote to her eldest daughter, Princess Victoria, who was herself pregnant for the first time, saying that she had always felt 'like a cow or a dog at such moments'. Other women greeted news of another pregnancy with resignation rather than delight. Lilla Howell, great-grandmother of the writer Frances Osborne and subject of her book *Lilla's Feast* (2005) had deliberately bounced on a bed to bring on a miscarriage at the turn of the twentieth century when finding herself pregnant for the second time. On finding herself pregnant yet again, she wrote to her sister-in-law Barbie:

> I wonder if you will be very much surprised to hear that I am in the family way again. Oh dear, dear, poor little me. Such is life – well, it can't be helped and I am trying to make the best of it (Osborne, *Lilla's Feast*, p. 158)

Lilla's remarks were probably prompted more by her fears of the pain and potential dangers of childbirth than by the difficulties of raising a second child. She had seen her sister and sister-in-law nearly lose their lives in childbirth and had lost at least one nephew in infancy by this point.

To find out something definite from the records about our ancestors' real experiences of pregnancy and childbirth we really have to wait until the early years of the twentieth century. In the census of 1911 (the so-called 'Fertility Census'), for the first time, married women were asked how many children had been born alive to them and how many of those children had survived. The disparity in the numbers in some cases can take the breath away. This census also asked for the number of years that a couple had been married – a statistic which was often fudged by respondents to hide cases where children had been born out of wedlock (see Image 14).

To 'hear' real mothers describing their experiences of pregnancy, childbirth and childrearing in the past, you should read the rare and fascinating accounts collected by Mary Llewellyn Davis (1861–1944), General Secretary of the Co-operative Women's Guild, in *No-One But A Woman Knows: Stories of Motherhood Before the War* (1915) and *Maternity: Letters from Working Women* (1915). The accounts make graphic reading, giving a no-holds-barred insight into the experience of motherhood at a time not long after the 1911 census was taken.

Davis collected together short written statements from working-class women (the wives of miners, platelayers and the like) about their experiences of motherhood and family life. The women ended their pieces by recording their husbands' weekly income followed by a tally of how many children they had had, how many miscarriages and how many stillbirths. The statistics make sorry reading: 'Wages 30s; seven children, two miscarriages'; 'Wages 17s 8d; nine children, six miscarriages'; 'Wages about 24s; six children, one still-born, several miscarriages'

One woman who had had six children and one miscarriage within six years recorded:

> In those six years, I never knew what it was to have a proper night's sleep, for if I had not a baby on the breast I was pregnant, and how could you expect children to be healthy, as I always seemed to be tired. If I sat down, I very often fell asleep through the day (Davis, *No-One But a Woman Knows*, pp. 42–3).

One of the main difficulties for our female ancestors when starting a family was a lack of information on anything from contraception and childbirth to feeding and weaning children. There were silences between husbands and wives on matters sexual and gynaecological and even older women in the family were reticent about sharing their experiences. As the anonymous mother already quoted put it:

> I very often ponder over this period of my life. I must not say anything about my mother now, because she is dead, but I cannot help thinking what might have been if she had told me (Davis, *No-One But a Woman Knows*, pp. 43).

For information about the practice of obstetrics at the time your ancestor was born see: http://www.elenagreene.com/childbirth.html. This site shows how the whole business of childbirth changed from century to century including such matters as who might have been present at the birth, the methods of delivery, types of pain relief available and the length of the mother's lying-in period.

A key question to ask yourself about your ancestor's experiences of childbirth is whether it might have been conducted by a doctor or a midwife. Age-old reliance on midwives was gradually overtaken from the end of the eighteenth century onwards by the introduction of male midwives or obstetricians. Male midwifery became the new fashion amongst the rich. If your ancestors were aristocratic or part of the rising middle classes, it is likely that they will have employed a doctor or obstetrician rather than a midwife to deliver their children. The vast majority of women of all classes gave birth at home until the mid-twentieth century, though in some areas, so-called, 'lying-in' hospitals were available for women who needed extra support, such as the wives of soldiers and sailors who might have been away when their children were born (see Image 18).

Alongside the promotion of male midwifery there was often a backlash against female midwives who were considered to be untrained, often drunk and generally too informal. Whilst doctors could use the new technology (i.e. forceps) in the delivery of babies, midwives relied on traditional methods. The result of the intervention of male doctors eventually, of course, was that childbirth moved further and further away from being perceived as a natural function and more towards a procedure that required hospitalisation and surgery. Ironically, whilst doctors might have saved some babies because of their superior medical expertise, it is generally agreed that many new-born babies and mothers who had just given birth died in the nineteenth century because of the spread of puerperal disease carried from the dissecting room to the birthing chamber on the hands of doctors.

Childbirth was a painful and dangerous experience, although chloroform as an anaesthetic was given widespread recognition after Queen Victoria used it in 1853 at the birth of Prince Leopold and in 1857 at the birth of Princess Beatrice. Between 1847 and 1876, five mothers per 1,000 live births died. If your ancestor made it through childbirth, and was in the upper or middle classes, she would have been expected to stay in bed for at least nine days (and in some cases for up to a month or six weeks) after childbirth. Most working-class women would, of course, probably have had to be up and about much earlier. The idea that a natural bond would be forged between a mother and child through breastfeeding was prevalent, and it was commonly believed that a woman's constant attendance on a child thereafter was beneficial. Mothers throughout the Victorian period and beyond weaned their children on 'pap' made from bread or flour mixed with water or milk, though manufactured baby foods appeared for the first time in the 1860s. As a child grew up, the mother's main tasks were to keep her children clean, clothed and fed. In women's magazines and advice books, her role as an educator of very young children and as a spiritual guide to the whole family, but especially the girls, was also emphasised.

In poorer families, older girls would be relied upon to assist their mother in bringing up younger brothers and sisters – a social phenomenon that, in many cases, adversely affected their school attendance and later access to employment. Of course, the higher up the social scale a woman was, the more likely she was to delegate her maternal duties to another woman who would be paid for her services. A 'monthly' or 'lying-in' nurse might arrive a month before the baby was born and would sometimes stay until three months afterwards (see Image 15). The nurse's task was to keep the bedroom clean, wait on the mother and deal with the baby during the night (including taking it to the mother to be breastfed or feeding it herself if it was bottle-fed). As the child grew older there were also often wet nurses (usually working-class women with their own babies, who were paid to breastfeed the child of a wealthy family), nursery maids and governesses.

The very horrors of childbirth and the wonder of surviving it at all contributed to the particular mystique which circulated around mothers in the late nineteenth and early twentieth centuries. If our female ancestors were worn down physically and mentally by their travails, they were also elevated by them to a place of special reverence within the family. The combination was potent, and one which contributed to the growing recognition of women as 'equal to but different from', rather than inferior to, their male counterparts.

CHAPTER 3

'Tiny Strangers': Infants

The youngest children in our family histories, those aged from birth to about three years, are often some of the most fascinating to investigate since they might have given rise to birth, baptism and, all too often, death and burial records within a very short space of time. The very precariousness of the existence of our infant ancestors is intriguing; we cannot but be aware that so many of them did not make it very far along life's path. And those that survived may have done so against terrible odds.

But can the swaddled baby in an old photograph tell us anything about the family from which it came? Is there anything more than the obvious to be gained from infant records? What kind of beliefs about babies and babyhood prevailed when our ancestors were in their tender years? Why might our infant ancestors have been given particular first names? And how can we find out who the godparents of a child were and why might this be important?

Infants in Photographs

In the early days of photography, long exposure times of 35 or more seconds meant that sitters had to keep still for relatively long stretches of time – a feat that couldn't be expected of a baby or a young child. After the discovery of a heat-ripening process for gelatin emulsions in 1878, much shorter exposure times became possible, though it was not until Kodak's introduction of the Box Brownie camera in 1900 (and its later widespread use amongst ordinary people), that snapshots came within the grasp of our ancestors. The new technology, coupled with the fact that photographers increasingly had more experience of how to keep a small child entertained meant that babies and infants were more likely to appear in family photographs – or as the central reason for family photographs – from the beginning of the twentieth century. And the prime position of youngsters in photographs at the turn of the century was not just a matter of practicalities. The end of the nineteenth century witnessed a new interest in the happiness and emotional well-being of the child. In brief, children, even very young ones, became more central to the idea of the family, no longer kept quite so much out of ear- and eyeshot as they had been during the High Victorian period (1860–85). Photographers, however, still particularly dreaded taking group photographs in which a baby or a young child appeared. Whilst those paying for the photograph naturally wanted the child to make a conspicuous point in the photograph, the chances were that the baby would come out as nothing more than 'a minute speck in the group'. This proved an added irritation for photographers, as Henry Peach Robinson succinctly put it, 'It is my experience that few people have any idea how small a baby is until they see it in the centre of a group of grown up persons' (Robinson, *The Studio and What to Do In It*, p. 75).

Look very carefully at old photographs that appear to have been taken of baby alone. As we have said, often mothers (and sometimes fathers), would hide behind curtains, chairs or a table and provide unseen support for the child. Photographers could get irritated with mothers when photographs were being taken and often preferred the assistance of nurses or other servants who more often did as they were told. As Robinson put it 'A nurse who knows her business is the best help you can have. Even she will sometimes want a standing portrait of a ten-month baby, but it is easier to tell the nurse she is an idiot than the mother' (Robinson, *The Studio and What to Do In It*, p. 102) (see Image 16). Some babies started to appear entirely on their own in front of the camera in the 1890s and from this time onwards you might find them in old photographs wrapped appealingly in rugs or fur. Very often photographs in which babies appear were taken to celebrate a christening, for whilst pregnancy and birth were very private experiences for our ancestors, baptisms were times of open and sometimes ostentatious celebration.

If you know from other records the year in which a baby was born, its presence can obviously help to date the photograph. Even more accurate dating may be achieved by guessing how old the baby is. As a rough guide babies who are sitting up are probably over six months old. If they are holding a toy, they might be seven or eight months; few babies can stand before ten months. A further way of dating a photograph from the presence of a baby is to look at his or her clothes. Baby clothes, like all other aspects of fashion in their past, had their own changing history (as is briefly described below). As a rough rule of thumb, however, the more heavily swaddled the baby is, the older the photograph.

The christening gown of Queen Victoria's first child Princess Victoria in 1841 was reported in the papers as having been made from Spitalfields silk with a Honiton lace overlay (the Queen recorded that Victoria junior looked 'very dear' in it) and other families around the nation, of course, copied the design. Christening robes were always white to indicate the innocence of the child before God. In the 1840s they were made from a cotton pique with a plain bodice, long sleeves and a full pleated skirt. Underwear was usually a flannel chemise or vest and cotton drawers. Despite the fact that, from the 1860s, many middle-class homes had their own sewing machine, mothers often chose to hand-sew their own christening robe for the birth of their first child. Princess Victoria's robe went on to be worn by sixty-two other babies in the royal family before being replaced by a similar garment in 2004. And whilst this was exceptional, the principle of passing on a gown to successive generations of a family was commonplace.

By the middle of the nineteenth century, the fine white embroidery known as Ayrshire work was common for baby clothes and, by the end of the century, this could involve elaborately decorated panels with lace and pintucks. Babies wore bonnets, again decorated with white-work embroidery and mothers would have carried them to church wrapped in a shawl. Wealthier families might have wrapped their babies in elaborate carrying capes made from wool or cashmere. The styles of babies clothing to some degree mimicked women's fashions of the time, so if you have an idea about the cut of fashion in a particular decade see if it is replicated in the clothes worn by the infant in your photograph.

Babies in photographs from the 1890s onwards will be less tightly swaddled. As very young babies, they might still wear long clothes but before they were very many months old they might be in smock-shaped dresses that reached only to the ankle. From the 1910s onwards fewer baby clothes were made at home and more were shop-bought. By the 1920s, informal romper suits and short dresses were commonplace on very young children. (See www.pinterest.com/ maklinens/vintage-1920-1940-children-clothing/ for plenty of examples that can be compared with those in your family photographs.)

Take a closer look at the photograph of a family baby. All the paraphernalia that surrounded him or her from prams to nursery furniture, to comforters and toys have their own histories. Whilst contraptions of one sort or another that acted as prams, for example, go back to the eighteenth century, so-called 'baby carriages' were popular among the wealthy only from the mid-nineteenth century. Interestingly, their development went hand-in-hand with the construction of pavements in urban and suburban areas. From the 1880s, mothers and nurses were encouraged to take their children out for a daily walk to expose them to light and air for reasons of health and hygiene. It was not, however, until the 1920s that deeper prams with larger wheels and brakes became more popular than carrying shawls (see Images 17 and 18). And as an example of how changes in fashion moved alongside technological changes, notice how your infant ancestor in the 1920s was probably pictured wearing a matching jacket and bonnet, perfect for being viewed over the top of his pram (see Image 18)!

Infants in the Family
Queen Victoria's two eldest children Princess Victoria (b. 1840) and Prince Albert Edward (b.1841) were born within the first two years of her marriage, the birth of her son being hailed in the press as the first occasion in English history upon which a reigning Queen had given birth to an heir (although technically Princess Victoria had actually held that position for a year before she was superseded). In a country unaccustomed to acquiring new generations of royals so readily, the births were greeted with political relief and popular rejoicing. When

Albert Edward was two weeks old, *The Derby Mercury* (24 November 1841) reported that a royal nursery adjoined his mother's sleeping chamber and that his father often took people to visit him there. The paper went on: 'The general opinion of all who have been admitted to a sight of the Royal infant is that he is a finer child than many healthy children of two months old.'

With the births of the royal babies began the Victorian's love affair with the baby, a phenomenon sometimes referred to as that of 'the cult of the baby'. The births of our own ancestors, for the first time recorded by the State and not just the Church in this period, happened against this background – factors which makes their lives, when foreshortened, somehow seem all the more pathetic.

Births
Your ancestor's birth certificate will obviously give you the date on which your ancestor was born. Birth certificates with exact times of birth may indicate multiple births (see the section on twins in the next chapter). Babies born in Scotland frequently had times of birth noted on their certificates even if they were single births. If your ancestor was the first child in the family, check to see if nine months had passed since the parents' marriage! As has been discussed in the previous chapter, couples, particularly in the rural lower classes, often did not marry until a child was actually on the way.

You can find out more about what was going on in the world, the country and the locality in which your ancestor was born by tapping their date of birth into the internet. To find out which famous people were born at around the same time or which significant events happened at around the time of the birth see www.historyorb.com/. The British Library history timeline gives the key events in art, literature, sciences, medicine, politics and other fields in each decade at www.bl.uk/timeline. Some fun websites (for example, www.paulsadowski.org/BirthDay.asp) can tell you a whole series of fascinating facts about your ancestor's date of birth. A child born on Friday 9 December 1892, for example, is likely to have been conceived on Friday 18 March 1892!

After civil registration began in England and Wales on 1 July 1837, births could be registered by the State. This meant that a registrar was paid actively to collect information on local births. Initially, there was no penalty for non-compliance (though there was a fine for late recording). As a result, about a third of births over the next forty years or so probably went unrecorded by the State, though new arrivals might well appear in parish baptism registers – indeed some parents mistakenly thought that baptism was a legal alternative to the civil registration of birth.

From 1874 onwards, you are more likely to find a certificate for your ancestor's birth. At this point, the onus on registering the birth was placed strictly on the parents or the owner of the house in which the child was born; the birth had to be registered within six weeks (forty-two days) on penalty of a £2 fine. In order to avoid this, parents who had left registering their children late would sometimes falsify the date of birth on a certificate by a matter of a few weeks. For this reason, it's always worth looking at the date of registration on a birth certificate. If it is exactly six weeks from the date of birth, this is perhaps a little too convenient and may suggest that the child was in fact born slightly earlier.

Baptisms
Before civil registration in 1837, the entries of our ancestors into the world were recorded only as baptisms in parish registers. Henceforth, the church records continued alongside the statutory ones. More and more of these Anglican parish records and the baptism records of Catholic churches and Nonconformist chapels are appearing online at the major commercial genealogical websites all the time. If you can't find a record of baptism for a child in the few weeks following the birth, remember that some children were baptised much later on in childhood.

When looking at the baptisms of babies in the parish records or the records of other places of worship, look out for those cases where several children within a family were baptised on the same day. Note also that there was an upsurge in the number of people getting baptised in 1836 and 1837, just before civil registration started. This was due to a mistaken, but popularly held, belief that babies who had not been baptised could not be registered by the State.

With very high rates of infant mortality, many babies died before they had even been baptised. Babies who were taken into the workhouse were baptised within fourteen days of arrival. Their names would be entered into both the workhouse register and the local parish register. The reason for the speed of baptism was that historically so many babies (and infants up to the age of five) died soon after entering the workhouse (even when they were being cared for by their mothers). In the early nineteenth century, many babies in care benefitted from legislation of the late eighteenth century (Hanway's Act, 1767) which made it compulsory for all infants (under the age of six) in parish care (initially in the London area) to be boarded out with a foster mother. In 1788, this was made a national imperative. However, whilst these Acts might have saved the lives of many babies, children were, of course, usually returned to the miseries of the workhouse once they were a little older.

Censuses
The infants in your family will have been included on the decennial censuses. Occasionally, there were babies within a household who had not yet been baptised or whose names had not been decided upon. In these cases, the enumerator might have written 'Baby' or 'Infant' rather than a first name. Be careful when considering the ages of babies as recorded in the census. Often a child under the age of one would be recorded as 'one year' old regardless of how many days, weeks or months old he or she actually was. On the other hand, there are some delightful examples of children recorded as being 'one day' or 'one week' old when the census was taken. Some enumerators were extra conscientious when it came to recording a baby's age entering, for example, '3 ½ months' or '1 ½ years.' Some wrote 'Un 1 yr' (under one year) or the word 'infant' to indicate an age less than twelve months.

Bear in mind that since the censuses were only taken every ten years, children were often born and then died in between censuses, so that their lives are not represented in these records at all. Lancashire millworker Lydia Cook, for example, had had six children by the time the 1871 census was taken but they had all died in infancy and hence she appears to be childless at this point. Only a patient search of all birth and death registrations in that area with her surname in the preceding decade have allowed the brief lives of those six children to come to light at all.

Oral History and Superstitions

Interviews with relatives which feature the arrival of a baby in the family might sometimes include details of superstitious practices that might have occurred at the time of a birth. Some of these practices were regional, but others held national sway. One of the most prevalent in the North and the South was the idea that a child's first movement should be upwards rather than downwards. Mothers and nurses were encouraged to take a child up a flight of stairs on its first journey after its birth – this was to ensure that its progress in life would be upwards. If there was no upstairs above the birthing room, the child might be carried up a pair of steps or even lifted high on a chair. Commenting on the birth of Stanley Baldwin, three times Conservative Prime Minister, at Bewdley, Worcestershire in August, 1867, E. J. D. Radclyffe (*Magic and Mind* [1932]) wrote, 'When Mr Baldwin was born, he was carried all the way upstairs by his nurse: at the top floor, she got a chair and climbed on that, that the baby might rise in life.'

There were other superstitions regarding the first clothes that a baby might wear. Particularly prevalent was the idea that it was bad luck to dress the baby in something new. It should first be wrapped in an old garment. To that end, a midwife might bring an old petticoat with her to the birth. In the Isle of Man, baby boys might be wrapped in some part of a man's clothing and girls in some of the mother's clothing, whilst elsewhere it was deemed lucky for a boy to wear female clothes and a girl male clothes as a first covering. Up and down the country, in Leeds, Lincolnshire, Bridgewater (Somerset) and Ayr, to name just a few places, when newly-born babies were taken to visit relatives for the first time, they were given gifts, commonly eggs, salt or bread as well as matches and silver coins which symbolised food, light and money, some of the main necessities in life.

Stillbirths and Infant Deaths

Sadly, of course, many babies born to our ancestors will have died at,

80

or around, the time of birth. In the past, stillbirths did not have to be reported and, since before 1874 you did not need a certificate to bury a newborn, such babies were often buried informally and without ceremony – the acknowledgement of their existence comes down to us, therefore, only through oral history.

Stillbirths in the nineteenth century were blamed upon a variety of causes from over-tight corsets to the 'intellectuality' of some mothers. The lack of reporting meant that a large number of issues that related to stillborns could not be properly investigated. Were some stillbirths the result of poor maternal health, or in fact infanticides that were covered up? Did they occur more often when doctors or when midwives were officiating at a birth? And how many babies, who actually lived for a few short hours or even days, were considered stillborn and thus lost altogether from history? It is impossible to know the answers to these questions. The compulsory registration of stillbirths began only in 1927 (1939 in Scotland) with the occurrences having to be registered within three weeks, causes of death were added in England and Wales only in 1960 (though from the start in Scotland), stillborn babies could only be named after 1983 and, even now, it is not possible to name them in retrospect.

Death certificates were, of course, correctly demanded for babies who lived for just a matter of hours, weeks or months. These might show a death from a disease such as cholera or smallpox. Check online to see if there was an epidemic of that kind of disease at the time of death (www.sciencemuseum.org.uk/broughttolife/themes/diseases. aspx provides useful information in this respect). There were, for instance, some terrible outbreaks of cholera in 1832 and 1849 and smallpox in 1837 and 1871–2 which claimed the lives of tens of thousands, including many babies.

Remarkably enough, it is actually possible to find out from archival records whether or not your infant ancestor received free vaccination (an aspect of public health policy) paid for by the poor rates. The 1840 Vaccination Act asked that Poor Law Guardians pay doctors to vaccinate every person within their Poor Law Union against smallpox. Babies were to be vaccinated at six weeks old unless they were too ill in which case the vaccination would be postponed. Vaccination officers completed report books or registers of vaccination (now sometimes held in local or county record offices the location of which can be ascertained through the website of the National Archives, www.nationalarchives.org), as well as certificates announcing whether or not a vaccination had been successful or postponed. Many children slipped through the net for one reason or another, but usefully, Boards of Guardians also kept records of which children had not been vaccinated. Vaccination was made compulsory in 1853, but it was still impossible to enforce the law fully. Parents who refused to comply could be fined. Subsequent vaccination laws in 1898 and 1907 made it easier for parents conscientiously to object to vaccinations.

Take note of the causes of death on your infant ancestor's death certificate. These might range from 'marasmus' to 'inanition', 'debility from birth', 'lack of breast milk' or simply 'starvation'. Teething was sometimes recorded as a cause of death, when a more correct explanation was probably poisoning by contaminated milk during the weaning process (see Image 19). Another common reason for infant death in the nineteenth century was the widespread use of narcotics (especially opium) and alcohol to keep babies quiet. Some babies overdosed, but many were simply so sedated that they failed to feed properly.

Thankfully, you will find that more of your ancestors survived infancy in the early years of the twentieth century. Improved public health facilities, vaccination, improvements in medicine and maternal health and the smaller size of families all contributed to an astonishing decline in infant mortality between 1900 and 1930.

Further Records of Babies – Baby Books
Recording the details of a newborn baby – height, weight, footprint, first tooth, first haircut and the like – may seem like a very modern phenomenon – but Baby Books in fact, first came into vogue at the end of the nineteenth century and were very popular by 1970. They might turn up among family papers or in second-hand bookstores. Some may be advertised for sale on-line at bookstores and auction sites such as www.abe.com and www.ebay.com, so it is worth having a quick search for any of the key names in your family (particularly if

they are unusual). The parts of a Baby Book which had to be filled in provided our literate and educated ancestors with a useful and immediate way of recording, categorising and organising their experiences as new parents. Moreover, it would appear that mothers and fathers of a hundred and more years ago had exactly the same desire to make memories concrete as we do today. Baby Books characteristically include places in which to keep material reminders of the baby's development: photographs, locks of hair and even baby teeth. There might also be tables in which the baby's height and weight were recorded every month, a space to draw the shape of the baby's head and places to note the appearance of his or her teeth and to trace his or her hands and feet. In addition, Baby Books often typically contained envelopes for the storage of cards, telegrams, letters and even valentines sent to the child, all of which may include further family history clues.

Titles such as A. O. Kaplan's *Baby's Biography* (1891) and the Reverend Illingworth Woodhouse's *Baby's Record: Mother's Notes About Her Baby* (1895) comprised a list of blank forms in which mothers could record the important details about their child's first years. In the 1920s, a number of prominent women produced a clutch of rather more sophisticated and detailed baby books aimed mainly at the upper classes. The Jewish child welfare reformer Eva Violet Isaacs (Marchioness of Reading), for example, came up with *The Little One's Log* (1927) which was published under her pen name, Eva Erleigh (see Image 20).

Lady Utica Beecham, the first wife of the composer Thomas Beecham (and from the same metropolitan social circle), designed *Our Baby* (1920). It was into a copy of this latter book that Jacqueline Hope-Nicholson mother of 'Charles Felix Otho Victor-Gabriel John Adrian Hope-Nicholson' penned the intimate details of her baby son's life in black ink. Felix, as the child was thankfully more simply known, was born on 21 July 1921 and was the son of William Hedley Kenelm Hope-Nicholson, a Barrister at Law at the Inner Temple. The family lived in Chelsea in a house (34 Tite Street) coincidentally earlier owned by Oscar Wilde. A Wikipedia article on Felix's father placed the family very firmly in the artistic and literary circles of 1920s

London. The Hope-Nicholsons, it seems, separated in 1937 and whilst Felix stayed in England with his mother, his two sisters went to live in France (at Beaulieu) with their father. The very full entries made by Jacqueline Hope-Nicholson in the baby book are explained away perhaps by the fact that she was a keen genealogist who knew what the value of such records would be for future generations.

The pre-printed parts of this Baby Book purported to teach readers the essence of a happy married life and how to be good parents. Lady Beecham instructed mothers on such diverse topics as a mother's thoughts during pregnancy, what she should eat, drink and wear and what entertainments she should allow herself. Further pages are devoted to breast-feeding, how to care for a baby's eyes and mouth, how to ensure it sleeps well, a chart of how and when the milk and permanent teeth grow, how to wash a baby, how to protect its food, the care of bottles, how to treat a number of common ailments such as bronchitis, and diarrhoea, children's clothing, the mother's voice, parental ideals, purity and honour, and education. In the same way as advice books and magazine articles, such extra material in a Baby Book can instantly throw open a window on how babies and babyhood were perceived at the time your ancestor was born.

The sections of the Hope-Nicholson Baby Book which were to be filled in included a startling number of useful genealogical details: the child's name, the year, month and day of the week on which the child was born, the time of birth, the physician's signature and address, the nurse's signature and address, place of birth, father's name, mother's name, father's occupation, father's birthplace, mother's birthplace, mother's name before marriage. Details of the christening included hour, day of the week, month and year, by whom the child was christened, the godfather(s) and godmother(s), the place of christening, names of siblings, date of Holy Confirmation, date of Holy Communion, date of Holy Matrimony, and addresses of 'Winter and Summer homes'.

There is also a miscellany of other information about baby Felix which is not strictly relevant in genealogical terms, but which nevertheless help to build up a picture of this immensely privileged child and his life. These include: The baby's symbols (i.e. its flower, birthstone, colour and zodiac sign), dates of incidents such as baby's first laugh, first step, first words, and 'pretty sayings', a record of 'baby's ailments', 'Baby's first prayer', 'Presents and birthdays' and 'Journeys made'. 'The book also gives handwritten dates of events much later in the child's life such as holy communion and marriage which might, if followed up, produce many different family history leads to other records and sources.

Filling in a Baby Book was primarily the task of the mother but other members of a family might also have added details. Indeed, it was common for a child himself to add information to his Baby Book in retrospect once he had grown up. In this way, Baby Books – unlike virtually any other source, except family bibles – are real family narratives. It's important to be aware that many hands might have been at work within them and that they might have recorded information with varying degrees of accuracy. You can learn something about the family into which the baby was born simply by noticing which sections of the baby book have been most consistently filled in, the health of the child or his physical and moral progress; his relationship with his parents; or his social engagements and holidays. Additionally, look out for entries that are not necessarily strictly factual, but which tell you something about the way the writer saw the world, for example in Felix's book, a 'Place of Birth' section reading, 'Mamma's blue and gold bedroom at More House, 34 Tite Street, Chelsea', puts a rather rosy romantic, not to mention aristocratic glow on the child's entry into the world reminding us that baby books are in some ways 'idealised biographies'.

Issue 1: Where did baby's name come from?
Unless your ancestors came from a culture other than Christian, they will probably have chosen first names for the babies in their family based not on their meaning but because they commemorated someone else in the family or because the name had appealing 'ornamental' properties (see Image 21).

Here are some strategies for finding out more:

• Begin by considering the sound and spelling of the name. Since the academic credentials of nineteenth-century census enumerators were not always what they might have been, spellings of names can be very sloppy. Saying a name out loud might produce some surprises. Thus, the apparently very unusual girl's name 'Felis' for example, recorded in the 1841 census for a child in Henstridge, Somerset, was actually a misspelling of 'Phillis' or 'Phyllis'. Likewise, the Lancashire girl's name 'Suranne' on a nineteenth-century census turned out to be a conflation of two baptismal names 'Sarah' and 'Anne' when the birth certificate was discovered.

• Some families were systematic in naming their children. A common pattern, for example, in England between 1700 and 1850 was to name baby boys in the following manner. The eldest would be named after the father's father, the second after the mother's father, the third after the father and the fourth after the father's eldest brother. If it's not immediately obvious where a child's name comes from, consider that he or she might have been named after a deceased great-grandparent (particularly if all the grandparents were still alive at the birth of the child). In one of several traditional Scottish naming patterns, the seventh to the tenth sons were named for the father's great-grandfathers. The tenth to the fourteenth sons were named for the mother's great-grandfathers. The seventh to the tenth daughters were named for the mother's great-grandmothers and the tenth to the fourteenth daughters were named for the father's great-grandmothers!

• Other unusual choices might turn out to have a family connection. Surnames were commonly recycled as first names or a mother's maiden name might be inserted as a child's middle name. This applied to both boys and girls. Richard Lovell Edgeworth (1744–1817), the nineteenth-century Anglo-Irish politician, writer and inventor, was so-called because his mother Jane's maiden name had been Lovell. He went on to use 'Lovell' as a first name for one of his sons (Lovell Edgeworth b. 1775).

• At other times, babies might have been named, not because of a family connection but because the names were familiar to the family from sermons in church or other cultural activity. Girls' names 'Mary' and 'Martha' are obvious examples, but 'Judith', 'Jemimah', 'Tabitha', 'Esther' and 'Zillah' also all come from the Bible. And for boys, whilst 'Joseph', 'John' and 'Paul' leap out as Biblically-inspired, you might need to do a bit more reading to locate 'Nathan', 'Obadiah' and 'Jabez'. Family history was often recorded by hand in the opening pages of the family bible, and it's not surprising, therefore that it was the source of many unusual names even in relatively uneducated families. Names of babies at the upper end of the social scale might be the result of a parent's (usually a father's) classical education. Popular examples of such names in the nineteenth century were 'Alexander' after Alexander III (the Great); and 'Roxana' after his wife.

• But, as we all know, very often, in family history research a name crops up that seems to make no sense at all. Such names went in and out of fashion much as they do today. Try typing the unusual name into the search box for English and Welsh Birth Indexes available at www.ancestry.co.uk or for Scottish Birth indexes at www.scotlandspeople.gov.uk. These indexes list the names of children born from the start of civil registration in 1837 to the present day. You can limit the search to a year or span of years and then compare the results for other periods. (NB: You can't do this analysis on some other of the BMD sites because these require you to input a surname as well.)

To take an example, such a search for the unusual boys' name 'Ezekiel' or 'Ezekial' shows that this was a first or middle name for just over 1,000 boys in 1845, but in 1900, as many as 18,000 boys were given that name. Even allowing for the growing population over the course of the nineteenth century, this it is quite an increase. To be called 'Ezekiel' at the end of the nineteenth century, it seems, was far more common than in the middle of the century.

Once you have some statistics like this to hand, you can make some educated guesses about why this situation had come about. One explanation for this example is that Ezekiel was a popular Jewish name. There were many more Jews living in Britain by the end of the nineteenth century than there were at its middle. Since the name 'Ezekiel' seems to crop up most often as a second or third name, it is reasonable to assume that it was the Hebrew name of many Jewish babies who also had a secular, English first name.

• A general search for your ancestor's unusual first name on www.ancestry.co.uk will show you how many people had that first name in a much wider collection of records (birth, marriage and death, censuses, military records, parish records and many others) at particular periods in history. These kinds of searches will give you a general feel for just how common your ancestor's first name (or combination of first names) actually was. It may turn out that the name is nowhere near as unusual as you at first thought! Alternatively, such a search may also show you that a particular name was common in a particular part of the country at a certain time.

• Try simply tapping your ancestor's first name into a search engine such as Google. This might show you that the name in question was popular at a particular time because it was the name of a member of the Royal Family, a literary character, a celebrity or national hero, a significant place, battle, or other term that captured something in the air at the time of the birth.

• There are plenty of places on the internet where you can quickly find out when historical events took place to back up a hunch about the origins of your ancestor's first name. If, for instance, your ancestor had the rather striking first or middle name 'Jubilee', you might assume that he or she was born in one of the two years when Queen Victoria was celebrating her lengthy sojourn on the throne, either 1887, her Golden Jubilee, or 1897, her Diamond Jubilee. The birth indexes confirm that more than 400,000 children born in one of those two years rejoiced in the first or middle name 'Jubilee'. Likewise many girls were called 'Adelaide' after the founding of the Southern Australian town of that name in 1836.

• To the same end, type your ancestor's unusual first name into the keyword search box of the British Newspaper Archive available at www.britishnewspaperarchive.co.uk or www.findmypast.co.uk. Look specifically for references to the name that occurred near in time to your ancestor's birth. For example, if your ancestor was named 'Alexandra' and was born in the 1860s, you will note that there are many references in contemporary newspapers to the marriage of the Danish Princess Alexandra and the Prince of Wales in 1863. Going back to the birth indexes, you will see that before this time, the name Alexandra was clocking up about 20,000 girls in England and Wales every year. But in 1865, the number had more than quadrupled to over 85,000!

• Several fads or crazes characterised the naming of babies from the mid-nineteenth century onwards. For example, the 1850s saw a new English interest in Scotland and Scots names for babies became more popular. Helping the trend along was Queen Victoria – a great lover of Scotland – who chose 'Duncan' (previously not a popular name for English boys) as a third name for her eighth child and fourth son Leopold in 1853. The Celtic revival of the late nineteenth and early twentieth centuries brought in a wave of Welsh names for English babies including 'Alan' and 'Cary' for boys and 'Bronwyn', 'Bethan' and 'Cecilia' for girls. Mediaeval names such as 'Albin', 'Bayard' and 'Bertram' were popular due to the artistic movement known as the Pre-Raphaelites from 1848 onwards. 'Albert', though a popular name in Britain in the medieval period, had fallen out of favour by the nineteenth century. Queen Victoria, of course, married an Albert and her eldest son was christened 'Albert Edward'. Both names immediately became very popular. The girls' names 'Alberta' and 'Edmunda' also made an appearance in this period.

• Our ancestors were occasionally moved to name their offspring after those in the public eye. Military men were a good source of inspiration. Many boys in the nineteenth century, for instance, were named 'Arthur' after Arthur

Wellesley, Duke of Wellington (1769–1852), victor of the Battle of Waterloo and later Prime Minister. The arts were another good source of names amongst our educated and metropolitan ancestors. 'Giselle', for example, became popular after the ballet of that name which was first performed in London in 1842. Check out also the names of famous nineteenth-century British actors and actresses online. Later in the 1910s and 1920s movie stars such as Hilda Bayley and Constance Benson provided more inspiration. Writers and the heroes and heroines of novels were also a source of names amongst the literate classes. 'Gwyneth', for example, became popular in the late Victorian period after the pseudonymous writer Gwyneth Vaughan (1852–1910) whose real name was Annie Harriet Hughes.

• The end of the nineteenth century saw an upsurge in girls named after flowers. Obvious ones such as 'Iris', 'Rose', 'Lily' or 'Lillian', 'Daisy' and 'Violet' perhaps need no further explanation than that they were gentle on the ear, but what about 'Myrtle', 'Oleander' or 'Petunia'? Check out a Victorian flower dictionary online to see if your ancestor's more unusual flower name is recorded and explained.

• Another avenue of research on unusual Christian names might be a world map or gazetteer. Some babies were given the names of the places in which they were born or with which their family had particular associations. Founder of modern nursing Florence Nightingale (1820–1910) was so called because she was born in the city of Florence, Italy. Her older sister Frances Parthenope (b. 1819) had been born at Parthenopolis, a Greek settlement near Naples. On the 1901 census there are 170 women with the name 'Christiania' (rather than Christina). This was, of course, the old name for Oslo, capital of Norway, a popular turn-of-the-century holiday destination!

• Other children were named after friends of the family. It is worth checking out marriage certificates for the names of the witnesses (sometimes good family friends who later became godparents to children of the union). The suffragette Nellie

(Emmeline) Hall, for example, born in 1895 in Eccles, Lancashire was named after her godmother, the much better-known political activist Emmeline Pankhurst (1858–1928). Finally, don't forget to scan the censuses for the names of your ancestors' neighbours. You never know – the source of an unusual first name might just have been living next door!

• There was a common superstition – of long standing – that a child, or at least the first child born to a couple, should not be named after a living parent. There was also great resistance to the idea of naming a baby after one which had already died. Having said this, there are, of course, numerous examples of both of these 'dangerous' naming practices in many of our family trees. As one contributor to *Notes and Queries* in 1888 (7th ser.VI 498) put it, 'There was a very common feeling in the eastern counties against naming children after brothers and sisters . . . who had previously died. My father was the third of his name in the family, and it was considered a proof of strong-mindedness in his parents going against the superstition.' For information on the naming of twins, see Chapter 4.

Issue 2: How might I find my ancestor's godparents?

If your ancestor's family was Anglican, Catholic or Orthodox Christian, the chances are that any babies born to them will have had nominated godparents. Nonconformist ancestors such as Methodists and Unitarians, on the other hand, considered the presence of a godparent as optional at baptisms. Baptists (and other religions which practised the baptism of adults rather than babies) did not require godparents to be present at baby-naming ceremonies. Jewish ancestors did not have godparents in the sense of spiritual guardians, though a Jewish family may have appointed friends of the family to be present when a child was named and when a boy was circumcised.

Traditionally, babies baptised in the Church of England have had three godparents, two of whom are the same sex as the child. Babies baptised in the Roman Catholic faith in the last 200 years have been required to have only one godparent, but more often have had two, one of each sex.

Godparents – or 'sponsors' (from the Latin for 'guarantor') as they have sometimes been known – were the spiritual guardians of children. As a minimum, they were expected to attend baptism ceremonies and to be involved in the religious life of a child. The godparent of a baby in your family might turn out to be quite unexpected – 'the Earl of Carnarvon was my grandmother's godfather' writes one contributor to Ancestry's message boards and goes on to ask eagerly how she might verify this fact and find out why such an august chap was chosen. Godparents were important; indeed, their actions and advice might have played a significant and long-lasting role in an ancestor's upbringing. If they were not already related to the parents, they might have come to seem like family with bonds of trust and affection developing between the different parties in ways very similar to family relationships.

Even if you are sure that the baby in your family had godparents, it may be difficult to find out who they actually were. Entries of baptism in parish registers did not usually require the names of godparents and neither did the birth certificates that replicated that information after the start of civil registration in 1837. Bear in mind that in Anglican churches, the parents of a child might also have been appointed as its godparents. This practice was barred in the Roman Catholic Church and in the churches of some other branches of Protestantism.

The names of a baby's godparents might be recorded on baptismal certificates which occasionally turn up amongst family papers. Alternatively, they might appear in family bibles, newspaper obituaries (of prominent people) and private documents such as letters and diaries. Godparents may additionally turn up in wills and other family papers as kindly benefactors and occasional guardians (though their role was never legal). Sentimental personal records of a baby's life such as Baby Books may be frustratingly non-specific over details such as the names of godparents. In our earlier-mentioned example, from the 1920s, the entry is tantalisingly vague – 'Those present at the christening – His parents, Grandparents, 4 of his Godparents, 5 great Aunts, 4 cousins and 10 friends, besides, of course, Lauretta and Nannie' (see Image 22). Occasionally the names of godparents will be inscribed on christening gifts which may have been passed down as family heirlooms. Godparents' names are additionally one of the pieces of family information that are frequently passed down in oral history, so don't forget to quiz elderly relatives about who these people might have been.

Whilst the godparents of today are very often friends of the family, in the past they were more likely to be close relations of the child by blood or marriage. Where this is the case, finding out who your ancestors' godparents were might turn out to be entirely the same quest as discovering a new branch of the family tree. Grandparents, aunts and uncles were all drafted in, sometimes several times over if there were a lot of children in the family. It is interesting to note that godparents were so much considered to be part of the family in some sections of earlier communities that they were forbidden by Catholic Church Law to have sexual relations with the parent of the child, or with the child him or herself (even if they were not actually related by blood) at the risk of committing incest! Indeed, the Catholic prohibition that prevented a godfather and a goddaughter having a sexual relationship only ended in 1983.

Although parents were free to choose whomsoever they liked to be the godparents of their children (providing these people had been baptised and brought up in the same faith), in practice some patterns emerge. Typically, the godparents of the first child might be the paternal grandfather and the maternal grandmother. The second child's godparents might then be the maternal grandfather and the paternal grandmother. Subsequent children often had godparents who were the parents' brothers and brothers-in-law, or sisters and sisters-in-law with a balance being kept between paternal and maternal lines. It was also common practice for older brothers and sisters to be made the godparents of younger children (in the Catholic Church there is currently a stipulation that godparents need to be at least fourteen years older than their godchildren).

Whether relatives or friends, the godparents of the baby in your family, in some cases, might have been very same people whose names are recorded as witnesses on your ancestors' marriage certificates. After all, many babies were born within the first year of marriage when family loyalties would have remained much the same as at the time of the wedding. It's also possible that if the baby's parents were godparents to another child in the family, then that child's parents might have been asked to be godparents to your ancestor. In close-knit but extended families, this kind of reciprocity of role was common.

Another clue to a baby's godparent might be his or her first or middle name. This practice could cut across gender lines. Queen Victoria's actual first name, for example, was 'Alexandrina' after one of her male godparents, the Emperor Alexander of Russia. Be aware in such cases that there might have been good reason why a parent chose to name a child after his or her godparent. Historical analysis of sixteenth-century wills has proved that godchildren who were named after their godparents were more likely to inherit their money than godchildren with other names!

Florence Nightingale was a popular choice as a godparent among her friends and family and several of her female godchildren were named after her. They included: Florence Ellen Monckton Milnes (daughter of a favourite suitor); Florence Paget (daughter of the Marquess of Anglesey); Florence Stewart McAlister (granddaughter of her good friend and collaborator Sir John McNeill); and (family member) Florence Nightingale Shore. The last of these sought to emulate her famous godmother by pursuing a career in nursing. A letter that Shore wrote to Nightingale states her desire 'to become a hospital nurse, probably inspired by your kind interest in being my godmother', and her 'ultimate hopes to become an Army nurse as you were'.

In other cases, godparents were drawn from a family's social network. The practice of asking well-connected friends to be the godparents of one's children was common in the mid-nineteenth century. Frederick Foster Hervey Quin, an aristocratic wit and raconteur, who founded the original London Homeopathic Hospital in Golden Square, Soho, in 1849 was godfather to one of Dickens's children. Another child, Walter, was the godchild of Dr John Elliotson, the prominent mesmerist, whom Dickens knew personally.

The chief role of godparents was religious. They were appointed primarily to guide a child through from baptism to adulthood in the

Christian faith. In the first instance, godparents played a key role in baptismal ceremonies with one of the godmothers often carrying the baby up the aisle ahead of the parents and holding it whilst it was named. At the baptismal font, the child's godfather(s) would traditionally stand to the right of the child and the godmother(s) to the left. A godparent might be expected to pray regularly for the child, to ensure that he or she attended church and Sunday school and had a bible. Godparents might also be expected to provide spiritual gifts on a child's birthday or the anniversary of his or her baptism. Their role was to continue until the child married. The spiritual relationship was reciprocal with the godparent opening up the possibility of eternal life to the godchild, and the godchild, by demonstrating his own virtuous life, finding favour for the godparents' souls in heaven.

A second role for the godparent was emotional. Godparents were in a sense considered to be the parents of a child's 'second birth' or baptism. The idea was that for a child to be 'reborn', he or she required new parents; and it was hoped that the godparents would pass on to the child some of their own personal qualities, just as parents did. Correspondingly, the godchild was expected to show respect for the godparent as he or she grew up.

You may discover that a godparent took care of one of the children in your family, or made his or her godchild a beneficiary of his will, but he or she had no legal obligation whatsoever to do so. A godparent would not even have been required by law to step into the breach if a child's parents had died. Fathers were responsible for their children's upbringing. If they died or became absent then it was the duty of the parish to care for the child. Mothers only acquired full and equal legal rights of access to a child from 1925, although many mothers, of course, took over when a father disappeared at earlier dates than that. Additionally, in the nineteenth and twentieth centuries, as today, parents often nominated legal guardians (who might have been people very different from the godparents of a child); or the child would be brought up by another family member in the case of parental death.

Finally, and importantly for family history, godparents were also gift-givers. From the mid-nineteenth century onwards presents might have included coins, medals or crosses, silverware including cups or porringers (small shallow bowls); and tooth cutters or rattles combining coral and bells. Many godparents would also have given a gift of money. According to the detailed list recorded by his mother in his baby book, 1920s well-to-do baby Felix Hope-Nicholson received at his christening '2 silver mugs, a gold seal, 2 silver knives, forks and spoons, an ivory bauble, 2 medals, a gold safety pin, 2 gold spoons, a set of gold comfit implements, 3 silver spoons, 2 silver napkin rings, 2 silver and mother of pearl spoons and forks, a crawling rug, Romney suit etc etc.' Such a list of christening presents amongst your family papers will give you an idea of the status of the social circles in which your ancestor moved. It might also explain the origins of some of your family heirlooms.

1. The wedding of Jack Symes and Alice Gillings, Clifton, York, 1927. From left to right, back row: Charles Avison (groom's brother-in-law), Phyllis Avison (groom's sister), Jack Symes (groom), Emmie Mayo (groom's sister), Joe Mayo (Groom's brother-in-law). Front row: Marjorie Avison (groom's niece), Elizabeth Symes (groom's mother), Alice Gillings (bride), Jenny Winstanley (groom's sister), Elsie Winstanley (groom's niece). In an added – but far from unusual – double connection, Charles Avison was also a first cousin of the bride. (Author's collection)

2. This young Edwardian father stands protectively behind his wife and child. In many photographs of married couples, men and women stood apart. Any touching shown usually indicated belonging or possession rather than romance or sexual attraction. (Author's collection)

"A CURLY HEAD WAS PRESSED CLOSE TO HIS."

3. 'Daddy time': from the mid-nineteenth century, many middle-class fathers spent far more time away from home than they had done in earlier generations. (*The Girl's Own Paper,* 9 April 1892)

Papa. " ALAS ! I CANNOT TELL HOW DEEPLY IT PAINS ME TO FIND THIS *Blasé* AIR OF INDIFFERENCE—THIS ICY, HEARTLESS DISDAIN, IN ONE SO YOUNG—SO FAIR ! NOR ARE YOU THE ONLY PERSON IN WHOM I HAVE PERCEIVED THESE SYMPTOMS ! THEY ARE RAPIDLY BECOMING THE FASHION OF THE DAY ! "
[*Papa is not mad, but has been left a few moments in charge of his baby, and is learning his part in a piece for a private performance.*

4. The Victorian father in this *Punch* cartoon has been left alone for a few minutes in charge of his baby. With no understanding of what is required, he spends the time rehearsing his part in a play, much to the perturbation of the watching servant. (*Punch or the London Charivari*, 15 January 1870)

5. The precocious child in this postcard speculates on how his father is faring in the First World War. (Author's collection)

6. With many men serving away from home during the First World War, relationships with children could be sporadic and uncertain. (Author's collection)

Chapter 1

CERTIFIED COPY of an   ENTRY OF BIRTH
Pursuant to the Births and   Deaths Registration Act 1953

Registration District   Yeovil

1855.   Birth in the Sub-district of   Martock   in the   County of Somerset

No.	When and where born	Name, if any	Sex	Name, and surname of father	Name, surname and maiden surname of mother	Occupation of father	Signature, description, and residence of informant	When registered	Signature of registrar	Name after
160	Eighteenth March 1855 Ash Martock	William	Boy	—	Emma Symes	—	X The mark of Emma Symes Mother Ash, Martock	Twenty Eighth April 1855	George Stuckey Registrar.	

Certified to be a true copy of an entry in a register in my custody.

Superintende[...]

7. The birth certificate of a boy named William in 1855. No father is recorded. On the 1861 census he appears to be named 'William Hurst' but in subsequent censuses and for the rest of his life generally he used his mother's surname 'Symes', claiming on his marriage certificate of 1884 that his father was one 'William Symes'. His real paternity remains a mystery. (Author's collection)

8. 'My father's eyes had closed upon the light of the world six months, when mine opened upon it.' Charles's Dickens's fictional character David Copperfield was a posthumous child; his fatherless situation acting as a catalyst for his further adventures. (Wikimedia Commons. From Charles Dickens, *The Personal History of David Copperfield* [Toronto: Musson Book Co., 1910], pp. 160–1)

9. A young woman of the Edwardian era, Ellen (from the Roughley or Stringfellow family) pictured showing her engagement ring to best advantage. (The Wigan World Website www.wiganworld.co.uk)

10. Mother's Joy: an Edwardian hand-tinted postcard showcasing the maternal bond at the heart of the domestic ideal. The mother is possibly an actress, and if so, the domestic set-up suggested by the child, goes some way to redeeming her dangerous association with the theatre. (Author's collection)

11. 'I was conducted to the nursery door': at the height of the Victorian period, middle- and upper-class mothers delegated some aspects of their maternal role to hired nannies and governesses. ('The True Story of a Nursery Governess', *The Girl's Own Paper* Vol VII, No 301 [3 October 1885])

12. The Victorian poet Elizabeth Barrett Browning with son 'Pen' (Robert Wiedemann Barrett Browning), her first and only child, born when she was 43. (Wikimedia commons. Courtesy of Eton College. Published 1860)

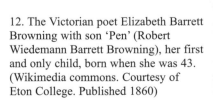

13. Victorian reformer Annie Besant (1847–1933), who published material on family limitation (contraception), was vilified and accused by *The Times* of writing an indecent, 'lewd, filthy, bawdy and obscene book'. (Frontispiece to Charlotte Despard, *Theosophy and the Woman's Movement* [Theosophical Publishing, 1913])

14. The pathos of statistics: Lancashire publican, Lydia Hilton, recorded that she had had fourteen live births on the 1911 (so-called 'Fertility') census, that she had lost ten and that only four of the babies had survived. (www.findmypast.co.uk)

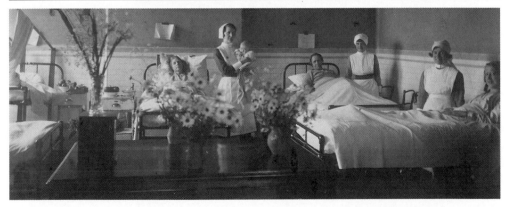

15. Although most mothers gave birth at home, there was sometimes the option of using a lying-in hospital. These institutions were renowned for being less safe than home because of the proximity of many other women in childbirth and the movement between them of the medical people who could pass on the deadly puerperal fever (only properly recognised as a contagious disease from the late 1840s). This unknown lying-in hospital of (probably) the 1930s was probably much safer than its Victorian predecessors. (Author's collection)

17. Young child in a pram, photographed by James Milne, Portrait and Landscape Photographer, St Ruth's, Arbroath, 1870s. The three wheels on this pram would have allowed it to circumvent byelaws which prevented four-wheeled vehicles using the pavements in some places. Such prams were common in middle-class families in the 1860s and 1870s. (Author's collection)

16. Babies in old photographs were often held by their mothers or by a nurse. When they were old enough to sit up alone, they might be tied around the waist to the back of a chair with a sash. (Author's collection)

18. The deep shape of this pram with its small wheels gives away the date (1944) of this photograph of a young child watching calves at Sevenoaks Cattle Market in Kent. Affordable, practical prams such as this one gave mothers across the social scale more mobility from the Second World War onwards. (Wikimedia Commons)

19. From 1908, Glaxo milk powder was being marketed in Britain as a substitute for mother's milk under the slogan, 'The Food That Builds Bonnie Babies.' This advert from *The Daily Mirror* of 25 November 1914 shows that it was rapidly becoming popular, despite some reservations about its efficacy: some babies were dying after being bottle-fed due to the lack of understanding about the need to sterilize bottles between feeds. (*The Daily Mirror*, 25 November 1914, www.britishnewspaperarchive.co.uk)

20. A sanitised representation of how babies came into the world graces the frontispiece of an upmarket baby book in the 1920s, *The Little One's Log, Baby's Record* (1927). (Eva Erleigh, *The Little One's Log: Baby's Record*, Illustrated by Ernest H. Shepard. Partridge [1927, 2nd impress, 1929]).

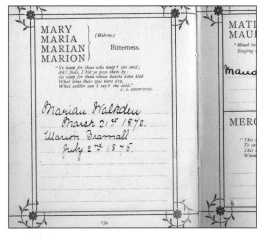

21. Victorian 'Birthday Books' like this one aimed to give parents a little more information about potential names for their children. (Anon, *Christian Names and What They Mean* [Marcus Ward and Co. 1885])

22. The entries in this baby book from the 1920s are not very helpful in that they don't actually name the godparents of the child, though they do tell us about other family members present at the christening. But the list of presents is fascinating and confirms the upper middle-class status of this child, Charles Felix Otho Victor Gabriel John Hope-Nicholson. (Lady Beecham, *Our Baby: A Mother's Companion and Record* [London: Leopold E. Hill, 1920])

23. A protective big sister places her arm just behind her brother to steady him, c. 1910s. The chunky knitwear on the little boy was a new fashion for the times, as were the shorter socks. The girl's dress is definitely in an age-appropriate style rather than a shorter version of a woman's clothing, but it is plain, indicative perhaps of wartime austerity. The ribbons are a bright touch common to the era. (Author's collection)

24. Three sisters in an unknown Edwardian family. The importance of having a male heir meant that many couples continued to produce children until a boy finally arrived – hence the large number of families with a top-heavy female contingent. (Author's collection)

25. Family of five paddling during the 1910s. The popular interest and delight in childhood went hand-in-hand with the development of seaside resorts and affordable seaside holidays. (Author's collection)

LITTLE JIM. 5.

The cottage door was open'd,
The collier's step was heard;
The mother and the father met,
Yet neither spake a word!

He knew that all was over—
He knew his child was dead;
He took the candle in his hand,
And walk'd towards the bed.

26. This hand-tinted postcard depicts a collier and his wife at the bedside of their dead child. Undated, (c.1900–30). So many children died in the nineteenth and early twentieth centuries, that it is very likely that any ancestor who survived to adulthood would have witnessed the death of one or more siblings in infancy. **(**Author's collection)

"AS THEY GATHERED ALL ROUND HER."

27. Older girls learnt to mother their younger siblings as families got bigger and bigger. ('As they all gathered round her', picture to story 'Courtleroy' by Anne Beale, *The Girl's Own Paper*, 6 February 1886)

Everybody's Loved by Someone.

"Everybody's loved by someone.
Everybody knows that's true,
Some have father and mother dear,
Sister and brother, too ;
All the time that I remember,
Since I was a mite so small,
I seem to be the only one
That nobody loves at all."

28. The importance of family or the lack of it was an ever-present matter of popular interest. Postcard sent from 'D and B' in Ulverston to Miss E. Thompson, Dalton-in-Furness, 1905. (Author's collection)

29. 'Those Troublesome Twins': twins in the family are always a source of fascination for the family historian, bringing to the fore issues of competition, rivalry, separation and loss. (*The Girls' Own Paper,* Vol IX, No 411, 12 November 1887)

30. The marriage of Ada Terrell and John Pickles, Manchester, 1928, showing the extended Terrell and Pickles families. The knee-length dresses of the bridal party (short but not as short as they had been earlier in the decade) together with the mob-cap type headdresses are typical of the year, as are the long trails of green foliage in the bridal bouquets. (Author's collection)

31. A birthday postcard sent between adult brothers, 'Frank' and 'Ernest,' during the First World War (in fact New Year's Day 1916): message reads: 'Wishing You Many Happy Returns Of The Day.' (Author's collection)

32. A brisk and frequent postal service in the early twentieth century ensured that fond aunts had no excuse for being out of touch with favourite nephews on important occasions. This card reads: To Master V. Sheppard, 35, Travers Road, Southgate, N14. 'Dear Little Vickie, Just a little card to wish you many happy returns of the day. With fondest love from Auntie Doll, Finsbury Park, 19th March, 1929'. (Author's collection)

33. These three young ladies (Marjorie Avison, Elsie Winstanley and Olive Gillings), pictured here in York in the 1920s twirling Japanese-style parasols, were all only children. Marjorie and Elsie were first cousins and Olive was an uncle's niece though marriage (and, therefore, an honorary cousin). Having got together at the marriage of the uncle (at which they were all bridesmaids), they remained closely in touch until they were elderly despite living as far apart as Manchester, Bognor Regis and Guildford. (Author's collection)

34. Silverpoint drawing of Edith Holman Hunt, by her husband. Due to the Marriage Act of 1835 (which forbad a man from marrying his deceased wife's sister in the UK) the union of the artist William Holman Hunt and Edith (Waugh) in 1873 had to take place in Switzerland. Holman Hunt had previously been married to Edith's sister Fanny. On the marriage, Edith's nephew, Cyril Benoni Hunt, also became her stepson. The couple faced strong opposition from both family and friends. (Birmingham Museum of Art, Wikimedia Commons)

35. & 36. First cousins the naturalist Charles Darwin (1809–82) and Emma (née Wedgwood) (1808–96) who married in January 1839. (Watercolours by George Richmond, 1830s and 1840. Wikimedia Commons)

37. In 1890, the Photographic Society of Geneva agreed with prominent physiognamists 'that we come to resemble those amongst whom we live by unconscious imitation of the expression of their features.' In a study of seventy-eight old couples and as many adult brothers and sisters, twenty-four of the former apparently resembled each other much more strongly than the latter. (Author's collection)

39. Changing times: this *Punch* cartoon from 1870 shows how the young were increasingly being portrayed as disrespectful towards the old. (*Punch or the London Charivari*, 18 June 1870)

38. 'The Green Leaf and the Sere'. Many Victorian paintings put elderly people on the periphery of the canvas, or situated in forests or remote countryside as if to emphasise their marginalisation from modern society. Writers and artists also used the supernatural, the gothic, witches and madness as methods of portraying the aged. (From the picture by M. Ellen Edwards, frontispiece of *The Girl's Own Annual*, 1887–8, The Leisure Hour Office, 1888)

40. Design of a workhouse for 300 paupers by the architect Sampson Kempthorne (1809–73) who designed workhouses in Abingdon, Andover, Bath, Crediton, Hastings and Newhaven. Men and women were clearly segregated as were boys, girls and the infirm. (Wikimedia Commons, from the *Annual Report of the Poor Law Commissioners* [1835], p. 412)

CENSUS OF ENGLAND AND WALES, 1911.

Before writing on this Schedule please read the Examples and the Instructions given on the other side of the paper, as well as the headings of the Columns. The entries should be written in Ink.

The contents of the Schedule will be treated as confidential. Strict care will be taken that no information is disclosed with regard to individual persons. The returns are not to be used for proof of age, or in connection with Old Age Pensions, or for any other purpose than the preparation of Statistical Tables.

Number of Schedule 164

NAME and SURNAME	RELATIONSHIP to Head of Family	AGE	PARTICULARS as to MARRIAGE					PROFESSION or OCCUPATION		BIRTHPLACE	NATIONALITY	INFIRMITY
1 George William Sheader	Head	46	married					Fisherman 5/1	Own Account	Yorkshire Scarborough		
2 Bertha Grace Sheader	Wife	44	married 21	6	4	2				Yorkshire Scarborough		
3 Thomas Mabel Sheader	Daughter	21	single							Yorkshire Scarborough		
4 George William Sheader	Son	17	single					Fisherman 5/1	Own Account	Yorkshire Scarborough		
5 ... Elizabeth Sheader	Daughter	14	—							Yorkshire Scarborough		
6 Margaret Alice Sheader	Daughter	7								Yorkshire Scarborough		
7 William Sheader	Great Grandfather	86	Widower							Yorkshire Scarborough		

Total: 3 4 7

I declare that this Schedule is correctly filled up to the best of my knowledge and belief.
Signature George William Sheader
Postal Address 37 Sand Side, Scarborough

7 Rooms

41. William Sheader, 86 years old, is described as the great-grandfather in this Scarborough fishing family, recorded on the 1911 census. The terminology is confusing. Family members were supposed to be described in terms of the relationship to the Heads of Households but William is unlikely to have been the great-grandfather of the head of this household. He is probably actually his grandfather and therefore great-grandfather only to the youngest generation living in the house. (www.thegenealogist.co.uk)

42. Elderly widow of the Laithwaite family, wearing a traditional shawl and cap (possibly of Welsh origin), taken probably in the 1860s. Such early photographs of very elderly people are thrilling; this lady may have been born as far back as the 1780s. (Wigan World Website, www.wiganworld.co.uk. With the permission of Ron Hunt)

43. At 96, Thomas Tattum was the oldest member of the community in Ashton-in-Makerfield on the day of the Queen's Coronation in 1953. Born in Baggilt, Wales in 1859, he had come to Ashton-in-Makerfield to work in Garswood Colliery where he also played lead cornet in the pit brass band. (Wigan World Website www. wiganworld.co.uk. With the permission of Ron Hunt)

44. Tennis Club, possibly Dewhirst's Mill Club, Skipton. The costumes and relaxed outdoor poses date this photograph to about 1930. These players were probably work colleagues as well as teammates. (Author's collection. With thanks to Mrs Mairead Mahon)

45. Card sent in friendship by 'Fred', produced by the Rotary Club, c. 1930, London, Message Reads: Glad hours to make life good for living/The love of Friends, well worth the giving,/Fair prospects for the years to be,/ Filled with true joy and Prosperity, by Helen Stewart. (Author's collection)

46. Your ancestor's neighbours may be an interesting source of information on your ancestors themselves. (Author's collection)

47. Girl Guides in Wharfedale, c. 1940s. The uniforms are very similar to those worn by Princesses Elizabeth and Margaret as guides during the Second World War – a fact which helps to date this photograph. (Author's collection. With thanks to Mrs Mairead Mahon)

48. Pages from the autograph book (1897–1901) of schoolgirl Nellie McCarthy (a.k.a. Ellen Clementina Higley, b. 1880), crammed full of names followed by nicknames such as 'Polt', 'Broad Bean' and 'Whiglets'. (With thanks to Mrs Pat Morant)

LIST of all PERSONS who SLEPT or ABODE in this INSTITUTION on the NIGHT of SUNDAY, MARCH 31st, 1901.

No.	NAME and SURNAME	RELATION to Head of Family or Position in the Institution	CONDITION as to Marriage	AGE last Birthday	PROFESSION or OCCUPATION	Employer, Worker, or Own Account	If Working at Home	WHERE BORN	
1	Sarah Vidler	servant	single	23	Laundress (domestic)			Hampshire	
2	Katharina Thomann	servant	single	30	Laundress (domestic)			Germany (German subject)	
3	Bertha Bailey		single	27	Teacher B.A. School			Madras India	
4	Mona Conlan	Scholar	single	25	Scholar Stu...			London	
5	Nellie McCarthy	Scholar	single	22	Scholar			London	
6	Evelyn Hopkins	"	single	17	Scholar			Barnet Middlesex	
7	Mary Lea Cray	"	single	16	Scholar			Shropshire	
8	Mary Gough	"	single	19	Scholar			Woodbridge Suffolk	
9	Kathleen Peard	"	single	14	Scholar			Epsom Surrey	
10	Lomi Dempster	"	single	15	Scholar			Hongkong (English subject)	
11	Margaret Jefford	"	single	15	Scholar			Poona India (E.S.)	
12	Dorothy Ramage	"	single	14	Scholar			Southampton Hants	
13	Helene Gransowsky	"	single	12	Scholar			Germany (German subject)	
14	Aline Dempster	"	single	11	Scholar			Hongkong (English subject)	
15	Mary Vailet	"	single	13	Scholar			Warrington Lancashire	
16	Annie Vailet	"	single	11	Scholar			Warrington Lancashire	
17	Jeanne Marie Vassal	"	single	18	Scholar			Algiers (French subject)	
18	Clara Parsons	"	single	13	Scholar			Leicester	
19	Margaret Parsons	"	single	12	Scholar			Leicester	
20	Barbara Penny	"	single	13	Scholar			Southampton	
21	Gertrude Penny	"	single	12	Scholar			Southampton	
22	Margaret Baglee	"	single	13	Scholar			Yorkshire	

49. The 1901 census reveals Ellen Clementina Higley (Nellie McCarthy) at St Mary's Roman Catholic Convent Boarding School in Ipswich. The other scholars listed here have the same names as the contributors to the autograph book, and the census reveals that they came from all over the world to study in East Anglia. (From www.ancestry.co.uk)

50. The Portico Library in Manchester holds a members' book which gives details of the addresses and occupations of some of its first Proprietors. James Pollitt, for example, was a 'calico and dimity manufacturer' at Top Bank Street, John Thacker, was a 'twists dealer' at 2 Palace Street and John Carr was a 'collector of taxes' at 18 Princess Street. (With the permission of the Librarian, Emma Marigliano)

CHAPTER 4

'A Burgeoning Brood':
Sons and Daughters

In the last quarter of the nineteenth century, children – that is, those under fifteen years of age – made up approximately 35 per cent of the population – a huge proportion. In the press, literature, photography and the arts, boys and girls came to be accorded a far more important place in public consciousness than had historically been the case. In the records, the details of how our young ancestors started out in the world are some of the most telling and poignant aspects of all our family histories. As family historian Sue Wilkes has pointed out, our 'ancestors' formative years were immensely important for their futures' (*Tracing Your Ancestors' Childhoods* [2013]).

What practical difficulties did children present for the photographer? What other aspects of family life become more apparent from a consideration of the children in a photograph? How did parents regard their children in the nineteenth and early twentieth centuries? What were the major landmarks in the history of education, child employment and child welfare that might have affected the children in your family? Was your ancestor's position in the family – as eldest, middle, youngest or only child significant? What did it mean to be a twin?

Sons and Daughters in Photographs
Children make some of the most compelling sitters in old photographs but they could be the bane of a photographer's work. Indeed, in the early days of photography, some studios refused to photograph children at all because of the difficulties they posed. Other early

97

photographers charged more for taking photographs of children under ten years old because of the additional skill required. In 1853, photographer Robert Framer of Brighton, for example, charged 1s 6d for a single portrait of a man or woman, but 2s 6d for a portrait of a child under 10, 7s 6d for a group of three children and 10s 6d for a family group of five. But as the number of photographic studios in each British city increased year on year and photographers found themselves thrown into competition with one another, they had to agree to take more challenging shots in order to make a living. Individual portraits or group shots of young children, and whole family groups, often with plenty of youngsters in evidence, became commonplace by the last decade of the nineteenth century (see Image 23).

Look out for certain special types of old photographs which feature children. These include those in which children of one gender only are featured. If you come across a photograph like this, bear in mind that you might not be seeing the whole family. In very large families, it was common for two photographs to be taken, one of the girls and one of the boys.

Keep your eyes peeled also for so-called 'Departure' photographs where a serviceman would pose with his wife and children prior to setting off for War (usually the First World War) or a so-called 'Separation' photograph in which the serviceman in the foreground is accompanied by a small section in the top corner portraying his children. In either case, the serviceman might take one copy of the photograph away with him whilst another remained with the family.

Childhood birthdays were celebrated in the Victorian period, but most families would not have been able to afford individual photographs of each child every year. If the child was an only child, or from a very wealthy background, it is worth speculating, however, whether your photograph was taken to mark an important birthday of some kind.

Henry Peach Robinson understood the intractability of children in the photographic studio, 'the fact is there can be little posing of a young child; you must do not what you would, but what the child will allow' (Robinson, *The Studio and What to Do In It*, p. 92). Typical problems were children who howled because they were totally unfamiliar with the strange world of the studio, and those who screamed and squirmed at the formal restraints under which they were sometimes placed, such as head and leg braces to help prevent them from moving and spoiling the photograph. And of course, there were children who couldn't or wouldn't pull the right expression, and who baited the photographer or fought with their parents.

Robinson relished the challenge posed by difficult child sitters: 'Analyse the problem as you would one in mathematics', he advised, '[because] there is something almost fascinating about a fractious three-year old who objects to have [sic] his portrait taken.' He went on to identify three particularly troublesome types of child sitter, the 'bold', the 'nervous' and the 'shy' and suggested how to deal with each of them. A bold child required photographing quickly before his confidence turned to bad behaviour. 'After a few exposures he will quietly slip off the chair or turn away from where you have placed him when you turn to go to the camera' (Robinson, *The Studio and What to Do In It*, p. 87). Once a child started to behave like this, Robinson recommended that the photograph should be abandoned and the child sent home and told to come back on another day.

Nervous children required gentle treatment and Robinson advised that the photographer should spend time introducing himself before the picture was taken and showing her (because it was usually girls who fell into this category) some of his earlier photographs. But it was *shyness* rather than fear that was the biggest obstacle when taking photographs of children. Those children who hid in the dresses of their mothers or nurses and refused to come out were pretty unbiddable. Here speed again was of the essence; the timid should not be given time to think.

By the end of the nineteenth century, many photographers' studios had an intermediate room between the reception area and the studio proper in which children could be calmed down or beguiled with toys before their picture was taken. Some toys, of course, made their way into the studio and into the photographs themselves. It was recommended that to start with, a single toy should be held in the photographer's pocket and made to squeak or rattle in order to attract the child's curiosity. This 'invisible performance' would be enough to get the child into a suitably interested and animated state of mind whilst preparing for the photograph.

But photographers had to be careful with noisy toys – children should not look as though they were straining to listen to something in a photograph. Discreetly deployed ticking watches, therefore, needed to be loud. Toys made from India rubber that squeaked were also very effective. In general anything that was 'comic or new' to the child was a good idea. A particular annoyance for the photographer was those mothers or nurses who, if given the run of the whole toy collection, would 'show them all at once or quickly one after another so that their power of use would be gone'. Robinson went on that 'if a child sees the toys belong to you, and can only be got through you, you will become a much more interesting person to him, and consequently have more power' (Robinson, *The Studio and What to Do In It*, p. 91). Though toys sometimes appeared on photographs, the emphasis was on simplicity rather than elaboration – photographers from the end of the nineteenth century, at least, were advised to focus on facial expression rather than props and composition.

Once under the spell of the photographer, a child might be lifted on to a table, made to stand on a moveable platform (so as not to be out of the photographer's field of vision), or made to rest his head in a brace. Getting a child to sit still was a tricky matter, but harder still was the task of getting him to maintain a suitable 'look'. Robinson had found that if he mentioned a part of the face to the child – an incorrectly open mouth, for example – the child would focus on that feature and 'proceed to contort it at once'. Far better for the photographer to keep silent, and to direct his subject by touch if necessary – advice that would not go down well with parents in a photoshoot of children today!

Photographs of children might alert you to a number of other issues highly relevant to your family history. One of these is the matter of 'birth spacing', that is, the amount of time that had elapsed between the birth of one child and the next (see Image 24). Witness also the poses struck by the different children in your family. Elder siblings often demonstrate both protection and control, with their arms on the shoulder of younger siblings or placed on the back of a chair on which a younger child is sitting.

Even children from relatively comfortable backgrounds would have owned very few outfits in the nineteenth century: perhaps two for weekdays and one, in which they were probably photographed, for Sunday best. Age differences between children in a family might roughly be deduced from the kinds of clothes they are wearing and are, of course, also an aid to dating photographs. The relative ages of sisters in photographs might be deduced by the length of the dresses they wore – with the hemlines of older girls being significantly longer. Another clue to the age of a girl might be the styling of her hair, with younger sisters wearing their locks down (loose or in ringlets) whilst their elder sisters wore it up.

For a full and more time-specific description of the kinds of clothes worn by both boys and girls in old photographs see any of the books by Jayne Shrimpton or Robert Pols mentioned in the bibliography. What follows is a brief resume of some key points.

Sisters

Perhaps the biggest difference between Victorian and twenty-first century girls' clothes was in the number of layers worn underneath – items not necessarily up for inspection in photographs. A young girl would wear a chemise (a loose-fitting shift), drawers (long knickers), stays (a softer version of a corset), stockings and at least two petticoats. In the 1850s and 1860s, fashionable little girls wore crinoline petticoats, like their mothers, with the important difference that their skirts were slightly shorter. In the 1870s and 1880s, much more restrictive narrow skirts became popular. The 1890s saw girls wearing loose-fitting dresses and separate skirts and blouses.

Groups of sisters can sometimes be identified in Victorian and Edwardian photographs by their matching outfits. There was a particular craze for dressing daughters alike in the mid-Victorian period (c. 1855–85), among the upper and middle classes, who were copying the daughters of Queen Victoria in this respect. Even sisters who were far apart in age could be portrayed in matching garb and young adults as well as small children also followed this trend. The matching could extend to hats, boots, jewellery and even to the mirror-like poses of the sitters.

Sometimes sisters would differentiate themselves from each other by a minor detail of dress such as a corsage worn on one side of the bodice or the other, or extra trimming. Whilst the fashion for matching dress predominated amongst the rich, working-class sisters were also sometimes portrayed in identical 'Sunday Best' outfits.

Brothers

Sets of brothers might also be dressed alike in old photographs regardless of age. Young boys, for example, might wear sailor suits and short trousers whilst older boys wore jackets and long trousers in the same colour and type of material. In photographs from the 1840s, 1850s and 1860s, look out for what might appear to be little sisters among the boys. Many young Victorian boys wore dresses (with fitted bodices and full knee-length skirts). Clues that the child is in fact a boy may be wide trousers under the dress, or a prominent collar.

For centuries, toddler boys had worn these dresses (instead of breeches or trousers). The most likely reason for this is that skirts made for easier changing of nappies and toileting of toddlers; breeches and trousers, by contrast, often had complicated fastenings. At around the age of five, breeching – the moment at which the boy first donned a pair of short trousers – took place. In the age of the camera, the moment of breeching might actually have been the occasion for which the photograph had been commissioned and might portray both the youngster in question as well as other children in the family.

From breeching onwards, young well-to-do boys of the Victorian period, would usually wear a version of the knickerbocker suit. This had a short dress (often a belted tunic with a diagonal front opening, brass buttons and braiding for decoration) complemented with baggy knee pants gathered or left open just below the knee. Fauntleroy suits (named after a character in the eponymous best-selling novel by Frances Hodgson Burnett 1885–6) were also very fashionable. These consisted of a velvet tunic or jacket with matching breeches and a lace collar. Boys' dresses were often in darker or brighter colours than those of girls' and more tailored, with metal, rather than fabric, covered buttons. Sailor suits, first seen on Queen Victoria's eldest son, Albert Edward, as early as the 1840s, had become extremely popular for both boys and girls by the 1890s.

Older brothers might be identified in photographs from the different styling of their clothes: with maturity, side openings on trousers were replaced with a front fly, buttons at the waist were replaced with braces, the length of trousers increased and tunics were replaced with shirts that buttoned down the front and which were covered by waistcoats or jackets. Boys in their early to mid-teens generally wore men's suits with long trousers, particularly when they had already entered the world of work.

Sons and Daughters in the Family

Our child ancestors in the Victorian period grew up under the auspices of a generally benevolent and sentimentalised view of children in society at large. From the late eighteenth century, the French philosopher Rousseau had put forward a view of the world that was child-centred, suggesting that youngsters should learn from nature rather than adults and questioning the idea of original sin; children were henceforth generally considered to have been born innocent and to be all too often corrupted by the workings of civilisation. The Romantic artists and poets of the early nineteenth century enhanced this view and by the Victorian and Edwardian periods, children were moving increasingly to the forefront of public adoration and concern (see Image 25).

Childhood for our ancestors was billed as the golden age of life, a time depicted in many novels, songs and poetry as happy and innocent. Of course, for many this was far from an accurate description of their young lives and none of the 'fairyfication' of Victorian and Edwardian childhood should put you off investigating the very real experiences of your ancestors as children which might have been anything but happy or innocent.

At the beginning of the nineteenth century, children's lives were, more or less, wholly dictated by the economic circumstances into which they had been born. But as the century progressed, whilst circumstances of birth remained the most important factor, a number of changes in the law meant that children acquired more rights in terms of education, employment and social welfare. Whilst in the industrialising world, life for many children had never been more difficult (their labour was seen as essential to the industrialising economy), for the first time in history, their cause was also being actively championed.

Rather than have their fortunes exclusively shaped by the wealth and social standing of their parents, in limited ways some Victorian children would be able to improve upon the circumstances of their birth because of the intervention of the State. Free education would ensure that they were literate and numerate, employment legislation would little-by-little improve their working conditions, and welfare legislation would help provide for those in the most desperate need and start to punish those who abused them. Such statutory changes were aimed at supporting 'respectable' families. Be aware that your own child ancestors lived against the background of these changes; they might have availed themselves of the opportunities offered by them, fallen foul of them, or bypassed them altogether.

The same three areas, education, employment and general welfare, were the matters which most pre-occupied our ancestors in respect of their sons and daughters, particularly where families were large and money short. A comprehensive account of our ancestors' experiences of childhood is given by Sue Wilkes in *Tracing Your Ancestors' Childhood* (Pen and Sword Books, 2013) which also gives a vast list of relevant resources for genealogists. However, a few key pieces of legislation can usefully be described here as starting points for investigating the young brothers and sisters in your family.

A Note on Children's Ages
Bear in mind when researching your child ancestors in records (particularly work-related ones) produced before the start of civil registration in 1837, that their ages might not be correct. In non-literate families, dates of birth might have been remembered only vaguely and there were often pressing economic reasons why a family might claim that a strapping boy of seven was in fact nine years old. In the absence

of birth certificates, doctors or surgeons were required to certify that children working in factories were old enough to do so, and they could easily be wrong.

Take care also when looking at the ages of sons and daughters in your family on the censuses from 1851 onwards. Children between the ages of two and five were often recorded as being a year older than their actual age (i.e. a child recorded as 'four' may well have actually been 'in her fourth year' and therefore actually only three). The other childhood age that should set alarm bells ringing is 15. Many older girls pretended that they had already reached the age of 15 in order to have a better chance of obtaining work as domestic servants.

Schooling
Censuses often designate young children as 'scholars', a catch-all phrase which usually indicates that they were receiving some form of education. Be careful, however, since some households may have claimed that children were at school when in fact they were only attending a Sunday School and were actually in paid employment for most of the week. In the early nineteenth century, if, how and where your ancestor was schooled, depended, as so much else in British history, on the size of the family income and whether the child was a boy or a girl.

Upper- and middle-class boys, for centuries, typically started private preparatory schools at the age of seven, before entering a fee-charging grammar or public school (such as Eton) at ten. University would follow at approximately 17. Their sisters, on the other hand, were most likely to be educated at home by governesses. Many new boys' boarding schools and grammar schools were created in the early Victorian period, with the provision of such schools for girls of a similar class only really picking up towards the end of the nineteenth century.

An ancestor who was a working-class child in the early nineteenth century is not at all likely to have attended school on a daily basis. Sunday Schools of many different denominations, however, existed from the 1780s. Additionally, Charity Schools, which had been around for centuries, were joined by British and Foreign Schools (which were

Christian but non-denominational) from 1808, and National Schools (which were strictly Anglican) from 1811. Many of these schools were run on the 'monitorial system' (devised independently by both Dr Andrew Bell and Joseph Lancaster) where classes were divided among and taught by pupil teachers or monitors. Typically the fees for attending such schools were tiny, usually just a few pence per week. There was no legal obligation to attend.

As the nineteenth century moved on, these schools were joined by so-called 'ragged schools' and 'industrial schools', both of which, though differently funded, were dedicated to the free education of destitute children. So successful were all these attempts at education that by 1861 an estimated 2.5 million out of a population of 2.75 million school-aged children could claim to have received some form of schooling. But it was not until the 1870s and 1880s that the major reforms in children's education took place and that we can claim with some confidence that all our young ancestors would have attended school on a daily basis.

In 1870, Forster's Elementary Education Act created a framework for compulsory state-sponsored schooling for children between the ages of five and 12 in England and Wales. There were some exceptions to this (at the discretion of individual School Boards) including those children in rural areas who were exempted from attendance whilst they helped bring in the harvest and undertook other agricultural tasks. The Education Act (Scotland) made similar provision north of the border in 1872 for children from five to 13 years. In 1880, a Second Elementary Education Act (1880) tightened these rules in England and Wales, finally making education compulsory for those of our ancestors aged between five and ten. From 1891, parents could no longer begrudge the money spent on their children's education, as schooling became free of charge. Our young working-class female ancestors, in particular, probably benefitted from this change.

If you wondering whether your ancestors were still at school or had left school at a particular time in the past, it might be helpful to know that the Elementary Education (School Attendance) Act of 1893 raised the minimum leaving age to 11, and a later amendment, in 1899, raised it to 12. The Fisher Education Act of 1918 (implemented 1921) raised the leaving age to 14 but it was not until the Education Act of 1944 (enforced 1947) that the leaving age went up to 15.

School admission registers and logbooks might have been retained by schools themselves or might be kept in local archives. Check the website of the National Archives (www.nationalarchives.org) for their location. Some have been transcribed and appear online. Other collections of school logs and registers, can be accessed through the online commercial genealogy sites (www.findmypast.co.uk, for example, has a large collection of transcribed records of nineteenth-century schools in its Manchester Collection). Admission registers will probably give you the date of your ancestor's admission into a school, his or her date of departure (especially if this was at an unusual time), and his or her address and parental contact details. Log books are less likely to include details about specific ancestors, focusing more on general information about the functioning of the school, but occasionally, they will mention those children who have been awarded school prizes, or who have been noted for matters of discipline, absenteeism, ill health and even death.

You never know, you might just be lucky and turn up an unexpected gem of information about an ancestor's family circumstances in a school log such as this one recorded on 25 April 1884 by Mary Anne Webster, the schoolmistress of Haworth Village School, 'Millie Harper has been away from school all the week until this afternoon on account of the death of her mother,' or this one made on 20 March 1878 by the headmaster of Stretton Handley Village School, Derbyshire, 'Had to punish Frank Handbury, William Parkes and Sarah Ann Hardy for taking a child's dinner'!

Employment
The census might provide information that your ancestor's young sons and daughters were working. If a type of employment such as glove-making or straw-plaiting is recorded, you can hazard a guess at the name of their employer either by consulting a book on the history of the local area, or more accurately, an historical directory for that area – many of these are available to view for free at www.historical directories.org. The largest employer of young girls was domestic

service (with over 89,000 girls giving this as their employment in the census of 1871). Boys in rural areas worked as agricultural labourers of one sort or another from as young as eight or nine.

The situation of children in employment improved as the nineteenth century moved on. For a full overview of the changes in employment legislation see: www.parliament.uk/about/living-heritage/transforming society/livinglearning/19thcentury. Factory Acts aimed to limit the number of hours worked by women and children and improve their working conditions more generally. In 1819, one such Act made it illegal to employ a child under the age of nine and limited the working day to twelve hours within 24, but this legislation applied only to cotton factories. In 1833, a Factory Act banned children under the age of 18 from working at night and limited children aged 13 to 18 to a 69-hour working week. The minimum working age for textile factories was set at nine years and children aged 9–13 were limited to a 48-hour week and were entitled to annual holidays; they also had to have at least two hours schooling a day. In 1842, the Mines Act banned girls of any age and boys under the age of ten from working in coal mines.

In 1844, another Factory Act brought in the so-called 'half-time system' for children whereby they might work half the day and be schooled the other half (look out for cases in the census where your ancestor might be described as a 'half-time' cotton worker and so on). In 1861, the age limit for boys working in mines was raised to 12. From the 1840s onwards, unregulated industries such as lacemaking were investigated by Lord Shaftesbury as part of a Royal Commission into Children's Employment. The Factory Extension Act of 1867 and the Workshops Regulation Act of the same year further limited the hours children could work and made more employers subject to inspections.

In 1873, the Agricultural Children's Act banned children from under the age of eight from working on the land. As the century moved on, there were a whole series of other Acts which raised the minimum working age and broadened the legislation to include other industries. In 1901, the minimum working age across all industries was fixed at 12 by the Factory and Workshops Act. Whilst all this legislation improved the position of children by challenging their exploitation in the workplace, some of it will have impacted hard on families in which the income generated by young sons and daughters was crucial to the family economy.

Welfare

As has already been mentioned in Chapters 1 and 2, a series of Acts (the Custody of Infants Acts 1839 and 1873 and the Guardianship of Infants Act 1886) granted mothers some power in the custody of their children in cases of divorce and separation, but probably relevant to more of our ancestors would have been the legislation determining welfare reform for children living in poverty.

The Poor Law Amendment Act of 1834 made provision for destitute children to enter the workhouse. If they were living in an area that was not the place of their father's 'settlement' (i.e. where he had been born), they would be removed to that area and placed in a workhouse there. Additionally, they would be segregated from those parents who had accompanied them into the workhouse and from siblings of the opposite sex, made to wear a uniform, given only a rudimentary education and put to work from a young age. A little older, and they would be apprenticed out to work in local businesses which were often none too happy to take them on. So unpopular was the introduction of the Poor Law that preposterous rumours about its operation circulated at street level. One such story suggested that any family entering the workhouse with more than three children would have to suffer them to be killed!

Whilst there was much reluctance of the part of some politicians to intervene into the heart of the family, so desperate was the condition of some children by the last decades of the nineteenth century, that there was also a strong movement in society to get involved. In 1884, the London Society for the Prevention of Cruelty to Children was established in Greenwich. By 1889, it had thirty-two branches throughout England, Wales and Scotland, funded inspectors who investigated reports of child abuse and neglect and had changed its name to the National Society for the Prevention of Cruelty to Children (NSPCC). Queen Victoria became its patron.

In 1889, the Prevention of Cruelty to, and Protection of Children Act 1889 (commonly known as the Children's Charter) was passed.

This enabled the state to intervene, for the first time, in relations between parents and children. Police could arrest anyone found ill-treating a child, and enter a home if a child was thought to be in danger. The Act included guidelines on the employment of children and outlawed begging. In 1894 the Act was amended and extended, to allow children to give evidence in court, and to allow the prosecution of those who failed to provide a sick child with medical attention. Any cases of child cruelty within your family in the past might be investigated through court records (search for the location of these at www.Nationalarchives.org) and newspaper accounts (www.british newspaperarchive.co.uk) (see Image 26).

In the twentieth century the health and education of children started to be taken more seriously as politicians and social reformers properly recognised that the future of the nation was built upon the future of its young people. As a response to this, in 1904 the Prevention of Cruelty to Children Act gave the NSPCC the right to intervene in child protection cases. The Children's Act 1908 established juvenile courts and introduced the registration of foster parents. The Punishment of Incest Act (1908) made sexual abuse within families a matter for the State rather than the Church and aimed to protect young girls from the unlawful sexual attentions of adult male blood relatives.

In the 1940s, two Acts of Parliament, finally tackled the deprivation suffered by some children at home and stressed the individuality of youngsters. The Family Allowances Act of 1945 (in operation from 1946) provided child benefit of five shillings per week for each child other than the eldest whilst the child was at school and up to the age of 18 if the child was either apprenticed or in full-time education. Later Acts increased the amounts paid to families. The Children Act of 1948 brought in a comprehensive childcare service, run by County Councils, for children either without parents or with parents who were unable to care for them for any reason, and paved the way for later work by social workers with deprived children within their homes. Although children had been adopted informally since time immemorial, it was not until 1926 that adoption became a legal process in England and Wales (1930 in Scotland and 1931 in Northern Ireland).

Children's problems were by no means at end by the 1950s, but it is thankfully true to say that, on the whole, most young people were in far less vulnerable a situation than they had been 150 years earlier.

Issue 1: Was my ancestor's position in the family pecking order significant?

Your ancestor's place in the family line-up will not be incidental to his or her life history. The number of children in the household and the way in which they were spaced out were probably the most significant factors in his or her young life and may well also have contributed to how he or she developed into adulthood. A further complicating factor occurred where one or both parents had been married before, brought children from a previous marriage into the new marriage, and then started a new family together, the children of what appears to have been one tightly-knit household might actually have been the step- or half-brothers and sisters of each other. Watch out for these.

In the eighteenth and early nineteenth centuries particularly, informal adoption and fostering of orphaned children from the community together with the taking-on of apprentices to work in family businesses meant that it was quite common to have several unrelated youngsters living in a household alongside the biological offspring of the parents in a sort of stepfamily arrangement. All of the above factors would have determined the tenor of life within the home, including how much space there was, issues of health, nutrition and hygiene, levels of income. They would also perhaps have shaped the kinds of relationships enjoyed between older and younger family members, those who were the 'natural' progeny of the mother, or the father, or both.

It is important when researching your family history to try and work out the exact size and shape of your ancestor's sibling group. The censuses of 1841–1911 will show you child siblings living at the same address at the same time. But, of course, it is possible that some children of the family were out of the house on the night that the census was taken, and they might therefore not appear at their normal address. It is also sometimes the case that some children in a family (occasionally several) may have been born and died between the ten-yearly censuses and will, therefore, not appear. Remember also that in big families, children could be sent away for prolonged periods to visit relatives or might also have lived in semi-permanent arrangements (including unofficial adoption arrangements) away from their families. So never assume that every child is accounted for when you are checking census returns.

Since it is physically possible for a woman to conceive at any time from four to six weeks after giving birth, there were many families in the nineteenth and early twentieth centuries where one child followed very quickly upon another. For many households, the age gaps between children were around 18 months to two years. Wild deviations from this pattern in your ancestor's family with ragged age gaps between the children are worth investigating further. Was one parent either absent or ill at one time or another, or did the mother possibly suffer miscarriages or stillbirths? Living children who might have filled the gaps might also have died as babies or youngsters.

The one census from which you will potentially be able to find out more about the particular circumstances of your family in this respect is the 1911 census (sometimes known as the Fertility Census) which required families, for the first time, to record how many live births there had been in their marriages and how many of those children were still surviving.

Larger Families
Children in different positions in the pecking order of a family will undoubtedly have experienced life in slightly different ways and it's worth speculating a little on how these patterns might have developed within your ancestor's family. Parents often had different (usually lower) expectations of their younger children to those that they had had of their older children. You should consider whether the size and shape of your ancestor's large family made for the likelihood of 'favourites' and of 'black sheep'. Bear in mind also that affections and energies could shift as family fortunes changed. If an elder son died, all the hopes and expectations that the family might have piled upon him might then have been transferred, for better or for worse, onto the next son in line.

In general in the nineteenth century, older brothers and sisters were very much involved in the hands-on care of younger ones, especially when parents were at work. This involvement may have involved everything from feeding youngsters to fastening their clothes and taking care of them when they were sick. Elder children also acted as caretakers, educators and playmates, or stood as go-betweens between the younger children and their parents. Sadly, nineteenth-century newspapers report thousands of incidents – falls, scalding, drinking disinfectant, burning or drowning – in which young children incurred fatal accidents when left in the care of siblings not much older than themselves. One such case was that of Elizabeth Dobson, the four-year-old daughter of 'waller' Joseph Dobson of Kendal who suffered fatal burns whilst drying her pinafore before a fire after being left in the charge of her seven-year-old sister and another nine-year-old girl. Her mother had left the home for just a few minutes on a short errand (*Westmorland Gazette*, 23 December 1854).

In large families, younger children would have watched their older brothers and sisters grow up and been affected by their life choices in terms of work and marriage. Some will have wanted to follow suit; others to make sure that they took a totally different path. Young children were expected to obey the authority of their elder siblings and often held older brothers in particular in high esteem (even if they were away from home). Older girls sometimes acted as surrogate mothers or teachers, and were very often given the special responsibility of hearing their younger siblings read (see Image 27). Some large families encouraged a pairing-off of siblings, with close associations developing between the two eldest children in a family, for example, and also frequently between the two youngest. Other siblings in large families may have fallen into groups or clusters depending on their age and their gender whilst the last child in a long line up was often treated like an only child especially if (as was often the case) there was a large age gap between the penultimate and the last birth.

Of course, some nineteenth-century families were so very large that a child at the end of the line would hardly have known his or her older siblings as children. Such was the case of the English actress Dame Madge Kendal (1848–1935):

> I am the twenty-second child of my parents. Yes, the twenty-second. My brother Tom, the author, was my father's eldest

son. I am the youngest of the family. I never knew my brother Tom except as a man grown up – such a great many brothers and sisters came between us. (Quotation from 'Dramatic Opinions', *Murray's Magazine*, in *The Cheltenham Chronicle*, 21 September 1889.

The pattern of children in your ancestor's family will have had significance for all sorts of domestic issues. For large families in small houses, there would have been constant human interaction to a degree that we can hardly imagine nowadays. Children of the same sex would most probably have slept together, and there would no doubt have been constant squabbles over toys, books and other possessions. Pressure on domestic space in the Victorian period meant that the childhoods of many of our ancestors were necessarily mostly spent outdoors, in the streets as far as the working classes were concerned and in gardens by those higher up the social scale.

And matters ran deeper. You may have witnessed within your family history evidence that there existed a feeling of moral obligation and respect for rights (forged between siblings in childhood) that was borne out in action as their lives unfolded.

If parents and older brothers and sisters respect the rights of the younger ones, a needed lesson is taught, and, in turn, they respect the rights of others, because they have learnt what it is to enjoy privileges. (Quotation from *Household Words* in the *Luton Times and Advertiser*, 13 February 1885.)

The gender of siblings as well as their respective ages will have been a crucial factor. Boys – though they will have had more opportunities than girls, at all social levels – will also have faced more difficult times in the sense that they will have had to move away from the family environment for the purposes of education and work, whilst girls will most probably have remained within it until marriage and even beyond. Girls, on the other hand, will have been required – again at all social levels – to service the needs of their brothers, from assisting them with their learning and doing their mending, to running errands for them.

If the evidence of private letters and diaries is anything to go by, upper and middle-class brothers and sisters from the late eighteenth century onwards became closer and less competitive than they had been in earlier ages and bonds of affection between childhood siblings grew ever deeper. It would seem that there was a new emphasis on the role of love in family life and parents emphasised the need for harmony and co-operation between their children. Your ancestor might have benefitted from the sense of warmth and security that a large busy family brought, but on the other hand, he or she might have felt claustrophobic in a situation where there was more concentration on the group than on the individual.

Our ancestors who came from large families will have had to learn to deal with shifting allegiances within the family group and may well have exercised skills in childhood with which we are unfamiliar – showing loyalty to their group, negotiating to get what they wanted, appreciating and offering support in times of need. They might also have had to strive hard to forge a sense of their own identity and autonomy.

In the middle and upper classes, whilst 'teenage' brothers might have been away at private schools or in military regiments, girls usually stayed at home until marriage and were, therefore, thrown upon each other's company for more lengthy periods with all the resulting intensity that that would have brought. As the mother of the writer Jane Austen and her sister Cassandra once remarked, 'If Cassandra were going to have her head cut off, Jane would insist on sharing her fate' (*Memoir*, by J. E. Austen-Leigh quoted in Constance Hill, *Jane Austen, Her Homes and her Friends* [John Lane, 1902], p. 34).

The relationships between the young sisters in your family might have to remain very much a matter of supposition due to a paucity of official information on the lives of females in the past, but records of the experiences of brothers are more likely to be discovered. Many sets of upper- and middle-class brothers, for example, were accepted into the same houses of public schools, the same university colleges and then the same sporting teams, all of which might yield fruitful results in archives and record offices. A prime example of this were the three Studd brothers, John Edward Kynaston (J. E. K.) (b.1858), George Brown (G. B.) (b. 1859) and Charles Thomas (C. T.) (1860) who studied first at Eton and then at Trinity College, Cambridge and who each captained the University cricket team. All three brothers also became born-again Christians after a conversion in 1878. A further four Studd brothers attended the same school and were all competent cricketers.

By the middle of the twentieth century, families tended to be smaller with the result (according to some psychologists), that the children within them competed more for parental affection. It has been suggested that there was an increase in sibling rivalry and jealousy particularly amongst young children in this period. Ancestors who were children in the 1930s and 1940s might have experienced a focus on themselves as individuals rather than on their relationships with siblings. They are more likely to have experienced separate beds and even bedrooms for each child, for example. Siblinghood, it seems, was no longer quite the intense domestic experience it had been in earlier generations.

Only children

If your ancestor was an only child – particularly if he or she came from the lower classes – he or she is likely to have felt a little unusual. As we have said, Victorian families – at all levels – tended to be big. Occasionally, however, middle-class families chose to have just one child in order to concentrate time and resources on his or her education. But other children were likely to have achieved their 'lonely only' status as a result of maternal death or the death of other siblings. There was a general feeling in society that to be an only child was an aberration that was in some way detrimental to the health and happiness of that child. An article in the *Luton Times and Advertiser* on 29 July 1876 imagined the parents of only children to be 'over-anxious' and went on:

> The sun will tan the only child; the rain will wet the only child; the cold will freeze the only child; the heat will burn the only child; horses will surely run away; cars [carriages] will certainly smash up; ice will surely break through; berries will poison; fruit will harm; bons-bons will spoil teeth; nuts will spoil complexion. Everything that is really enjoyable, and which five or six children share together and have 'fun' with must be kept carefully away from the only child.

116

In a general climate of marital fruitfulness, only children tended to be pitied and even shunned. The late nineteenth-century American child psychologist, Granville Stanley Hall, indeed, went so far as to say that being an only child was' a disease in itself' (*Of Peculiar and Exceptional Children* [1896]) (see Image 28).

The deep unpopularity of families with only one child continued in fact until the third decade of the twentieth century. At this point, more married couples started to actively choose to limit their families. Difficult economic times between the two World Wars led some parents to feel that they could afford only one child. With increasing equality in the workplace and a generally more emancipated view of life, many women chose to go back to work after one child. Chief amongst the reasons for the new smaller families, of course, was the better availability of reliable and inexpensive contraceptives from the 1930s onwards.

With no challenges from other siblings, however, only children (especially boys) in the past did have some advantages. Vast estates could be held together by the uncontested rights of a single heir and, even in modest families, the passing-on of property and effects without dilution may have given individuals the ability to invest in projects that would otherwise have been out of their reach.

Issue 2: What did it mean to be a twin?

Perhaps a pair of faces as alike as two peas in a pod stare out at you from a faded photograph, or a Birth Cerrificate arrives from the General Register Office with an actual time of birth recorded upon it. Either of these clues might be the first indication you have that there were twins in your family.

Long before the introduction of artificial methods of conception such as IVF, as many as one in 80 births resulted in twins. The number of twins in England and Wales appears to have nearly doubled between 1841 (when there are 9,272 mentions on the census) and 1901 (when there are 17,678 references). Of course, the population in general rose dramatically during that period. But it is also true that historically instances of twins have increased in times of economic growth and nutritional bounty such as the late Victorian period (see Image 29).

Such statistics suggest that it is fairly likely that somewhere within your family tree, you will come across at least one set of twins or a multiple birth. Consider the first names of your family twins carefully, you may find that they were named to reflect their twin status. They may, for instance, have names that begin with the same letter (and sometimes first syllable) such as 'Mary' and 'Marion', or that end with the same syllable, such as 'Johnny' and 'Holly'. They may take the names of twin characters from mythology or literature such as 'Romulus' and 'Remus', 'Apollo' and 'Artemis', 'Cassandra' and 'Helenus' or the Biblical 'Jacob' and 'Esau'. Other twins' names such as 'Amy' and 'May' are anagrams of each other, as are 'Mary' and 'Myra'. Names may have the same meaning in two different languages, for example, 'Eve' and 'Zoe' which both mean 'life' ('Eve' in Hebrew and 'Zoe' in Greek). Or they may have opposite meanings, for example – 'Melanie' meaning 'dark' and 'Phoebe' meaning 'light' both in Greek.

It is common to talk about twins 'following on the mother's side of their family' and 'skipping a generation'. Today, knowledge about genetics shows that there is some truth in these statements. If your female ancestor had a mother who was a twin, she may have inherited from her a 'hyperovulation' gene (that is, a gene that made her release more than one egg at once). This means that she would have had a reasonable likelihood of having twins herself. This pattern, of course, gives the impression that twins follow on the mother's side and skip a generation. On the other hand, your male ancestor may have inherited the same special gene from a mother who was a twin, but this would have had no effect on his propensity for fathering twins. However, if he had a daughter who inherited the hyperovulation gene from him then she might well have gone on to have twins. The matter of whether or not twins run in families (i.e. whether a family has a genetic reason for producing twins) is only applicable to non-identical twins (conception of identical twins occurs at random).

As well as genetics, there are a number of other factors that might possibly have been at play in increasing the likelihood of twins in your family in the past. Mothers giving birth in their late thirties and forties, for instance, tended to be more likely to have twins and so did those who had several other children already. More controversially, it is now thought that twins are more likely to have been born to mothers with a high dairy or animal-product content in their diet. During the Second World War and other periods where dairy products were harder to come by, the rate of twin births dropped. Other (less convincing) theories suggest that heavier and taller women are more likely to have had twins, as are those who conceived whilst breastfeeding!

Don't assume that your twin ancestors were identical. Birth certificates can't give you this information and even photographic evidence may be deceptive; fraternal twins may look very similar. Identical (monozygotic) twins occur when one egg is fertilized and splits into two within two weeks. The resulting twins will be of the same sex and will be genetically identical. If two eggs are released at the same time and fertilized by separate sperm, the resulting twins will be non-identical, fraternal, or dizygotic. They will be no more alike than any other siblings. All twins who are male and female are non-identical. Unfortunately, it is impossible to tell whether or not twins in the past were identical or non-identical without DNA evidence.

The twins in your family may have done nothing of particular note but as you trace their histories, there will always be the intriguing question of whether their lives mirrored each other as they grew up. It may be, for example, that they married at about the same time (they may even have had a double marriage), had similar numbers of children, made the same geographical moves or worked in the same sort of employment. The *Hull Daily Mail* of 5 June 1936, for example, reported that when twin sisters Miss Mary Elizabeth Snowdon and Miss Isobel Milnthorpe Snowdon, of the old Manor House, Bramhope, near Leeds, married together in Bramhope Church, 'they were dressed alike in moon-white satin and also wore similar travelling dresses when they left for their honeymoon'. Alternatively, twins may surprise you. You may be struck – far more than you would be with ordinary siblings – by the enormous differences in their fortunes.

In addition, the very 'twinship' of twins may have led to some very special outcomes in your family history. The health of your ancestral twins, for example, may be a matter that merits further investigation. Many twins (and indeed sets of twins) died before reaching adulthood. Often one or both died at birth. Annie and Lilly Symes (who appear to have been identical from photographic records) born on 9 December

1892, at 12.30pm and 12.55pm respectively (and, at the time, the fourth and fifth of five children) were both born with health problems. Lilly, born with hydrocephalus ('water on the brain'), died at the age of 13 months from pertussis (whooping cough) and bronchial pneumonia, whilst Annie, who had walked with callipers from toddlerhood, died at 12 years from pulmonary tuberculosis.

Twins tended to be smaller and weaker than single-birth children and were, therefore, more vulnerable in historical periods when infant mortality was high anyway. But the high death toll was also perhaps due to the fact that many twins were born to older mothers (Annie and Lilly's mother was 37 at the time of their birth), and would, therefore, have had a higher chance of inheriting chromosomal abnormalities. This resulted in the birth of some sets of twins with physical and mental deformities and other health problems. Remember also that the mothers of twins are more likely to have suffered health problems in pregnancy than other mothers. And the death of a mother in childbirth was certainly more common with multiple than single births.

It's also worth reflecting on how your family finances might have been affected by the existence of twins. In Britain, inheritance laws were guided by 'male preference primogeniture' – that is, the eldest male would always inherit capital and estates in preference to his younger brothers. Where twins were concerned, an estate might be lost because of the matter of twenty minutes between the birth of one brother and another. And if, in a pair of twins, a girl was born before a boy, it's possible that – though the elder – she lost out quite dramatically when property came to be inherited.

There may be other economic consequences of having twins that are relevant to your family history. If you are searching census records, for instance, look out for one twin disappearing from the family home at some point. Don't assume necessarily that the child died. If the family was poor, it's possible that he or she might have been adopted by another family or by another member of the same extended family as a means of spreading the cost. Modern methods of searching the censuses online mean that – providing the child did not change his or her name – you should be able to locate the missing twin, wherever he or she might be, simply by typing their name and (if you have it) their year of birth into the search box of the relevant census on one of the online commercial genealogical sites.

As has been noted earlier, the birth certificates of twins include the exact time of birth. This was done in order that elder and younger children could be distinguished for inheritance purposes. So, if you order a birth certificate and find that there is a time recorded against the date of birth, it is very likely that more than one child was born alive at the birth. Remember, however, that early registrations of birth are not consistent. Some registrars did not bother to put the times of births of twins in the registers at all whilst others put times against all the registrations (not just those of twins). Scottish birth certificates nearly always record the time of birth, even for single births. If one of a pair of twins was stillborn, then the live-born twin would probably not have a time of birth recorded at the registration of birth. Remember that until July 1927 there were no registrations at all (either of birth or death) of a stillborn child.

Don't assume brothers and sisters were twins when they were not. The 1840 census rounded people's ages down to the nearest five years – thus making many siblings appear to be the same age. Also siblings may be recorded as the same age on the census, but they may not be twins. Remember that two children may be born to the same mother at opposite ends of the same year.

It is finally salutary to remember that some mothers had a propensity for multiple births. Queen Victoria was the great-grandmother of two sets of twins both born to her granddaughter Princess Margarete of Prussia. Margarete already had two sons from single births before having the two sets of twins, the first in 1896 (Philipp and Wolfgang) and the second in 1901 (Richard and Christoph). The old Queen (who was rarely amused) apparently saw the funny side in the sudden increase in the numbers of her great-grandchildren shortly before her own death in 1901. But few women probably could match the fecundity of Mrs McQueen of Muckeanston, Near Thornhill, Cumbria who was delivered in October 1857 of triplets, then in November 1858 of twins and then again in September 1860 of twins. Seven children within three years! (*Westmorland Gazette*, Cumbria, 22 September 1860).

CHAPTER 5

'Kinds of Kin': Adult Siblings, Aunts, Uncles and Cousins

For many of our ancestors, relationships with siblings were probably the longest-lasting connections of their lives, vastly outspanning their relationships with their parents, husbands or wives and their own children. In addition, as historian Leonore Davidoff has so succinctly put it, 'Even when they had drifted apart, siblings behaviours, accomplishments and failures were psychologically and emotionally significant to the others' (Davidoff, *Thicker than Water*, p. 133). Moreover, relationships with the spouses of brothers and sisters (sisters- and brothers-in-law) and their children (nephews and nieces), could also be deeply significant by virtue particularly of the many years such a connection might last.

On what occasions and with what difficulties did photographers take pictures of the extended family? What roles were played in your Victorian and early twentieth-century family by brothers and sisters when they became adult? What did it mean to be an uncle or an aunt or a cousin? Why were certain relationships between members of an extended family, such as that between a man and his deceased wife's sister, prohibited? And why were marriages between cousins not only allowed but even encouraged in some sections of the community?

Adult Siblings, Aunts, Uncles and Cousins in Photographs

You are more likely to have group photographs of the extended family (including aunts, uncles and cousins) from the end of the nineteenth century, than from the 1850s and 1860s. Greater skill was required to take a photograph of a large number of people than of an individual, and group photographs were therefore either unavailable or extremely expensive in the early years of photography. Where groups were portrayed in the earlier period, they tended to be small. From the 1880s onwards, however, the widespread use of faster-drying photographic plates meant that larger groups became more common in photographs.

Late Victorian and Edwardian families were renowned for their clan-like gatherings on occasions such as christenings and weddings. Family group photographs were taken in studios but also in all manner of other outdoor locations, such as fields, gardens and back yards – so don't let the setting put you off recognising the relationships between those portrayed. Many of our ancestors will also have attached importance to family traditions at certain times of the year such as the 'Boxing Day Walk' or the 'May Day family picnic'. By the last decade of the nineteenth century, these outdoor occasions, featuring a number of branches and generations of the family, were being assiduously photographed both by professional photographers and by amateurs within the family circle.

Group photographs of weddings are particularly interesting in that they may bring together many faces from diverse branches of the family – even those who lived at a distance – all in one picture (see Image 30). It is on these photographs that we sometimes glimpse family members who have otherwise eluded the camera. Sometimes the exact relationships between family members can be guessed at from the way they have been positioned in the photograph, bride's brothers on one side, groom's brothers on the other side, for example (although there were no specific rules on this). From the 1890s onwards, many more members of the family might have been part of the nucleus of the wedding party itself, dressed as bridesmaids, flowergirls, groomsmen and ushers. For further help with dating group photographs of weddings you should consult the dedicated chapter in Jayne Shrimpton's book, *How to Get The Most From Family Pictures* (Society of Genealogists Enterprises Ltd, 2011), or Avril Lansdell, *Wedding Fashions, 1860-1860* (Shire, 1986), which look at changes in wedding attire and customs.

If your ancestor was a person of note, the details of his or her wedding might have been written up in a local or national newspaper, searchable by keyword at www.britishnewspaperarchive.co.uk or through www.findmypast.co.uk. Such reports can be very useful in identifying the relationships between family members on group photographs since they often give the names of the principal guests and the people playing a part in the wedding service. Bear in mind, however, that the weddings of more ordinary families are unlikely to have been reported in the press until well into the twentieth century.

In 1891, photographer Henry Peach Robinson mused on the difficulties of taking successful group photographs. With extended families, some of the problems were technical, as they were with all groups of people (see Chapter 7 on Friends, Neighbours and Club Associates for more on this), but with families there was the added problem of trying to control a group of people who knew each other intimately and between whom there were many overlapping lines of connection, well-known clashes of personality and sometimes emotional tension.

Robinson suggested that there was always 'one funny man' in a group who needed to be dealt with firmly from the start of the shoot. This character within family photographs was probably an uncle known for his teasing of the women and children. Robinson advised confronting this fellow directly: 'So, you are the funny man are you? If I can get on with you, I can easily manage all the rest. If you will kindly suppress yourself for a few minutes and let me have my turn, I shall be much obliged' (Robinson, *The Studio and What to Do In It,* p. 82). The result of this, according to Robinson would either be that the joker would turn out to be a good fellow who would do all he could to help you, or he would sulk. Whichever outcome occurred, the photographer would then, declared Robinson, be able to take the photograph without further problems!

Adult Siblings, Aunts, Uncles and Cousins in the Family
The further back you are able to go in the nineteenth century with your family tree, the more likely you are to become aware of the closeness of your extended family in the past. Try to work out the geographical proximity of your ancestors to the other branches of their family from census records or from trade directories (brothers or cousins might

have run adjacent businesses, for example). You might well end up realising that several different closely-connected family branches must have worked, played, travelled, worshipped and celebrated family occasions together – particularly if they came from a rural area.

Your family's various branches might well have shared a home, material goods, the same social and emotional circles, and even (if they were connected by business interests – as many were) the same vicissitudes of fortune. If you are wondering, for example, how an ancestor met his or her future marriage partner, consider carefully whether he or she was a distant cousin, or the friend of one of your ancestor's siblings. Many courtships began this way. Also, don't be too surprised if the same surnames keep cropping up again and again as they join your family tree. There were many instances of pairs (or groups) of brothers marrying pairs (or groups) of sisters.

One very common family configuration that you might come across when investigating your family on the census, is that of an adult sibling living in the house with a married couple. On census night 1881, over one million adults aged between 30 and 50 were living in a household including a sibling (Davidoff, *Thicker than Water*, p. 140). When elder siblings married and had children, their younger sisters and brothers (who might now be teenagers or young adults) were often recruited to help in the new household. Young uncles, for instance, might have become apprentices in the family business, whilst young aunts might have become mothers' helps or companions. If the census enumerator was doing his job properly, he would have recorded the correct designation of these extra relatives by describing their relationship to the head of household (i.e. 'sister', 'brother-in law,' 'brother' or 'sister-in-law'), but watch out also for those cases where the blood or marital relationship is not made clear, where people who are actually siblings of the householder or his spouse are, for example, described as 'visitors' or 'assistants', or under the role that they played in the household, 'gardener', 'housekeeper', 'stableboy', 'nanny' or the like. If their surname was different from that of the head of the family, it's easy to miss the connection.

Newspaper reports occasionally throw up an example of where such a mixing of the nuclear and extended family did not work out.

Such was the case of John Shepherd, a gardener who lived with his brother James, a market gardener and his family in Hull in 1890. One evening John took to his bed at 5pm and soon after shouted downstairs, 'I have killed myself'. At this, his niece, Jessie, and nephew ran upstairs to find him bleeding from a wound in his throat inflicted by a razor. John survived but went on to have a stroke and suffered from a 'desponding frame of mind' (*Hull Daily Mail*, 24 February 1890). Of course, press reports give a skewed view of such matters and had no cause to recount the thousands of arrangements up and down the country in which members of extended families happily co-existed.

Another common pattern in the nineteenth and early twentieth centuries was for adult siblings to set up households not that far distant from one another or from the parental home. It is always worth scrolling down through census pages immediately before and after those on which your ancestors appear just to see whether the same surname (or any other family surname) turns up. But be careful – identical surnames do not necessarily indicate a close family connection.

Further evidence of the close connections between adult siblings might be found on marriage or death certificates. On marriage certificates, look out for brothers and sisters or brothers-in-law and sisters-in-law of the bride and groom who might have been witnesses to the event. On death certificates, where ancestors were widowed, adult siblings are very likely to have been the informants of the event. Further evidence of the closeness of other members of the family might come from letters, diaries or even oral history in which the marriage partners of siblings might even be referred to as 'sister' or 'brother' regardless of the lack of a blood connection. This was a world in which even as distant a relation as a brother's wife's sister counted as kin.

This situation was not unchanging, of course. As the nineteenth century went on, more and more individual branches of families moved into the cities and did not take their wider family with them. For those who moved away, industrial urban life provided a far larger pool of people from whom to choose a marriage partner, and the very dense network of familial relationships enjoyed by those in the rural community therefore did indeed start to break up over time.

But even where one member of a family or one branch had moved away, there were plenty of means of keeping in touch with extended family back home. New communication systems including the establishment of the railways in the 1830s and the Penny Post in 1841 ensured that aunts and uncles and cousins were never more than a few hours or at most a couple of days away. After 1870, once photographs were easier to produce and came down in price, they were within the reach of the pockets of even the poorest in society and, accompanied by a letter, were a powerful means of reminding family members in one place of those in another.

Adult Brothers
Researching adult brothers can be a very rewarding experience for the family historian, since if you find one brother in the records of a workplace, club or special interest group, you are highly likely to find details of another. Additionally, adult brothers might have served together on committees or boards of commercial, professional or scientific associations, or even officiated in the same place of worship.

If you are wondering how a male ancestor managed to finance a new enterprise, you might need to look no further than his brother. In the nineteenth century, when the banking industry was in its infancy, your ancestor might have considered it safer to borrow money from a brother than from a financial institution. Additionally, some men took over the care of their brothers' families completely in times of adversity. The author Charles Dickens (1812–70), for instance, excelled in the care of his younger brothers. Frederick (b. 1820) lived with him during the early years of his marriage; Albert (b. 1822) (a civil engineer and sanitary inspector) died in 1860 and his family was thereafter helped financially by Charles. And when a third brother, Augustus (b.1827), left his blind wife for another woman and then died himself, the author provided financial support for both women.

Adult brothers have always done business together, but in the Industrial Revolution (1780–1850) there was a burgeoning of such business enterprise. Safely founded on deep trust – at least in theory – brotherly partnerships were perhaps more able than other sorts of partnership to focus on navigating the fluctuating economic currents of the times. It has even been suggested that formal partnerships between brothers were more prevalent than those between fathers and sons in the nineteenth century, perhaps a reflection of the fact that the vast pace of technological change was easier to manage between partners of the same generation.

The brothers in your family might have brought different but complementary qualities to growing enterprises. In the village of Street in Somerset, for example, Quaker Cyrus Clark ran a tannery making sheepskin rugs. But it was his brother James who, in 1825, had the brainwave to transform the off-cuts of material into slippers and later shoes. From this, the world-renowned Clark's footwear business was born. Further north, William Hesketh Lever's great business acumen and marketing skills combined with his brother James's back office role enabled the two of them in 1885 to set up Lever Brothers (the forerunner of Unilever) – originally a small soap manufacturing business in Warrington.

And there are numerous other examples (big and small) of successful fraternal business relationships that sometimes were replicated across several generations. In early eighteenth-century Birmingham, for example, the industrialists and entrepreneurs brothers Benjamin and John Mander set up a cluster of businesses concerned with paints, lacquers, japanning, chemical manufacturing and varnishing. A hundred years later, another pair of brothers from a later generation of the same family, Charles Benjamin Mander and Samuel Small Mander, focused on varnishing (and later still on inks and printing), creating the highly successful and world-renowned manufacturing company Mander Brothers.

Legal records (including wills) to be found in county archives and local record offices show how the unparalleled loyalty and trust between brothers frequently meant that they acted as guarantors for each other in business endeavours and that they helped each other out financially in times of crisis. Of course, such close degrees of intimacy mingled with business interests sometimes brought their own issues. Certain Bible stories (Cain and Abel, Jacob and Esau, Joseph and his eleven brothers), repeated often in Church, would have ensured that our nineteenth and early twentieth-century ancestors were well attuned to the potential dangers of the breaking of the brotherly bond.

Disagreements between real brothers were often fuelled by the law of (male preference) primogeniture which held that the eldest male child in a family inherited the vast bulk of its wealth – a situation which often left younger brothers in upper and middle-class families struggling to find careers in the Army and the Church. A sudden death in a family could send the whole situation into a tailspin with relationships between siblings and their lifestyles changing overnight. Court records highlight the frequency of such disputes between brothers over land and property.

Nineteenth-century newspapers were quick to pick up on a fraternal fracas, especially where it involved blood, money and sex – the key ingredients in a familial drama. The case of watchmaker Felix Henry Leon Lecluse and his brother Alphonse in 1894 included at least two of these:

> **Wounding a Brother**: At the central criminal court, Felix Lecluse, pleaded guilty to a minor count charging him with unlawfully wounding his brother in Soho on January 25th. The brothers carried out a jewellery business, and family differences arose respecting their father's will. On the day in question the prisoner, without the slightest warning, fired a pistol at his brother, wounding him in the face. Lecluse was sentenced to three months hard labour and bound over for 12 months. (*Sheffield Evening Telegraph*, 7 March 1894)

This case was all the more interesting from the point of view of the relationships between brothers since it was witnessed and reported to the police by a third Lecluse brother.

In the first half of the twentieth century, came a new and significant aspect to the fraternal relationship. Brothers who entered the services developed bonds that undoubtedly would have been strengthened by their shared experiences of action in the First and Second World Wars (see Image 31). Many families lost more than one son, but the Souls brothers from Great Rissington, Gloucestershire were exceptionally unlucky in that all five boys lost their lives in the first conflict. Albert and Walter joined the 2nd Battalion of the Worcestershire Regiment at the outbreak of the War in 1914 and fought in the Battle of Loos in September 1915. Fred, Alf and Arthur enlisted originally in the 16th Cheshires, a bantam regiment. Albert and Walter transferred to the 5th Brigade Machine Gun Corps in January 1916 and Albert was killed in March. Walter died unexpectedly from an embolism in his leg after the Battle of the Somme later in the year. Fred was recorded missing in action in the same battle. Alfred was killed at Ploegsteert Wood in Flanders in early 1918. His twin Arthur died in April. The boys' mother, Annie Souls, who got a shilling a week from the government for each of her dead sons, is reported to have kept a candle burning in her window in case Fred ever returned.

Adult Sisters
Whatever their relationship as children, the testing time for sisters came when they were old enough to be betrothed. You should consider carefully the age gaps between the young women in your family, when and whom they married, where they ended up living, whether or not they had children and the ways in which their lives might have followed a pattern of continual mergence and divergence. Victorian letters and diaries reveal that adult sisters often experienced deep pain when they were separated from each other, even by pleasant events such as courtship and marriage. From the wedding day onwards, the lives of sisters (which had previously been almost interchangeable) could become widely divergent depending on the wealth, background and character of the prospective husbands.

Some women never married, of course – and there are many instances in the censuses of sets of middle-class sisters (sometimes with female cousins and unmarried nieces) living together to minimise expenses and probably supported by small annuities bequeathed from their parents' estates, by investments and rents from property that had originally belonged to their parents or, more often, by the efforts of their working brothers (see Image 30).

The unmarried state was something to be avoided wherever possible, however, and it was important in families of good social standing for girls to get married in order of age and to marry men with similar social aspirations. The five daughters of Mrs Bennet in Jane Austen's *Pride and Prejudice* (pub. 1813), for example, are a constant worry to their mother since all of them are 'out' (i.e. old enough to appear in public at balls and dances) and not one of them is married, but it is Jane, the eldest, whom she seeks to marry off first. The situation of a younger sister marrying before an older one was considered embarrassing and something to be avoided, since a married woman automatically attained seniority over her older unmarried sisters.

Sometimes sets of sisters all married well and became the centre of successful extended family networks. Alice, Georgiana, Agnes and Louisa Macdonald, four of the seven daughters of a lower middle-class Methodist Minister, leapt from obscurity when they got hitched. Georgiana and Agnes married the famous painters Edward Burne-Jones and Edward Poynter (President of the Royal Academy) respectively, whilst Alice became the mother of the future Poet Laureate, Rudyard Kipling and Louisa the mother of future Prime Minister, Stanley Baldwin. Other groups of sisters did not make such equal marriages and spent a lifetime envying each other. Whilst Ada Jennings, great aunt of the novelist Frances Osborne, married a highly successful officer and diplomat, for example, her twin sister Lilla had to make do with a rather more ordinary British military officer, Ernie Howell – it was a distinction which rankled all their lives. And other distinctions to do with economic circumstances, numbers of children born, numbers of children who survived, widowhood, separation and remarriage were issues that might have affected the adult sisters in your families, drawing them together or creating tensions that might profitably be added into your family story.

In the twentieth century, the British public were enthralled by several high-profile sets of sisters whose energies inspired or set them against each other. The Pankhurst sorority, Sylvia, Christabel and Adela, for instance, adopted different stances (from the peaceful to the militant) in their quest to obtain the vote for women, whilst sisters Vanessa Bell and Virginia Woolf produced unusual and startling works of art and literature. Meanwhile, the complex political situation of the mid-twentieth century is often described through the antics of one of the oddest of all groups of upper-class sisters – the six Mitford girls – who ranged in sympathy from Fascist Diana to Communist Jessica.

Less apparent in the records than their male counterparts, some of what we know about sisters in the past may have been passed down to us only in the form of hearsay and we should be all the warier of the information for that reason. Watch out for family stories in which groups of sisters are differentiated only by their supposedly different physical characteristics ('the beauty', or 'the Plain Jane'); or their marital status and propensity for producing children, 'the spinster', 'the mother of ten'. Other descriptions may be equally distorting; Queen Victoria's five daughters have recently been described, for instance, as 'vivacious, intelligent Vicky; sensitive, altruistic Alice; dutiful, dull Lenchen (Helena); artistic, rebellious Louise; and shy baby sister Beatrice' (Review of Jerrold M. Packard, *Victoria's Daughters* [1999] by Wendy Smith, www.amazon.com). In real life, their personalities were probably far more complex than these reductive labels suggest.

Adult Brothers and Sisters

The relationships between adult siblings of different genders present different common patterns which might be worth investigating further in your own family histories.

Some sisters, bound to stay unmarried and at home, idolized their brothers who were out in the world, whilst many brothers will have thought of their unmarried sisters as pure examples of domestic perfection. In the unequal (sexist) world of the nineteenth and early twentieth centuries, however, sister-brother relationships could also be marked by antagonism and rivalry. Lancashire letter-writer Ellen Weeton (1776–1849) constantly felt envious of the disproportionate amount of money spent on her brother's education and lifestyle which she partly had to fund by working as a schoolteacher and governess. And some brothers correspondingly resented the supposed 'ease' of their sisters' domestic lives whilst they were sent out into the world to earn a living.

A common scenario was that of a young unmarried sister spending long periods away from the parental home whilst she gave assistance of one kind or another in the home of a married sister or brother. The brother (or brother-in-law) provided a home and a purpose for the young woman whilst she offered help with the household chores, the children or the running of a family enterprise (services which may have gone unrecorded on the censuses). Since the surnames of unmarried sisters will be same as that of their married brothers, take care not to confuse them with wives when reading the census. Don't assume either that sisters were always the dependent partner in these relationships – sometimes an unmarried sister might have loaned capital to a brother or brother-in-law or otherwise supported his business.

Unmarried older brothers in your family might have acted as companions, travel escorts or repositories of advice on legal matters, marriage negotiations or financial affairs to their younger sisters. And it is not at all unusual to see a sister acting as a housekeeper to an unmarried brother in a professional position such as a clergyman, physician, lawyer or banker. There were many such scenarios where a sister accompanied her brother to take up a position in the Empire, for example, as a missionary in South Africa or a member of the Indian Civil Service. It must undoubtedly have sometimes been the case that such an arrangement covered up for the homosexuality of the brother, or indeed of the sister, but it is worth remembering that these arrangements might have lasted for a good number of years and then have been brought to an end by the marriage of either one or both of the siblings. Even after a brother's nuptials, some sisters remained famously intimate with their brothers in ways that may seem strange to us today. Dorothy Wordsworth, for instance, adored her brother William and continued to live with the family long after the poet married in 1802 and had children.

The First World War was to change the way in which sibling relationships were experienced. In some senses, brothers and sisters had never been more different – with the young men daily facing the possibility of losing their lives in ways hitherto unimaginable. On the other hand, war brought with it more sexual equality in terms of employment, more tolerance, and more sense of shared endeavour and purpose between the sexes.

Uncles and Aunts

Where parents maintained relationships with their siblings in adulthood, their children, of course, benefitted from their connections with aunts and uncles. Far from being a shadowy background figure (or 'second-degree relative') in your family story, an aunt or uncle might have played a very significant part. It's worth remembering that aunts, uncles and cousins may have drifted in and out of your direct ancestors' lives in much the same way as parents and siblings did over the course of many years and decades.

Relationships with aunts and uncles who had married into the family would also have been important, providing familiarity combined with an extra element of distance which might have been useful at certain times in a family's emotional life. But more significant, certainly, would have been the relationships with 'blood' aunts and uncles who may have looked, sounded and even moved like parents, and who had been brought up in the same atmosphere with the same values and beliefs (see Image 32).

What these relationships could provide for children within families in psychological terms was both 'sameness' and 'difference' (Davidoff, *Thicker Than Water*, p. 35). Being with adults who were very much like their parents, but not their parents, might have been either threatening or liberating for our ancestors when they were young. The homes of aunts and uncles might have been almost as familiar to these children as their own homes. Certainly they would have provided a fascinating contrast – frequently like but unlike – the homes in which they had been brought up.

The divisions between siblings, parents and aunts and uncles could become blurred in some circumstances. Where there were many children widespread in age in a family, older children might find that they were the same ages as their aunts and uncles. Younger children, whose grandparents or even parents had died, might view aunts and uncles as stand-in parents. Since there was no automatic legal aspect to the relationship between an aunt/uncle and nephew/niece, these relationships were bound simply by a sense of duty, morality and affection. Where aunts and uncles strayed from their accepted avuncular role – in cases of neglect, brutality, incest or even just plain lack of concern – the newspapers and, one suspects, the law also, came down heavily upon them.

If your ancestor appears to be living in the household of an aunt and uncle on one of the censuses, it is possible that this might have been a permanent living arrangement. With high maternal mortality rates, many children in the past were entirely brought up by their deceased parents' brothers or sisters. The eighteenth-century historian Edward Gibbon (1737–94), for example, described how as a youngster he was 'neglected by his mother and starved by his nurse', despite the fact that he was the only surviving of seven children. After his mother's death, he was sent to live with his Aunt Kitty (Catherine Porten) in the Westminster School boarding house which she owned. Amongst other things, Aunty Kitty gave Gibbon a taste for books which he described as being 'the pleasure and glory of [his] life'.

But your ancestors might also have been staying only temporarily with an aunt or uncle when the census was taken. Children who were at British boarding schools often stayed with aunts and uncles at holiday times rather than returning to their parents who were stationed overseas. Alternatively, and lower down the social scale, they might have been spending time with an aunt or uncle whilst their nuclear family coped with a trying situation of one sort or another – the infectious illness of another member of the family, for example, or a new birth.

Aunts and uncles might have been significant in the transfer of skills to the new generation. Uncles might, for instance, have introduced their nephews to outdoor and masculine pursuits such as walking, sailing, fishing, shooting and mountaineering (see Image 34). Nineteenth-century newspapers sadly report many cases of fatalities where an uncle and nephew (often of not dissimilar ages) drowned in fishing boats or met their end together in other similar accidents. Very often aunts provided practical help in a family when a child was born, or soon afterwards. They might also have been responsible for the instruction of young children and older girls in the reading, needlework or other household arts that the mother was too hard-pressed to impart.

Aunts and uncles also frequently played a key role in the economic life of a family. If they lived in other parts of the country, or indeed in other countries, they might have been the first point of contact for grown-up nieces and nephews who had travelled or emigrated overseas for work or to settle. They might have helped to place and promote nephews and nieces' husbands in employment, or paid apprenticeship premiums or school or college fees. A favourite nephew might have been taken to work in a business, professional practice or commercial enterprise alongside an uncle. Assistant bootseller Jack Symes (1894–1968), for example, worked alongside his uncle Charlie Terrell in a Freeman, Hardy and Willis boot and shoe shop in Pontefract in the years before the First World War, before taking on his own branch of the same chain in Liverpool when the War was over.

And don't assume that it was only uncles who were able to help their younger relatives to secure jobs. Aunts too could be well connected and in a good position to call upon members of the extended family who might be in business and over whom they might have some influence. Less often, an aunt with an important position of her own might have been instrumental in securing employment for a niece or nephew. This, for example, was the case with Anne Jemima Clough who was the Principal of Newnham College, Cambridge from 1880 and who appointed her niece Blanche Athena ('Thena') Clough as her secretary in later years.

If your ancestor appears to have inherited a significant sum of money, land or other valuable item at some point, consider the fact that it might have been left to him or her by an aunt or uncle (especially if the latter were childless). It was in thanks for such an act of generosity that E. M. Forster (1879–1970), wrote *Marianne Thornton*, a memoir to his 'bachelor' great-aunt who had died when he was just seven leaving him the then enormous sum of £8,000 (£753,240 in today's money). After the Married Women's Property Acts of 1870, 1882 and 1893, women were much more in control of their own finances within their marriages. This meant that far more married aunts were able to give away money in their lifetimes if they so wished in the latter part of the nineteenth century.

If you suspect that a rich aunt or uncle might have left your ancestor a fortune, search for his or her will at www.ancestry.co.uk. The National Calendar of Wills made between 1858 and 1966 will give a brief summary of the people to whom the money was left. To obtain a copy of the actual will (for a fee), you can visit the Central Probate Registry (First Avenue House, Holborn, London) in person. You are advised to make an appointment beforehand. Alternatively, order the will via the website www.justice.gov.uk/courts/probate/copies-of-grants-wills. Older wills made before 1858 may be held in local or National Archives. See the National Wills Index at www.origins.net. In addition to leaving legacies to nephews and nieces, aunts often left personal possessions, particularly jewellery to nieces that had special meaning. Bear in mind, also that a parent might have left provision in a will for his or her brother or sister to be a guardian to the children in the event of his or her death.

Aunts and uncles might also have had a powerful influence on your ancestor in terms of passing on ideas and beliefs. If you are wondering why an ancestor suddenly converted from one religious denomination to another, became devout, or more temperate, or espoused a strange scientific idea of some sort, you might need to look no further than an aunt or uncle who had trodden the same path at an earlier date (see Image 36). Some Victorian 'spinster aunts' (and indeed some married ones) gravitated naturally towards the developing Women's Movement, campaigning for better educational and working opportunities for women and many young nieces will have followed in their footsteps.

Aunts and uncles might have inhabited very different social worlds from their nieces and nephews and, by doing, so might have introduced them to different people, ideas or ways of living than those they were used to from their own parents. Some fostered within their nieces and nephews a taste for adventure, education or creativity, for example (see Image 32). The writer P. G. Wodehouse spent his childhood amongst a group of creative aunts at the family home of Cheyney Court (Worcestershire). One of these, his Aunt Mary (Deane), for example, wrote a novel entitled *Mr Zinzan of Bath* (1891) and her sister, Wodehouse's Aunt Louisa, illustrated it. Certainly Wodehouse was fascinated by the influence of his aunts. In his novels, the character of Bertie Wooster's Aunt Agatha was a ghastly creation of whom he remarked: 'We run to height a bit in our family and there's about five foot nine of Aunt Agatha, topped off with a beaky nose, an eagle eye, and a lot of great hair, and the general effect is pretty formidable!'

In a culture that sentimentalised childhood, any adult who

contributed to the fond memories associated with that time was regarded with affection and, if nothing else, consider that aunts and uncles might have played an important part in the emotional life of your ancestor. Aunts, in particular, were in the fortunate position of being able to guide, warn and teach their nephews and nieces without overpowering them with motherly affection or overloading them with maternal baggage. Aunts were, after all, the closest adult females to a young person after their mothers. It has been suggested that when the Marriage Act of 1753 made it illegal for anyone under the age of 21 to marry without the consent of their parents, there were often difficult waters to negotiate in a family. Youngsters frequently fell in love without the approval of their parents, and it would often be the aunt, rather than any other family member, who stepped in to broker a resolution.

With so many women widowed, or left unmarried after the First and Second World Wars, our ancestors' 'spinster' siblings were on the increase in the first half of the twentieth century with the result that thousands of elderly maiden aunts were coming to the ends of their lives in the 1950s and 1960s. Many of these women had broken new ground in the professions of teaching, medicine and the like by avoiding marriage and motherhood altogether – even if it were not by their own choice. These women provided a huge inspiration for many women in younger generations wishing to branch out in their own careers or to take a path different from that of the traditional wife and mother.

Finally, bear in mind the importance of aunts and uncles in the telling and retelling of the stories from your family history. Many family historians owe a great debt to these not-so-distant relations who retained intimate knowledge of earlier generations of our families and kept the papers and heirlooms that accompanied them.

Cousins
Given the large size of most families in the mid-nineteenth century, cousins could be vast in numbers and widely disparate in age, with relationships between them ranging from the quasi-parental to the near equal (see Image 33). Whatever else your ancestors shared with their cousins, their chief point of similarity was their mutual ancestry.

Whilst the focus of this section is on first cousins (those with whom your ancestors shared the same grandparents), other cousin relationships might also have been important. Second cousins shared great-grandparents (but not grandparents). Third cousins share great-great-grandparents (but not great-grandparents or grandparents) etc. When the word 'removed' is used to describe a relationship, it indicates that the two people are from different generations. Your mother's cousin is one generation different from you, hence, she is your first cousin once removed. Your grandmother's first cousin, would be your first cousin twice removed.

English is different from some other languages in that it does not have single terms to differentiate between cousins on different sides of the family. You may, therefore, find these terms helpful when discussing the cousins in your family tree: 'parallel' or 'ortho-cousins' (the children of your mother's sister or your father's brother) and 'cross-cousins' (the children of your mother's brother or your father's sister). It's worth remembering that since many sets of brothers and sisters married each other in the past, some of their progeny would have been related twice over and were strictly speaking 'double first cousins'.

At the very least, there might have been strong bonds of affections between the cousins in your family. As Queen Victoria wrote in her journal from Windsor Castle in 1848 about the departure of her half-sister Feodore and her children: 'It gave us a great pang to see the carriage drive off, these partings are very painful, for our children too, the separation from their dear cousins is sad' (www.queenvictorias journals.org, 14 November 1848).

Cousins will physically have come together in the past on various family occasions (see Image 33). If your ancestor is living with an aunt or uncle on the census, consider the fact that he or she might have been drafted in as a companion to that relative's only child, or to a child of theirs very different in age from its brothers and sisters. In a world in which relationships between young people of opposite genders were carefully monitored and chaperoned, there was a welcome freedom of behaviours between young people of opposite genders who were cousins:

You call them by their Christian names; you romp with them; you take them out for long walks, make them presents, perhaps even kiss them. It is very nice, but not in the least naughty. Ah! What a blessing that is! Parents look at the way these cousins love one another, and never think of offering an objection. It is the received way of treating a cousin. (*The Southern Reporter* [Selkirk] 17 October 1878)

And this article went further in suggesting that male cousins could be very useful in the maturation of a young girl. 'A cousin is such an excellent whetstone upon which to sharpen the points of coquetry for use against the outside world.'

In the families of our ancestors, boy cousins might have entered a family business together, and girl cousins might have attended social events and family gatherings jointly. Those in the upper echelons of society might have 'come out' (i.e. entered society at the same dance). And many cousin relationships lasted a lifetime, not only in terms of affection, but also in terms of economics, with cousins frequently running small shops, businesses or schools together.

Issue 1: Why didn't Father marry Aunty?

One situation that faced many widowed fathers in the nineteenth century was a potential remarriage after a first wife had died. In 1835, a Marriage Act absolutely prohibited a man (in the United Kingdom or its colonies) from marrying the sister of his deceased wife. The same prohibition had existed in Scotland since the Scottish Marriage Act of 1567. This prohibition derived from a doctrine of Canon Law whereby those who were already connected by a family marriage were regarded as being related to each other in a way which made marriage between them improper (and indeed incestuous). Marriages which had already taken place before 1835 but which had contravened this law remained authorised. One such marriage was that between writer Jane Austen's younger brother Charles Austen and his deceased first wife's older sister (Harriet Palmer) which lasted from 1820 until his death in 1852.

The law forbidding marriage between father and aunt may have caused a dilemma for your male ancestor. When wives died (as we have seen so many did in childbirth), many a husband might have considered that the caring hand of her sister, a figure already known to his children, would make a better second marriage partner than a stranger. It's possible, for instance, that the Reverend Patrick Brontë (1777–1861), would have married his wife's sister 'Aunt Elizabeth Branwell' after his wife (Maria)'s death in 1821, had the prohibitory Marriage Act not been in place. Nevertheless Aunt Branwell came from her home in Penzance to live at the Brontë parsonage in Yorkshire until her death in 1842, and effectively brought up the Brontë children as a mother would have done. Tongues may or may not have wagged in Haworth!

The debate about whether or not a man's marriage to his deceased wife's sister should be allowed continued throughout the nineteenth century, with barely a year passing when it wasn't raised in the Houses of Parliament. The only men successfully to marry their wives' sisters in this period were rich enough to do so abroad where the law was different. These included the painters William Holman Hunt and John Collier who tied the knot in Switzerland (in 1873) and Norway (in 1889) respectively (see Image 34).

As early as 1842, a Marriage to a Deceased Wife's Sister Bill was introduced into the Commons but it was heavily defeated and the row intensified later in the century. One factor in support of revising the law was the popularly perceived 'surplus of women' in the population (from about 1850), which has been mentioned earlier. It was argued that more of these extra women would have the chance to marry if they were able to replace their deceased sisters. This reasoning, however, did not find favour.

It was only in 1907 that the Deceased Wife's Sister's Marriage Act finally allowed men to marry their late wives' sisters, although clergy were still allowed to refuse to conduct such a marriage if they so chose. It took the First World War, however, to remove the stigma attached to marriage between a man and the wife of his dead brother. The Deceased Brother's Widow's Marriage Act was passed in 1921 in England and Wales (and in 1924 was applied to Northern Ireland).

Issue 2: Could cousins marry?
Discovering that your great-grandfather married his cousin can be a delightful moment providing a sense of satisfaction and giving an impression of symmetry to your family tree. Such consanguineous marriages in the past were quite common in some communities, but the union might have met with as much opposition as joy.

If your ancestors were Roman Catholics, it is highly unlikely that you will find any cousin marriages on your family tree. From 1215, marriages to first, second and third cousins were expressly forbidden by the Catholic Church (this replaced an earlier ruling which forbade anyone marrying even those as far distant as sixth cousins). In 1917, the rule was reduced by Pope Benedict XV to a ban on marrying first and second cousins only, and, in 1983, this was reduced still further to first cousins. In the past, marriages to cousins among the Catholic community have only gone ahead only with a papal dispensation (which often had to be bought). Any Catholic who unwittingly married a close relative without a dispensation could obtain an annulment.

Your Protestant ancestors, on the other hand, might well have been married to their cousins or other near relatives. Anglicanism has allowed cousin marriage since the reign of Henry VIII and many Non-conformist religions such as Quakerism, and Unitarianism have actively encouraged the marriage of cousins, as has Judaism. During the nineteenth century, in particular, many middle-class Nonconformists followed the example of the nobility in marrying their cousins.

There are many reasons why your ancestors might have married their cousins. One important – but often overlooked one – is the fact that people travelled less far to find their marriage partners in the past. In small and remote village communities, tying the knot with your first cousin was possibly one of very few marital options. In cases where extended families had migrated from one part of the country to another, or from one country to another, cousin marriage could be a way of consolidating a sense of cultural identity that might otherwise have been lost.

As banking and other commercial dynasties were created in the nineteenth century, newly wealthy families hoped to consolidate financial success by intermarriage. Prime examples occurred within the Rothschild family (Jewish multinational bankers). Between 1824 and 1877, thirty male members of this family married cousins. In 1839 James Rothschild explained that children in the family had been brought up 'with the sense that their love is to be confined to members of the family, that their attachment for one another would prevent them from getting any ideas of marrying anyone other than one of the family so that the fortune would stay inside the family' (Kuper, *Incest and Influence*, p. 124). Many other high-ranking people including merchants, barristers, judges, clergymen, bishops, top civil servants, writers and scientists married cousins in the same period.

As a lifestyle choice, marrying your cousin had quite a lot going for it. Arguably it strengthened family ties, maintained family structure, gave the marriage greater stability and helped it to last longer. Prenuptial negotiations often went more smoothly when they were conducted with near kin rather than total strangers. Those who fell on hard times during their marriage might have been more likely to receive assistance of a number of kinds – from money and goods to patronage and advice – if they were related to their in-laws by blood as well as by marriage. It has even been suggested that in the intensely private world of the Victorian home, marrying your cousin was a way of diverting sexual interest away from even closer members of the family (namely brothers and sisters)!

Some advocates of cousin marriage in the nineteenth century went so far as to say that the health risks of marrying a cousin were fewer than those involved in marrying a partner whose bloodline you didn't really know. Certainly it seemed that fertility rates amongst couples who were cousins were high – though this may have been due, in part, to the fact that many such couples married at a relatively young age.

The practice of cousin marriage got the seal of royal approval on 10 February 1840 when Queen Victoria married Prince Albert. Victoria's mother, Victoria Maria Louisa, was the sister of Albert's father Ernest III, the Duke of Saxe Coburg and Gotha. Albert and Victoria were both born in 1819 with Victoria being three months older than Albert. Though marriages between cousins were common amongst members of European royalty, this one was rather different in that it was based primarily on love and not on economic or strategic considerations.

There were other well-known cousin marriages too. In January 1839, the naturalist Charles Darwin married his first cousin Emma Wedgwood (a daughter of the famous pottery dynasty) (see Images 35 and 36). Charles's mother, Susannah Darwin, was the sister of Emma's father, Josiah Wedgwood II, and the cousins had socialised together as children. In 1831, Charles came to Emma's home, Maer Hall in Staffordshire, to ask advice about the invitation he had had to sail as a naturalist on the exploratory voyage of the *Beagle*. Rumour has it that it was Emma's father (Charles's uncle) who persuaded Charles's father to let him go on the trip. Throughout the five years he was away from home, Charles sent letters home to the extended family – a fact which meant that cousin Emma always knew a great deal about what was happening to him. When he returned to England in 1836, Charles headed straight to Maer (and Emma) again to tell tales of his voyage. The Darwin–Wedgwood marriage was very successful, with Charles reminding Emma on his deathbed never to forget what a good wife she had been to him.

By the late nineteenth century, marrying a cousin (and a first cousin at that) was already a very well-established tradition in Britain, particularly amongst the upper and upper-middle classes. Nevertheless, like every trend, cousin marriage had its detractors and the issue was a point of hot debate among churchmen, politicians and ordinary people. The focus of the arguments centred on the children of consanguineous marriages whom, it was widely believed, potentially had a higher chance of ill health and deformity than those of the rest of the population.

Some of the well-known examples of cousin marriage at first glance seem to bear this out. Queen Victoria and Prince Albert had nine children. One son, Leopold (b. 1853) had haemophilia and died aged 31 after a fall in Cannes. Two of Victoria and Albert's daughters, Alice and Beatrice, were also carriers of the disease. The Queen was reportedly very concerned that the many intermarriages of the royal family had in some way 'weakened their blood' and wished that it might be revitalised. In fact, today we know that haemophilia is caused by a mutated gene inherited from the mother and has nothing whatsoever to do with the issue of consanguineous marriage.

The Darwins meanwhile had ten children. One, Mary Eleanor (b. 1842) survived only three weeks, and another, Charles Waring (b. 1856), who might well have been suffering from Down's syndrome (as mentioned in Chapter 2), died at the age of two from scarlet fever. A beloved eldest daughter, Anne Elizabeth (b. 1841), also died young (at the age of 10) from tuberculosis. Charles Darwin was concerned that his own chronic ill health and the mortality of the children might have been due to the multiple intermarriages between his wife's family and his own, including the union of the Darwins' grandparents, Sarah Wedgwood and Josiah Wedgwood who had also been first cousins. These concerns about the results of inbreeding (based on first-hand experience) were no idle musings on Darwin's part; they in fact helped to strengthen his increasing conviction in the idea of evolution.

The royal family and the Darwins were prominent examples of individual cousin marriages, but detractors were more concerned about cases where intermarriage was repeated many times within a small community. The practice of marrying first cousins, for example, was rampant in some remote areas, particularly the Highlands and Islands of Scotland. A study in 1865 by Arthur Mitchell, Deputy Commissioner for Lunacy in Scotland, suggested that 14 per cent of 'idiot' (mentally-handicapped) children were the progeny of near relations; that in 44 per cent of families with more than one mentally-handicapped child, the parents were related; and that 6 per cent of the parents of deaf mutes were kin. Mitchell acknowledged that environmental factors could also play a part in these statistics but felt that cousin marriage reinforced 'evil influences'. In fact, modern medical science now tells us that the risks of abnormalities in children born to cousins – even first cousins – are very small. It does concede, however, that because it takes two people with the same recessive gene to have a child with a particular disease, marrying within your own family does increase the odds of that happening. And multiple intermarriages within a family may create greater problems still.

By the last decades of the nineteenth century, there was a backlash against the practice of cousin marriage. In July 1870, during the second reading of the Census Act 1871, the MP for Maidstone, Sir John Lubbock – a friend and fellow scientist of Charles Darwin – proposed that the next census should include a question about whether or not householders were married to a first cousin. Had this question been allowed, our task as family historians might have been a lot simpler as interconnections between families would have been more obvious in census records! As it was, the suggestion provoked uproar in the Commons. MPs who were in favour of adding the question commented (without any evidence it must be said) that consanguineous marriages resulted in decreased fertility and a tendency to malformations resulting from a lowering of 'vital powers'. See the debate in Hansard at www.hansard.millbanksystems.com. One MP even volunteered the information that he knew of a case of a marriage of first cousins in which there were twelve children of whom six 'ended up in a lunatic asylum'.

Those opposing the motion, however, said they did not want the offspring of consanguineous marriages being held up to 'inspection' by scientists since this might stigmatise the resulting children for life. It was also argued that householders asked about the issue might lie on the census forms. If they had married a first cousin and their children were 'healthy and sound-minded' then they might acknowledge their relationship, if, however, their children were unhealthy or there were no children at all, they might conceal the nature of their marriage. At the end of the lively debate, the proposition of adding a question on cousin-marriage to the census was soundly defeated.

After the failed Parliamentary debate of 1870, George Darwin (son of Charles and himself, therefore, the offspring of a first-cousin marriage) independently set about the task of investigating just how many people in the general population had married their first cousins. He used marriage records, press announcements of marriage and questionnaires in what was one of the first ever statistical studies of a social issue. He concluded (perhaps not very accurately) that first cousin marriages accounted for 4.5 per cent of marriages within the aristocracy, 3.5 per cent of marriages within the landed gentry and the upper-middle classes, and 2.25 per cent of marriages among the rural population. Amongst all the classes in London, the percentage of first cousin marriages was about 1.15 per cent. George Darwin also wrote to the heads of several lunatic asylums to try to ascertain how many of their inmates were the progeny of first cousin marriages. The results suggested that only 3–4 per cent fell into this category – a figure which led Darwin to conclude that 'as far as insanity and idiocy go, no evil has been shown to accrue from consanguineous marriages' (quoted in Kuper, *Incest and Influence*, p. 98).

Unsurprisingly, the debate about first-cousin marriage has continued to twist this way and that. From the early twentieth century onwards, however, your ancestors are less likely to have married their cousins. This is partly due to the vast numbers of young men killed in the First World War (something which made the whole business of finding any marriage partner at all more difficult) and partly due to the fact that there was growing medical opposition to the idea of consanguineous relationships in the 1920s.

> The experts emphatically condemn such unions on the grounds that within them lurk the danger of physical and mental deterioration. (*Dundee Evening Telegraph*, 6 September 1922)

As the twentieth century progressed, families also began to operate differently with the networks of cousins and second cousins becoming ever less important to the nuclear family. Marriages of first cousins naturally dropped away, though they have never been formally outlawed.

CHAPTER 6

'Of Advancing Years': Grandparents and Great-grandparents

It is sometimes suggested that most people died prematurely in the Victorian period, but actually if your ancestor lived to three score years and ten or beyond, he or she would not have felt unduly unusual. Old people (that is those over 65) made up about 6–7 per cent of the population of England fairly consistently right through the nineteenth century. Thenceforth, their numbers (and proportion) in the population have been steadily rising.

How was old age portrayed in family photographs? How were the elderly perceived in the nineteenth and early twentieth centuries? How did our ancestors survive in their old age? Were very elderly people really as old as they said they were in the records? And what was the particular situation of the most vulnerable adults in society, elderly widows?

Grandparents and Great-grandparents in Photographs
Often seated whilst others stand, the oldest family members in some photographs might be people who were actually only middle-aged. Without the benefit of modern cosmetics, twentieth-century dental expertise and even hair dye, people tended to look much older than they actually were and there is very little chance, as there would be with a photograph nowadays, of mistaking a 65-year-old for a 45-year-old in a picture from the past (in fact, the reverse is more likely to have been the case). Additionally, props, clothing and pose might all contribute to making an ancestor look even older than he or she actually was.

Elderly people were actually some of the easiest to photograph, if Henry Peach Robinson is to be believed:

Old ladies and gentlemen are, as a rule, among my most obliging and kindly sitters. They do as requested, sit where they are placed, and when asked to sit quiet for the few seconds necessary, it is sometimes difficult to get them moving again, so anxious are they not to spoil the picture and give trouble . . .

Old men usually make admirable photographs. There is a gravity about old age which seems to suit photography. White hair may be a technical difficulty, but it is to be got over by judicious lighting and manipulation, and difficulty ought to lend a zest to all arts. Old people are usually steady without much effort, and, as a rule, they do not care so much how they look as young people do, and therefore are free from the self-conscious look that so sadly mars nearly all portraits, whether painted or photographed. Seated positions, in arm-chairs for preference, seem to be most suitable for age. (Robinson, *The Studio and What to Do In It*, p. 61)

Like Robinson, most nineteenth-century photographers treated old people in the studio with the kind of reverence that they could expect more generally in society. Rather than trying to minimise their age, as many photographers do today, they wanted to suggest the wisdom, experience and grandeur of advanced years. On the whole, elderly sitters accepted this treatment, but there were always exceptions. Robinson described an elderly marchioness who had been 'the favourite toast of sixty years ago, but who was so dilapidated and limp that she had to be shaken occasionally by her attendant'. In order to stop her mouth from sagging, this old lady insisted on keeping a biscuit in her mouth while Robinson exposed the plate!

Family occasions were a time to portray all the layers of a family simultaneously and it was common in the nineteenth century, as it is today, for great-grandparents, grandparents, parents and children to all be portrayed together on birthdays, anniversaries, at weddings and after funerals. Three-generation or four-generation photographs were a popular Victorian convention, in which the first grandchild, or great-grandchild, was photographed with its parent, grandparent and great-grandparent, the eldest generation usually holding the baby. The

149

pride in the co-existence of many generations was occasionally echoed in nineteenth-century newspaper reports:

> There is residing in Edinburgh, a child one year old who has a living father and mother, two grandfathers, and two grandmothers, four great grandfathers and four great-grandmothers, four aunts and five uncles, thirteen grandaunts and eight granduncles. (*Morpeth Herald*, 19 August 1871)

Multi-generational photographs commonly featured either all the female line or all the male line of a family. Since high mortality in adulthood meant that often a generation was wiped out before its proper turn had come, photographs in which every generation was present really did signify something of a family achievement in the past.

If your grandparent or great-grandparent ancestor is portrayed alone in a photograph in her best clothing, it's worth considering whether the photograph might have been taken to mark a significant birthday such as a 60th, 70th or 80th. Photographs featuring grandparents or great-grandparents as couples might have been taken to celebrate significant wedding anniversaries; 25th and 50th wedding anniversaries were celebrated from the late nineteenth century onwards (from the 1930s, people also often celebrated their first, 10th, 20th and 70th anniversaries as well) (see Image 37). Look out too for photographs of older sibling groups. On occasion, these were doctored so that the images of those siblings who were already deceased were grafted on to those still living in order to complete a family group.

The dress of elderly family members in older photographs is, unfortunately, less of an aid to helping us date the image than are the fashion choices of the younger generation. Older people did not keep up with clothing trends in the way that younger people did and thus might well be wearing clothes that are many years out of date. There are, however, a few aspects of dress and posture which are a definite giveaway to a person's superior age. In photographs from the later Victorian period, for example, older women can be identified by the wearing of indoor caps and their dresses, though in the same general shape as those of younger women of their day, may be looser in style and less elaborate in design.

Grandparents and Great-grandparents in the Family

From 1870 onwards with improvements both in the medical sciences and in public health, life expectancy started to increase. Middle-aged people were less likely to die from infectious diseases such as cholera or smallpox, for example, and thus might more frequently sally on into old age. But more than this, old age was becoming almost fashionable by the last three decades of the nineteenth century. After all, the country was presided over by an aging Queen whose whole revered persona was built upon ideas of seniority, sombre behaviour and family values.

When the Queen's daughter, Princess Victoria, became a grandmother in 1878, Victoria in turn became a great-grandmother at the very young age of 59 and the papers were quick to spot the sensational potential in this state of affairs:

> It will make some middle-aged people feel very old . . . to hear that the Princess Royal, who was born within their remembrance, is on the point of becoming a grandmother. Her daughter, the hereditary Princess of Saxe-Meiningen, is expecting her confinement next month, so that, if all goes well, her Majesty the Queen will be a great-grandmother before she is 60. Up to this time, no Queen of England has ever lived to see her great-grandchildren, but her Majesty may now reasonably hope to be a great-great grandmother and to see her grandchildren's grandchildren. (*Staffordshire Sentinel*, 16 January 1879)

With the birth of her first great-grandchild, Queen Victoria had become something of an emblem of the aging process itself – and it is worth remembering that she went on to live for another twenty-two years after this newspaper article appeared, a fact which made old age in the last twenty years of the nineteenth century more visible in the media and more generally discussed

Certainly, old age seems to have got more and more attention at this time with greater numbers of aged people appearing in paintings, photographs and novels than ever before (see Images 38 and 39). There circulated an idea in the nineteenth century that a virtuous life would be a guarantee of a contented old age. And for some members of the upper and middle classes, certainly, old age could indeed be the crown of a prosperous life. Continued health, longevity and finally submission to a natural death were regarded by some philosophers as worldly rewards for proper conduct, whilst infirmity and sickness in old age were seen as punishment for intemperance and undesirable behaviour. Of course, all too frequently the quality of our grandparent ancestors' old age was not remotely dependent on how morally they had led their lives, but on their good or bad fortune, or more particularly, their material wealth.

In fact, for many of our elderly ancestors the nineteenth and early twentieth centuries were a time of great precariousness in terms of health and finances. Paradoxically, although killer diseases were on the wane, this did not actually mean that the overall general health of the Victorian population improved. A higher proportion of elderly people in the population meant a higher incidence of those illnesses that particularly affected the elderly, including bronchitis, rheumatism, senility, and visual and other sensory impairments. Thus, whilst the delightful elderly ladies in Mrs Gaskell's novel *Cranford* (1851) affirmed and celebrated the joys of old age, some of the characters in the novels of Charles Dickens were in a pitiable condition reflective of the parlous economic state of many elderly people in British society.

When considering the longevity of your ancestors, it is worth remembering that it was only in the early twentieth century that *most* people started to live into old age, and that death in childhood, youth and middle age started to become shocking rather than 'par for the course'. Indeed, in 1900, your ancestor was still extremely unlikely to live to extreme old age: only seventy-four people in Britain reached the age of 100 that year as opposed to the 3,000 people who made it to a century in the year 2000.

If you take a look at a census in which an elderly relative appears, you will be confronted by the question of how they might have supported themselves in their latter years: whether they were still working, being supported by the family or living in some sort of private, charitable or public institution. All this will very much depend on whether they lived in a city or in a rural location, their class status, their ethnicity and what they had done for a living earlier in their lifetime. Elderly female relatives faced, if anything, greater challenges still. Whilst assistance from the State was increasing during the nineteenth century, it was incomplete and often highly inadequate. There was, therefore, always concern about the fate of family members in their final stretch of life.

Work

Before the advent of old-age pensions in 1908, and in many cases for long afterwards besides, most old people in the past had to continue to work until they were no longer able to do so. It is worth bearing in mind generally that in the nineteenth century it was, therefore, *physical fitness* rather than chronological age that determined what one's life was like materially.

The chances are that your elderly ancestor will have had to carry on working way past what we now consider to be 'retirement age'. According to an audit by the family history service Ancestry (based on 1,007 records from the 1891 census), over 57 per cent of adults continued to work past the age of 65 in the last decade of the nineteenth century. For men, the figure was as high as 88 per cent and for women 33 per cent. Some men were still working in highly physical jobs as farmers and miners well into their eighties and even, in some cases, their nineties. Where younger generations had moved away, you might find that the older people in your family remained behind in a village or country town where they helped make up the rural workforce. Women too might have carried on working as servants, laundresses, cooks and cleaners.

In some cases, these experiences will have been positive. In areas of so called 'proto-industrial' activity, elderly people could take part alongside other family members in employments such as weaving, knitting and gloving. Here the pace and hours of work could be determined by the worker, something which facilitated the productive contribution of older people to the household. In this configuration, grandparents might still maintain a role in the economic decision-making of the household. They could also usefully teach members of the younger generation the skills required in the family business and help out with childcare when parents had to work.

But much of the story of the older workforce in the past is depressing. You should think carefully about the job descriptions of elderly people as given on the censuses. With increasing age, many people moved into less secure, lower-skilled and worse-paid casual jobs or jobs in declining industries. Older factory workers who became ill or who could simply not keep up with the pace of the machines or the longer working day had to find other ways of earning a living. Many older people in cities carried on in their factory work for as long as was possible and then moved into lighter, more menial jobs such as charring, sweeping and street cleaning.

Bear in mind too that older people were also often the first to become unemployed in economic downturns and their work could be marginal, casual, degrading and exhausting. The changes brought about by industrialisation – the need for flexibility and rapid adaptation in the workplace, the demands of new technology, the problems of living in overcrowded accommodation and more besides – probably adversely affected the elderly more than any other group in the population. The Victorian era was perhaps the age when (more than for any other previous generation), the elderly were forced to learn a great deal from the middle generation in order to survive. Inevitably, many failed to rise to the challenge.

Family Support
For those too infirm or ill to work, there was little public welfare provision, as we shall see below. But your non-working elderly ancestors must have obtained money, meals, clothes, shelter and other sorts of household help from somewhere. The census might reveal that older members of your family moved to live with their children, or that a single daughter had stayed at home – perhaps forfeiting her own marriage prospects in the process – to look after her elderly parents. With the high mortality rates amongst adult men and women, it was fairly common for young adults to find themselves looking after their grandparents when their parents had passed away.

There were many cases where young families migrated from the countryside to the town and took their elderly folk along with them (either at the start of the business or later on once the junior part of the family had become established). In the 1880s, for example, most of the adult sons and daughters of the Terrell family from Henstridge in Somerset moved to Manchester to work as cooks, street cleaners and in the boot and shoe trade. Here they married and had children of their own. Initially, they left behind their elderly parents and youngest brother. In time, however, the older generation were sent for and came up to live near their children in Beswick.

Don't be too surprised – or censorious – if you find that the young people in your family left the elderly permanently behind when they moved to the towns to take up work in the industrial period. Although multi-generational households in the past were far more common than they are today with many large Victorian houses sheltering several generations of the same family, they were far less common in England than they were in other parts of Europe (see Image 40).

The older people in your Victorian family may well have been marginalised and left in vulnerable situations. In families where children grew up and moved away to work – especially where families were small in the first place – grandparents of the Victorian era and early nineteenth century must have lost their control over the overall family budget and family decision-making processes in ways that earlier generations had rarely done previously. Even where children grew up but stayed in the local vicinity, they were often in separate dwelling places to their parents and the central hub of family life usually shifted away from the grandparents' home to that of one of their married progeny.

Moreover, because of the high numbers of people of all ages dying prematurely in the Victorian era, an elderly couple could not rely on the fact that any young member of their family would be there to help them out when they needed it. Many elderly people were not cared for by their offspring, not because the children had moved away, but because they had predeceased them. Finally, some old people themselves, it seems, wished for a degree of independence, another factor which led to some of them spending their last years separately from the younger generation. It's worth noting that if your ancestor was from a family that had immigrated to Britain from Eastern Europe or Italy, for example, the younger generation is far more likely to have looked after the older one within the same household than if the family had lived in Britain for generations.

Religious and Private Charities
At the end of their working lives, some of our elderly ancestors would have benefitted from the attentions of religious or private charities. These might have been ancient in origin or have been newly started by local wealthy philanthropists disheartened by the fate of the elderly poor in their neighbourhoods. Inspired by the general air of munificence surrounding the Golden Jubilee celebrations for Queen Victoria, Mr Ellis Kerry of Crouch Street, Colchester wrote to his local paper on 17 February 1887:

> ... we should erect and endow a certain number of almshouses for respectable elderly people, who have perhaps given their best years and done their share of good in the Borough, yet have nothing to look for in their old age but 'The House' [i.e. the Workhouse], or semi-starvation in a cottage, the rent of which swamps the greater part of their little pittance. What more welcome gift in Honour of our kind-hearted Queen than homes for those of her subjects who have honestly toiled but are now past toiling? (*Essex Standard*, 19 February 1887)

It is worth checking in local and county archives, trade directories and local history books to find out what sorts of charities might have been in operation in the areas in which your ancestors lived. The location of records in the form of account books, minutes and Charity Commission reports might be found by searching the website of the National Archives (www.nationalarchives.org).

There were also a large number of national and local charitable organisations specifically attached to professions. An example of one of these was the Governesses' Benevolent Institution founded in 1841 by the Reverend David Laing. This provided a number of services for women who worked or had worked as governesses, including temporary financial assistance, a Provident Fund (or type of pension), a system of registration, a home for governesses who were between engagements and an asylum for aged governesses in Kentish Town.

The *Annual Reports* of the Institution chart what happened to some governesses who came by way of the Institution in old age. Obtaining an annuity (or yearly pension) was actually no easy matter. In 1848, there were eighty-four would-be annuitants chasing three £15 annuities. One plea for financial help was as follows:

Mrs Arabella H., aged 69. Became a governess on being left a widow at four-and-twenty, and has, ever since been engaged in tuition, but has been entirely ruined by bad debts, and the dishonesty of her solicitor who absconded with £1,200. Her advanced age prevents her gaining any employment, her health is giving way under her trials and privations, and she has no income whatever now. Nov.1846 (*Governesses' Benevolent Institution Annual Reports* [1852, published 1853])

Bear in mind that charitable help for elderly people in the form of annuities, accommodation (including almshouses) or other kinds of assistance tended to be arbitrarily given, small-scale and very locally distributed and despite their best efforts, charitable organisations themselves could not meet the needs of a rapidly expanding nineteenth-century population. Most of our ancestors, therefore, would have known they could not be counted upon.

Friendly Societies
It is possible that your elderly ancestor had the foresight to plan for his or her old age. If he or she was wealthy this might have involved sensible financial planning and a squirrelling-away of some monies which could then be drawn upon in later life. A popular method of saving for old age amongst the skilled and unskilled working-classes, on the other hand, was by joining a so-called Friendly Society. Members identified strongly with their society, often going through initiation ceremonies and using secret passwords and signs. You may find regalia, banners, certificates, sashes or emblems associated with a friendly society amongst inherited family items.

Friendly societies sprang up all over the country in both urban and rural areas. As early as 1806, there were thirteen such societies in the city of Lancaster alone. Women were usually excluded from membership although there were some female-only friendly societies too. The idea was to enable the working classes to help themselves through a mutual savings scheme. Meeting usually every month, often in a public house, members of friendly societies would be required to pay a small subscription. This then could be drawn upon at times when a contributor was unable to work because of sickness. Of course, many of these periods of sickness occurred when the worker was elderly, There were also some societies (such as the South Gloucestershire Friendly Society) which paid out a pension when workers were simply too old to work.

Friendly Societies were popular because they did not carry the stigma attached to the Poor Law Unions (state-funded aid), nor any of its penalties (paupers were not allowed to vote even after working men were enfranchised by the Representation of the People Act of 1867, for example), and because the levels of benefit paid out were higher. If you suspect that a Friendly Society was instrumental in helping your elderly ancestor in times of hardship, you should look to find the location of the records of the Society in question via the National Archives (www.nationalarchives.org). It's possible that you might come across minute books and membership books which will indicate the amounts paid by your ancestor and whether or not he or she ever drew upon the resources, for how long and for what reason.

The variety of types of Friendly Society was enormous with their different clientele and different purposes sometimes apparent in their titles. Family historians with an ancestor who lived in Lancashire, might, for example, spend some time puzzling over which of these many Friendly Societies he or she might have belonged to:

Some of the Friendly Societies of Lancashire have rather odd names: Thus, there is the Backbone Friendly Society, The Unanimous Sick and Burial Society, The Liberal Permanent Friendly Society, The Young King Charles Friendly Society, The Blooming Rose Friendly Sick and Burial Society, The Persevering Magnificent Sick and Burial Society, The Brotherly Knot, The Pool of Bethesda Friendly Society, The Honest View Sick and Burial Society, The Offspring of Love

Lodge of the Manchester Unity of Oddfellows, the Female Druids, The Female Foresters, The Independent Odd Females, The Dove Tent of Female Rechabites, The Beloved Lodge of Female Druids, &c. (*The Illustrated Times*, London, 12 October 1867)

Public Relief

If your elderly ancestor was not working, nor being wholly supported by the younger generations of the family or by private or religious charity or by a Friendly Society, he or she might have received some sort of public or state-funded relief. Following the 1832 Royal Commission into the Operation of the Poor Law headed by social reformer Edwin Chadwick, the 1834 Poor Law Amendment Act divided England and Wales into districts known as unions, expressly to tackle the problems of poverty – and, necessarily, therefore, of the elderly poor. The Poor Law Provision in Scotland was different and separate and revised by the Scottish Poor Law Act of 1845.

Names of recipients of a Poor Law Pension, also known as 'outdoor relief' (since it did not pay for accommodation), can be found in Poor Law records for local areas kept in local, county or national record offices. These locations may be searched via the National Archives website (www.nationalarchives.org). The Archives and Special Collections of the Mitchell Library in Glasgow, for example, contain over one million applications for poor relief made by residents of Glasgow and the West of Scotland, giving fascinating details about the ins and outs of domestic life for poor families in the region. Outdoor relief consisted of meals plus a small allowance. It allowed some old people to remain in their own homes or in that of another member of the family.

In the worst cases of poverty, an elderly ancestor will have been admitted to a workhouse (see Image 40). If he or she happened to be in such an institution at the time when one of the ten-yearly censuses was taken, his or her details will be amongst those of other members of that institution. You should also check for the location of the relevant workhouse records on the National Archives website. Entering such an institution would have involved an upsetting reduction of autonomy a relinquishing of personal belongings, and a loss of contact with friends and family. Conditions were frequently crowded and unsanitary, the work repetitive and heavy, leisure time unfulfilling, nursing provision poor and the food uninspiring to say the least. Some workhouses had adjoining 'workhouse infirmaries' which housed the incapacitated poor, very many of whom were elderly. Though your ancestor is unlikely to have relished the idea of going into the workhouse, older inmates did have some advantages over the young. Whilst younger couples were sex-segregated, for example, in some instances after 1847 married couples over 60 could stay together.

If you are interested in finding out the exact mechanics of poor relief inside or outside the workhouse, remember that it was organised and financed through local taxes and thus subject to considerable regional variation. It is worth reading up on how the Poor Law was implemented in the area in which you are interested and there are many local history books devoted to this subject.

Edwin Chadwick's *Report on the Sanitary Condition of the Labouring Population* in 1842 led eventually to some public health reforms which affected old people, but it did not tackle old age or indeed poverty in general directly. Sadly, as a result primarily of inertia on the part of the State, one in eight women aged 75 and over were still to be found in London workhouses in 1851. Forty years later, in the 1890s, this proportion had increased to the point that about a third of the population of workhouses were elderly men and women with the figures being higher in London. In 1901, 10 per cent of English men and 6 per cent of women aged 75 and over were in workhouses and there was still no state pension provision (figures from Pat Thane, *The Long History of Old Age* [2005]). It is to be hoped that if your ancestor was admitted to a workhouse, he or she was regarded rather better than this old lady who, as her long life drew to a close in 1907, was reported by the newspapers solely in terms of what she had cost the State:

Sarah Bramley, an inmate of the Nottingham workhouse, who is 108 years old, is seriously ill and is not expected to live many days. She was born in Nottingham in 1799 and entered the workhouse 44 years ago. Her maintenance has cost the Guardians over £900. (*Portsmouth Evening News*, 24 December 1907)

You might find an elderly relative described as 'a lunatic' on a census form and it is possible that he or she spent his or her final years not at home or in a workhouse but in a lunatic asylum. The locations of the records of these institutions can again be found via the website of the National Archives, www.nationalarchives.org. 'Lunatic' was a general catch all term for people with mental impairment (and didn't carry the intense negative connotations that it does today). In the case of older people, lunatic usually implied nothing more than the fact that the person was suffering from 'senile dementia' (a phrase first used in 1835) and joined, as the nineteenth century progressed, by terminology such as 'senile epilepsy', 'senile melancholia' and 'senile mania'. The suitability of a lunatic asylum for old people who were simply suffering the mental decay of old age, rather than a more serious psychotic illness, was much debated in the nineteenth century.

Old Age Pensions
In 1894, the social reformer Charles Booth published a report into the state of old people (*The Aged Poor in England and Wales*), in which he advocated a universal state-funded pension for the elderly. At this point, his cries went unheeded. By the early years of the twentieth century, however, it was generally acknowledged that there had been a sufficient weakening of family ties between elderly people and their working children to a degree that might seriously affect the former group, especially women, who might have been out of the workforce for long periods and unable to save.

In 1908, in response to these fears, the Liberal government passed the Old Age Pensions Act which was quickly followed by the institution of the State Pension Scheme (enacted from 1 August 1908). Don't assume, however, that your elderly ancestor would have definitely benefitted from a pension at this point. To have been considered eligible, he or she would have had to be over the age of 70, and earning less than £31 and 10 shillings a year (that is, 12 shillings weekly). He or she would also have had to undergo a character test to ensure that he or she had a history of employment, had been a British citizen for at least ten years, was of sound mind, was not receiving poor relief, had not been in prison during the previous decade, and had not been convicted of drunkenness. The pension was 5 shillings a week for individuals and 7s 6d for married couples.

This was a pension only for the very poorest and the longest-lived. It was, of course, set deliberately low – as an incentive to families to contribute to the upkeep of their elderly members. Few of our ancestors will have qualified and indeed *The Times* reported on 13 January 1909 that only 596,038 pensions had been granted, mostly to poor women. The pension was a far cry from the universal old age pension that had been advocated by Charles Booth more than a decade earlier but it was non-contributory, and it was a start.

After the First World War, in 1919, the amount of the weekly pension was increased to 10 shillings for individuals. In 1925 the Contributory Pensions Act extended the National Health Insurance scheme (established 1911) to provide pensions for people between the ages of 65 and 70 who had made contributions. This Act affected mainly male manual workers (higher-paid, white-collar workers were excluded). Employed single women could contribute, but paid lower contributions and received lower benefits on the often incorrect assumption that they had fewer responsibilities. Many such women amongst our ancestors will, in fact, have supported siblings or older relatives. The insurance pension was flat-rate and fixed at the same low level as the non-contributory pension.

In the 1920s and 1930s, many of our male ancestors who were white-collar workers may also have benefitted from occupational or private pensions at retirement at around the ages 60–65. State officials and high-status employees in the private sector had lower retirement ages than the state pension age. In general in terms of pensions, women fared worse than men because many were compelled on marriage to give up the kinds of employment in which occupational pensions were available and to take instead lump-sum marriage gratuities (these were mainly women who worked in jobs in the public sector, in post-offices, banks and the like).

In 1935, the National Spinsters' Pensions Association was formed, drawing attention to the particular problems of unmarried women leaving the workforce. These women had had restricted job opportunities, lower pay and fewer opportunities for saving than men, as well as suffering generally poorer health than men after the age of 55. Additionally many were caring for elderly relatives alongside a job, or had been forced to leave employment in order to care for elderly relatives. In 1940, the pensionable age for women was reduced from 65 to 60. But the level of pension remained very low.

The Government surveyed pensioners during the Second World War and found appalling levels of poverty, especially among females. In 1940 Supplementary Assistance, a means-tested boost to the already means-tested pension, was introduced. One-third of all pensioners immediately qualified for this, again mostly female. In 1946, the National Insurance Act finally introduced a contributory State Pension for all, at 60 for women and 65 for men. The initial amount received by our ancestors at this time would have been £1.30 a week for a single person and £2.10 for a married couple.

Over the course of the nineteenth and early twentieth centuries, public relief for the poor moved slowly away from the jurisdiction of the localities towards a more centralised benefits system. It was not, however, until 1948 that the situation for most of our elderly ancestors improved when the Poor Law System was finally completely replaced by government initiatives including the new National Health Service, Comprehensive National Insurance Scheme and The National Assistance System (a safety net for those members of society who had not paid National Insurance contributions).

Health
If your elderly ancestor was ill during the nineteenth century – particularly if the illness was chronic or incurable, such as rheumatism or arthritis – you can probably save yourself the bother of looking up his or her admission to hospital in archived medical records as it is very unlikely to have happened. As our ancestors' death certificates will testify, most elderly people died at home in their own beds. A key factor in the deaths of old people could be the weather, with public

health sources in Bristol November 1886 reporting, for instance, that thirty of the ninety-six deaths in the city the previous week had been of elderly people and continuing:

> The rise in the mortality was owing to the numbers of deaths among elderly people on account of the very cold weather which has recently prevailed. I expect a further increase in mortality from the same cause. (*The Western Daily Press*, 26 November 1886)

The general health of elderly people was very far down the pecking order in terms of the State's priorities in the Victorian period. Public money (tax – used for the building of new State-run hospitals) as well as money privately donated by individuals (for the upkeep of voluntary hospitals), was mainly reinvested into health services targeted at the young and more productive workforce. Indeed, the Admissions regulations for some hospitals expressly forbad the admittance of elderly people and many institutions specialised in the diseases least likely to affect them. Historians of old age have noted that English hospital records of the Victorian period show a gross underrepresentation of elderly patients relative to their higher medical needs compared to younger people.

Hospitals in the nineteenth century were required to produce positive publishable results in the form of cures. Thus, whilst large amounts of public money were ploughed into vaccination against and treatment of infectious diseases (from which the elderly did undoubtedly benefit to a small degree), very little scientific or medical attention was being paid to the kinds of infirmities of old age which will have afflicted the oldest people in society. As historian Pat Thane has put it, 'sadly to say, in the nineteenth century, Britain's hospital provision rather ignored its old people' (Thane, *The Long History of Old Age*, p. 238).

Hearteningly, however, our grandparent ancestors are increasingly likely to have been admitted to hospitals for a whole range of complaints in the early twentieth century. To start with, a new field of medicine entirely devoted to the ageing population came into being: the term 'geriatrics' was, in fact, first used in 1909. But it was not until the inauguration of the National Health Service in 1948 – almost at the end of the period covered by this book – that the health of Britain's old people was really taken seriously. At this point, for the first time in history, people suffering from mundane but disabling conditions (impaired hearing, failing eyesight, dental and podiatric problems) could for the first time be treated for free.

Improvements in welfare provision, health treatment, income, diet, public health and hygiene meant that it was much more common for our grandparent ancestors to live into extreme old age by 1950 than it had been at the beginning of the twentieth century. Hair colourants, cheaper fashions and better information about maintaining health all contributed to the increasingly youthful appearance of elderly people. On the other hand, of course, the proportion of older people in the population steadily increased in the first half of the century and with it, the suffering of more people from chronic illnesses and from conditions such as Alzheimer's.

Sadly, the treatment of our elderly ancestors at different historical periods by the State seems to have been very much dependent on the relative proportions of old and young people in society at any one time. When the birth rate fell around the time of the First World War, the value of the elderly in society rose, when the birth rate went up again (i.e. between the two World Wars) the status of the elderly fell again. Our assessment of our ancestors in old age needs to be carried out with this background of factors in mind.

Issue 1: Was my ancestor really as old as the records say?
As has been suggested, don't be too surprised to find ancestors on death certificates and censuses who lived to a good old age. Although average life expectancy was much lower in the nineteenth and early twentieth centuries than it is now – 47 (for men) and 51 (for women) in 1900 as opposed to 76 (for men) and 81 (for women) in 1991 – this doesn't mean that most people died in middle age. Calculations of life expectancy were influenced by very high infant death rates which inevitably brought down the 'mean' age of death. In fact, those of our ancestors who managed to survive infancy had a pretty good chance of living to 60 and beyond. Certain geographical areas such as

Falkland, Fife were proud of their proclivity for maintaining an elderly population:

> Our attention was drawn by one of our neighbours the other day, to the numbers of great-grandfathers and great-grandmothers in Falkland, when, says, our correspondent, upon writing down their names, we found that there were no fewer than nine great-grandfathers and fifteen great-grandmothers, and we question if any other place of a similar size could number so many. (*Dunfermline Saturday Press*, 27 August 1859)

Where couples married at young ages over several generations, a household might find itself either headed by or caring for a great-grandparent. In the censuses, great-grandparents are usually described as the 'heads of families' until they are about 65. After this, they will appear as the 'mother' or 'father' 'grandmother' or 'grandfather' of the Head of Household. Where they are recorded as 'great-grandmother' or 'great-grandfather,' this is probably a mistake on the part of the enumerator since they are unlikely to have held this relationship to the Head of Household (see Image 41).

Consider carefully the given ages of your oldest ancestors on the census. A Government Report into the 1881 census (www.vision ofbritain.org.uk/) expressed a wariness about some of the ages given by older members of the population. Significantly, very elderly persons, it suggested, were tending to overestimate their age. The report on the 1881 census advised future enumerators to put little trust in 'anyone stating their age as a multiple of 5 or 10 over 85'. And those stating that they had reached the ripe old age of a hundred were to be treated with extra scepticism; very few people, conceded the report, would actually be 'entitled to centenarian honours', despite the fact that nearly 150 British citizens claimed to have reached that point. *The Aberdeen Evening Press* of 4 January 1894 threw doubt on one claim by a man that he was 116 years of age; 'It would be interesting to learn on what evidence this averment is based; for, it is a remarkable fact that, whereas up to a certain point, mankind is ashamed of its years and tries to decrease them by *taradiddling*, after that point has been passed, it becomes ashamed of its youth, and seeks to make itself out older by the same methods.'

Failing memories obviously played a part in this and few of our ancestors would have bothered to check civil registration documents or parish records to double-check their date of birth before filling in a census form. There may also have been an element of boasting in the padding of figures as suggested above; those in their eighties had good reason to feel a little special, and adding a few years to their age might well have added to their standing in the community (see Image 42).

There was a particular problem of elderly people exaggerating their ages in rural Ireland after the introduction of the means-tested pension for UK residents over the age of 70 (including Ireland) on New Year's Day 1909. As the registration of births in Ireland had not been compulsory during the vital period and many registers of baptism or marriage could not be traced, pension officers were forced to accept the evidence of ages shown in family Bibles, on marriage certificates and insurance policies. They were also encouraged to study the appearance of claimants' carefully. Word got round that the officers would be impressed if aged claimants said they could remember 'the night of the big wind' (6–7 January 1839) – a memory which supposedly might help confirm that the respondent was at least 72 years old in 1909. But English pension officers were understandably on their guard against the vagueness of these aspirant Irish pensioners.

By the 1930s, however, with improved longevity for many, some of the scepticism of officialdom had disappeared and journalists were happy to celebrate very long lives. The 101-year-old Mrs Elizabeth Jeffrey of Hartland featured in *The Exeter and Plymouth Gazette* on 12 August 1932, attested to the extraordinary changes that had taken place in society during her lifetime and commented particularly on the development of machinery. The paper added, 'She has specially had in mind its effect on the farming industry. In her young days, corn was reaped by hooks and a picturesque and pleasing thing it must have been to see the regular and auxiliary farmhands engaged in their task. Nowadays, a machine, drawn by horses, or perhaps a motor, does the work with monotonous whirr, but no doubt with effectiveness and celerity.' Those whose lives spanned the greater part of the period covered by this book had certainly seen some extraordinary changes within their lifetimes (see Image 43).

Issue 2: How did widows manage in old age?

At first glance, elderly widows might not seem the most attractive subjects to investigate on the family tree. Indeed, the lonely, dour women in black often remain ignored by family historians who are under the misapprehension that their lives can't yield anything of interest. Far from it: widows of all ages actually made up a huge proportion of the nineteenth- and early twentieth-century populations (they were far more numerous, for example, than women who never married). In 1851, there were three-quarters of a million widows in Britain (in a population of twenty million). Men who became widowers (especially after the deaths of wives in childbirth) unfortunately remain outside the scope of this section.

Unlike married women and even spinsters, widows are fairly visible in old documents since they had a definite legal status when these other women did not. As has been explained in Chapter 2, in the nineteenth century (until the passing of the Married Women's Property Acts of 1870, 1882 and 1893) married women had few legal rights to the ownership of personal property and had no rights to dispose of property through wills. All this changed on the death of their husbands. 'In widowhood,' as one historian has put it, 'women were reborn as independent actors.' They had the right to own property, run businesses and to dispose of their assets via a will. They appeared in court on their own behalf, and headed households in the census. All this means that there are far more records available to help you in tracing the life of your widowed ancestor than there are to help you when researching married women in the distant past. Widowhood was not just the provenance of the elderly, of course, but nevertheless there was something particularly poignant about the situation of a woman who lost her husband in old age.

Unless she wrote particularly personal letters or kept a diary which has been preserved, you will never know how your elderly ancestor actually felt upon losing her husband, but, if she was a Victorian, it is more than likely that she tried to emulate the reserved and terribly

British stoicism of her widowed monarch. Queen Victoria's protracted mourning for her husband Prince Albert began in 1861 when she was only 42 but already a grandmother twice over. She described her feelings on losing him thus: 'I am an utterly broken-hearted and crushed widow of forty-two. I must live on (and I will do nothing to make me worse than I am), it is henceforth for our poor fatherless children – for my unhappy country, which has lost all in losing him – and in only doing what I know and feel he would wish.' (Letter to King Leopold of the Belgians, 20 December 1861)

Unsurprisingly, the expressions adopted by elderly widows in Victorian and Edwardian photographs are uniformly sombre or wistful. Look carefully at your elderly ancestor's accessories, her umbrella, for instance, which, if deep black, might indicate recent widowhood. You should also look out in photographs for any reminders of her deceased husband. Some widows sat in front of portraits of their dead spouses. Some touched jet lockets around their necks, others held letters edged in black, and many carried small bouquets of lillies or forget-me-nots. Queen Victoria – a leader in this as in all aspects of mourning – was often photographed with a bust of the late Prince Albert in the background.

The widows in your family will also be identifiable from their clothing since they were expected to dress to indicate mourning for at least twenty-eight months and sometimes up to four years after their spouses' death. The entire ensemble was colloquially known as 'widow's weeds' (from the Old English 'waed' meaning 'garment'). There were three distinct periods of mourning. *Full mourning* (usually worn for a year and a day) demanded unrelieved black clothing. Look out for dresses that are more than usually heavy and concealing in dull-surfaced fabrics such as plain bombazine (a mixture of silk and wool), parametta, merino wool, cashmere and, most popularly, crepe. It was thought proper that the hair was completely covered. Special caps and bonnets were also worn (sometimes made of white crepe). Veils were also popular.

During the period of *secondary mourning* (which lasted about nine months), a widow might wear somewhat fancier fabrics, provided they were still black, and might add fabric trims made from black velvet, silk, lace ribbons and jet. In the final six months of *half mourning*, widows might wear grey, white, purple or violet in addition to black. Every change was subtle and gradual, beginning firstly with trims of these colours (in the shape of rosettes, bows, belts, and streamers) added to the black dresses. As the mourning period moved on, hats and bonnets became more trimmed and fancy, whilst veils became shorter until they were eventually removed altogether

Look out also in family photographs for mourning jewellery. Newly-widowed women would probably avoid jewellery of any kind. But, in the later stages of mourning, all manner of jewellery including necklaces, brooches, watches, bracelets and rings of black jet was worn. Mourning buttons of black jet were sometimes sewn on to garments. Some items included compartments in which a lock of the dead husband's hair might be placed. When in half mourning, widows might wear black jet jewellery relieved with a little silver to lighten the effect. Poorer people had jewellery of black glass made to look like jet.

Whilst widows might have taken the period of mourning very seriously, the state of widowhood was by no means universally awful. One newspaper voiced the common feeling that life for a widow could, sometimes, in fact, be better than life for a married woman:

> There are widows and widows. There are those who are bereaved and those who are released; those who lose their support, and those whose chains are broken; those who are sunk in desolation; and those who wake up into freedom. (*The Western Daily Press* [quoting from *The Saturday Review*], 15 February 1869)

Your elderly widowed ancestor will have had a kind and quality of life very much dependent on the new state of her finances – usually a lowering thereof – after her husband's death. A number of different possibilities were on offer.

Many women who had lost their husbands remarried (10 per cent of all marriages in 1850 involved a widow) and the press often joked about these so-called 'hawk widows', 'she has no notion of a perpetuity of weeds, and though she may have cleared her half-century with a margin besides, thinks the suggestive orange-blossoms of the bride infinitely more desirable than the fruitless heliotrope of the widow' (*The Western Daily Press* [quoting from *The Saturday Review*], 15 February 1869). But, despite the confidence of this assertion, older widows were actually far less likely to remarry than women who had been bereaved in their twenties and thirties.

Some widows were left enough money on their husbands' deaths to survive or even to live comfortably without remarrying. You will find them on censuses and other records described as 'gentlewomen' or 'living off independent means'. In the nineteenth century, even if a husband died intestate (without a will), his widow would be entitled to half his estate under the Dower Act of 1833; the other half would be divided amongst his legal relatives (of whom she was not counted as a member). If the couple had children, the children would be entitled to two-thirds of the estate and the widow a third. Under the Equitable Jointure system (popular in the second half of the nineteenth century amongst the middle classes), a woman's father could bargain (before she was married) for how much she would receive if she were to be widowed.

In 1851, there were 117,000 women living off independent means, mainly in the South of England and in metropolitan areas. Large numbers of such genteel ladies were also to be found in the spa towns of Bath, Brighton and Cheltenham. Other widows relied on the goodwill of other family members for economic help. Many widows lived off annuities derived from investments in public or other funds and there is evidence to suggest that some such women were quite active in financial decision-making processes.

Widows with less to live off and still in possession of their health, might have succeeded their husbands as owners and managers of small businesses. Many elderly widows ran lodging houses or became chaperones, sometimes finding that their widowhood conferred a certain respectability. If you suspect that your nineteenth-century widow ancestor ran a business, you may potentially discover its name and location in a trade directory. Many of these can now be searched online at www.historicaldirectories.org.

Widows who had no supportive kin, no inheritance and no business, might have found themselves the recipients of charity. This could come from individual benefactors, former employers or societies of one sort or another and might take the form of accommodation, a yearly stipend or other goods. Nineteenth-century newspapers are full of reports of Christmas teas and other festive occasions to which the elderly widows of a parish might have been exclusively invited. It is worth asking in your local library or County Record Office what form charity for widows might have taken in the area in which you are interested. It was not until 1897, that a national charity was set up to help widows. The Charity for Distressed Gentlefolk was begun by Elizabeth Finn with the aim of helping middle-class widows by providing them with small grants and loans. Correspondence and papers for this organisation are held at the London Metropolitan Archives (http://www.cityoflondon.gov. uk/lma), but bear in mind it helped only a handful of widowed women.

Those widows beyond the reach of charity for one reason or another, would, after the Poor Law Amendment Act of 1834, have become some of the most pitiable and vulnerable inmates of workhouses. But, perhaps surprisingly, widows in the early twentieth century were some of those who benefitted most from the first State Pensions introduced by David Lloyd George with the Old Age Pensions Act of 1908. This indeed had partly been drawn up with the needs of elderly and unsupported women in mind. Since they could hardly have been expected to contribute anything to a pension, as many of them might not have worked, or not have worked for long enough or in well-paid enough jobs, the first pensions were non-contributory. Women, including many widows, could claim between 10 pence and 25 pence a week from the age of 70 on a means-tested basis from 1 January 1909.

Widows of British Army and Navy officers were entitled to various benefits at different stages in history. Information relating to army and navy widows (1660–1913) are kept at the National Archives: www. nationalarchives.org. In 1925, State Widows' and Orphans' Pensions were introduced (acknowledging the issue of poverty amongst women whose marriages had ended due to bereavement). The widows' pension was paid to all widows of insured men with children under the age of 14 at the time of the husband's death. It was set at the same low level as the old-age pension and was payable for life. Protest followed that this was unfair to women widowed at older ages who might have been out of the labour market for many years caring for a husband and children and who would find it difficult to support themselves, especially amid the high unemployment of the 1920s. In 1929 entitlement to the Widows' Pension was extended to all widows of insured men from the age of 55. This assisted a substantial group of poor older women.

The economic situation of widows continued to be difficult until at least the middle of the twentieth century. The demographics were not in their favour. In many first marriages women married men, on average, four or five years older than themselves. Since women tended to outlive men by three or four years, this meant that there was often a financial shortfall at the end of a woman's life of nearly a decade. Women who had been married to men with occupational pensions could not necessarily expect to inherit all or any of that pension on their husbands' deaths. As a result of all these factors, how your female ancestor fared at the end of her life is likely to be something that deserves your curiosity and, more often than not, your sympathy.

CHAPTER 7

Beyond the Family: Friends, Neighbours and Club Associates

Most of our interest as family historians obviously lies in the blood and marriage relationships of our ancestors, but, in our quest to understand more about these shadowy names in the records, we shouldn't neglect to investigate the wider circles in which they mixed. Friends, neighbours and associates of all kinds will have contributed to their day-to-day life experiences and knowing a little more about these other people, may help us better to imagine what an ancestor himself or herself was like and explain some of the life decisions that he or she took.

What can we learn from photographs in which our ancestors are pictured alongside friends, neighbours or fellow members of clubs or organisations? What aspects of our ancestors' friendships should we be interested in? What constituted neighbourliness and what can our ancestors' neighbours reveal about our ancestors themselves? To which kinds of organisations and clubs might our ancestors have belonged? What can private records of social interactions yield? And what might we find out about our ancestors from the records of clubs and organisations?

Friends, Neighbours and Club Associates in Photographs
Group photographs of your ancestors might show them posing with friends, partying in the street with neighbours at times of national celebration, or standing shoulder-to-shoulder in more formal pictures with workmates or other members of the clubs and societies to which they belonged. Throughout the nineteenth and twentieth centuries, the

range of organisations of which our male and female ancestors were members were more numerous and more varied than ever before. A quick flick through old group photographs online shows rifle clubs, football clubs, clubs for model boats and model aircraft, dominoes and darts teams, tennis, hockey and polo teams, guides, brownies and scouts, to name but the most obvious. There were also clubs with political affiliations, ex-servicemen's clubs, and religious groups connected to churches and chapels, synagogues and the like.

Just as with extended family, photographs of other sorts of groups posed plenty of problems for the photographer in the early days. In 1858, a dozen young girls (aged between eight and seventeen) from an industrial school in North London making dolls' house furniture were taken for a day out to a local country house in Romford:

> In the course of the day a son of the house desired to take a photograph of the party. They were arranged – some standing, some sitting, some with flowers. The difficulty was that, if one held a flower, all the others wished to hold one also, which the young artist declared to be against the rules of composition. The children wished Miss O. P. Q. to come into the group; and then each wanted to be taken sitting by her side. When all was settled, great misfortune got among the chemicals, and the photograph did not succeed. ('Ragged Robin', *Household Words*, Volume XIII [17 May 1856], p. 419)

In 1891, photographer Henry Peach Robinson suggested that larger groups were best photographed outside where the sitters would not be cramped and where the exposure would be much quicker. For best results, sitters, he said, should be arranged in a 'pyramid shape' or in 'a series of pyramid shapes'. Where there was no natural differentiation of height, the photographer might aim to create that effect by positioning some of the sitters either on a bank or a step, or bending over as if talking to the others. Whilst a group might include many people of varying appearances and stature, 'there should always be a oneness in the group; the string should run through all the beads, but should be more felt than seen (Robinson, *The Studio and What to Do In It*, p. 84).

Robinson further recommended that all the sitters be positioned out of the glare of the sun, that shining leaves (which created white spots) should not appear and that a broad expanse of light such as a blank wall should be in the background. Group pictures should be taken quickly and efforts should be made to ensure that every 'face [. . .] present a favourable portrait independent of the others'. As has already been mentioned, the availability and success of the group photograph was greatly aided by the introduction of highly-sensitive gelatin dry plates from the late 1870s onwards. These vastly reduced exposure times – making it easier to capture a group that might otherwise present too many moving variables. The gelatin plates also allowed for the use of lenses with a greater depth of focus, which meant that all the individuals in a group who were naturally on 'different planes' could be in focus at the same time.

Photography, even in the late Victorian period, was new enough to attract comment in the press. Newspaper accounts of a club's activities, therefore, might give the names of those present as well as more information about the circumstances in which a photograph was taken. In early August 1883, for example, forty-two members of The All Saint's Rambling Club, from Derby met at Irongate, went by train to Miller's Dale, visited Chee Torr, Cressbrook Dale and Monsall Dale before arriving in Bakewell where they 'partook of a knife and fork tea at 4pm'. After a short church service:

> Two photographs of the entire party were taken by Mr H. Arnold Bemrose. Amongst other members of the party were Mr H. H. Bemrose, J. P., and Mrs Bemrose and family, Councillor Symons and Mrs Symons, Mr Frost, Mr Frost jun., Mr and Mrs Broad and Mr C. Hefford. (*Derby Daily Telegraph*, 8 August 1883)

Whilst nineteenth-century photographs of club groups tend to be formal and solemnly posed, those from the first decades of the twentieth-century are often much more relaxed and more suggestive of the activity in question. There is also more likely to be a mixing of the sexes in pictures of groups such as swimming or tennis parties from the 1920s onwards (see Image 44).

Further help in dating old photographs of groups might be available online. Many clubs and societies that are still extant have their own websites which will give the dates at which they were founded and key dates in their histories such as when membership rules changed to allow the admission of women. School, university and military uniforms in group photographs might be successfully identified from a number of dedicated books or websites (see the bibliography for more details).

Friends, Neighbours and Club Associates and the Family
As the example of the All Saints' Rambling Club, Derbyshire (above) shows, social contacts with friends, neighbours and members of other organisations might well have involved more than one member of the same family and might have lasted for generations. Any information you can glean about an ancestor's social connections might, therefore, also be a key to understanding more about your family in general.

Friends
Friendships in the past, as today, usually flourished between people who lived or worked in close proximity to each other, who met regularly and without formality and who had opportunities to share ideas and personal feelings. On the whole, our ancestors tended to make friends with those with whom they shared common backgrounds or interests, or with whom they shared similar demographics (age, occupation, gender, class or ethnicity). Location (or a shared experience of place) was a common factor that linked people in the past. Thus a migrant from Cornwall to London in the late nineteenth century, might have been more likely to start a friendship with another migrant from the South-West to the city than with someone who had been born in the city.

Your ancestor's relationships with friends will have been important to their emotional lives, upheld, as such relationships are today by bonds of affection, sympathy, mutual understanding, compassion and trust. The dense interplay of meetings between friends are mostly lost to history, of course, but there is plenty of evidence of them in the kinds of records that crop up in family papers, letters, postcards and

177

diaries, to name only the most obvious. Whilst women might be absent from many 'official' records from the past, it is in the field of private correspondence with friends that they really take their place in history.

If you find evidence of an ancestor's friendships, try to work out what the points of connection between the two parties might have been. Looking up the details of the lives of friends in censuses and certificates might indicate a number of different kinds of connection between them including birthplace, occupation or even language spoken, or size and ages of family. Look out for friendships which continued throughout a life history, and be aware of how they might have come to encompass other members of a family as time went on. Friends gave gifts which might still be amongst inherited family possessions, they also exchanged favours, lent money to each other and honoured obligations. Friends may have helped your ancestors to obtain employment or accommodation, or advised them on everything and anything from relationships, finances and education, to motherhood or planting a garden (see Image 45).

In the following example of a friendship conducted almost exclusively by letter between two women in the early nineteenth century, the similarities between the two partners in the friendship are not obvious at first glance but become clearer with more background knowledge. The Irish writer Maria Lovell Edgeworth had a friendship (of well over twenty years duration) with American housewife Rachel Mordecai Lazarus, despite the fact that the two women had different religions (Maria was Protestant – though 'rational' in outlook – and Rachel Jewish); were of widely divergent ages (Maria was the elder by twenty years); had a different domestic status (Maria was unmarried and childless, although she had many younger siblings, and Rachel married with seven stepchildren and four children of her own); and occupied vastly different positions in society (Maria was famous and Rachel not so).

On closer inspection it's obvious that Maria and Rachel were more probably friends not because of their differences but because of the similarities between their family situations. They were both the eldest daughters of large extended families, both had lost their mothers as children, both were closely attached to their fathers and surrounded by young children in whose education they shared a passionate interest. Their many letters to each other show a real sense of their shared experiences and a desire to learn from each other's educational methods. The women sent seeds to each other and even, on one occasion, a parrot was sent by Rachel to Maria, though unfortunately it died on the long journey across the Atlantic!

With the unremarkable Rachel Lazarus, Maria Edgeworth had unexpectedly found a meeting of 'hearts and minds', and it was a connection which would extend outwards to encompass many other members of both families. On Rachel's death, her sister Ellen continued to write to Maria. When Maria died, Ellen wrote to her step-mother and half-sisters. On Ellen's death, another half-sister of Rachel took over writing to Maria's sisters and niece, and later Rachel's niece and great-niece continued the correspondence with Maria's half-sister. All in all the correspondence between the two families lasted 127 years and included dozens, if not hundreds, of letters.

Bear in mind that some relationships, described as 'friendships' in private documents such as letters and diaries, might have gone further, of course. It is impossible to say whether co-habiting non-related couples of the same sex (as seen in the census) were just friends or in fact were homosexual partners. In 1885, the British Parliament enacted Section 11 of the Criminal Law Amendment Act which prohibited 'acts of gross indecency' between men. The only official evidence we have then of male homosexuality is that of court records relating to men who breached the law. Lesbianism in the past, on the other hand, was never a criminal offence and is consequently even more difficult to unearth in the records. Nevertheless, it is undoubtedly the case that gay relationships, male and female, frequently masqueraded as friendships in the past. Oscar Wilde's 'friendship' with Lord Alfred Douglas (1870–1945) in the 1890s, for example, was actually a full-blown homosexual affair and a number of so called 'romantic friendships' between women such as that between (Marguerite) Radclyffe Hall (1880–1943) and Una Troubridge (1887–1963) were undoubtedly lesbian in nature.

Neighbours
Equally as relevant as friends to the story of our ancestors might be

those with whom they had less intense or affectionate relationships. Neighbours were not a mere backdrop to your ancestors' lives and might actually have been involved in them in numerous practical ways. These are the people to whom your family would have spoken most frequently on a daily basis, the ones who would have informally minded their children, sat with their sick and helped to lay out their dead. In times when shops closed early and telephones didn't exist, it was to the neighbours that your ancestors would go if they ran out of food, or needed physical or emotional assistance of any kind. Your ancestors will have shared many experiences with their neighbours – from diseases and unemployment to weekend pastimes, holidays and festivals. Neighbours are also the people next to whom your ancestors probably sat in church, and with whom they drank and played sport at local clubs and pubs. And it's beside the neighbours too that your ancestors will probably be buried (see Image 46).

And don't forget that it is highly likely, especially in rural communities, that some of the neighbours might have been related to your ancestors by blood and/or marriage. The historian Claudia Nelson reminds us that in the nineteenth century, 'England was full of villages in which generations of intermarriage had resulted in a community tied together by a complex network of blood relationships' (Nelson, *Family Ties in Victorian England*, p. 134). Where neighbours were also relations they were often tied together not only by bonds of duty, loyalty and affection, that, in themselves, might have been stronger than those experienced today, but also by economic, business, religious and political affiliations.

Related or not, information about your ancestors' closest neighbours may be gleaned most easily from the decennial censuses 1841–1911. From 1861 onwards, the censuses for England and Wales recorded whether houses in an area were inhabited or uninhabited. In theory, you should be able to get a feel for exactly how populated your ancestors' street and neighbourhood actually was. To discover more about your ancestors' neighbours scroll down the census pages on which your ancestors appear and visit the pages immediately before and after them.

Censuses asked for the place of birth of everyone living in a house.

It is interesting to compare birthplaces of all the inhabitants of a street. In late nineteenth-century Manchester – a city to which thousands migrated – it is hardly surprising to find that the adult inhabitants of a single street were all born elsewhere in places such as Cheshire, Lancashire and Derbyshire, or even further afield. Alternatively, you might find that your ancestors' neighbours all hail from a similar area far away. Many inhabitants of particular Irish villages, for instance, came and settled in England's big industrial cities and it was natural that they would want to live close to those who had been neighbours at home.

Comparing the employment of your ancestor with those of his immediate neighbours (as recorded on the census) can be an illuminating exercise. Trade directories are another good source of information about local businesses and their proprietors. Many of these are searchable online at www.historicaldirectories.org and will give you the names of people running businesses adjacent to those run by your family and with whom they would have been in daily contact. Such directories tend to be organised in several different ways (alphabetically, under type of business and – crucially for the study of neighbours – as building by building indexes of streets). Ask yourself whether the neighbours were in the same basic income bracket as your ancestors or not? Did they share other experiences such as taking in lodgers, running a workshop together, or sharing the use of another building?

It's pleasant to think of our ancestors gossiping with their neighbours across hedges and fences. But remember that, especially in the growing industrial cities, many languages might have been spoken within a small geographical area. Manchester, for example, had an influx of people for whom Russian, German and Italian were first languages. Some Scottish censuses actually asked whether or not residents could speak Gaelic. It is interesting to compare neighbours in this respect. Residents who could not speak the language of the rest of their community might have been very isolated.

If you are researching ancestors who fought in the First World War, it is worth scrolling down through the 1911 census as well as looking at military records on the online commercial genealogy sites. Many

young male neighbours and friends joined up together – a phenomenon actively encouraged by the Secretary of State for War, Lord Kitchener, in the early days of the conflict. Kitchener believed that more men would join the army if they thought that they would be fighting alongside friends, neighbours and work colleagues ('Pals') rather than being allocated to regular army regiments.

The most famous and tragic example of such a regiment was probably 'The Accrington Pals,' a battalion made up of a large number of young working-class men from the Northern towns of Accrington, Burnley, Blackburn and Chorley, who answered Kitchener's call for volunteers and became the 11th Battalion of the East Lancashire Regiment. On 1 July 1916 – the first day of the infamous battle of the Somme – the Accrington Pals advanced on the French village of Serre, but within a short time 235 men were killed and 350 were wounded. There is an appalling irony in the fact that the young men whose names had appeared close to each other in the 1911 Census were soon lying next to each other in the earth of France.

Club Associates

Beyond the neighbours, it's also worth spending some time contemplating your ancestor's wider social circles. The fact is that (for many of our male ancestors particularly) time away from work was often split between home and a club of some sort. 'Leisure' time does not necessarily mean 'lost' time to the family historian since many of these organisations kept detailed records of their members, from dates of admission and cessation of membership, to dates of birth, addresses, relationship to other club members, employment details and subscriptions. If your ancestor was an active participant in the management of any club or organisation, it is possible that you might find out even more about him or her – including perhaps his or her actions or even opinions – from the minutes of meetings.

Obituaries in professional journals, or (from the 1930s onwards) of ordinary people in local newspapers might list associations with which your ancestor was involved or interests that he or she pursued. In 1936, for example, the obituary of Mrs Helen Elizabeth Grimes in the *Leamington Spa Courier*, included references to Stoneleigh Tennis

Club, Kenilworth Hall Stables, Stoneleigh Cricket and Football Club and the Parochial Council of Stoneleigh, any of which might provide more information on the life of this lady (27 November 1936). Alternatively, amongst inherited belongings and family memorabilia you might find certificates or prizes obtained from interest groups such as temperance associations or cycling clubs. Old ties, blazers and badges that bear the insignia of a favourite club might turn up in attics and garages (see Image 47). Look out too amongst ornaments and silverware for forgotten club prizes, such as the Robertson Silver Inkstand presented to winners of a tournament at Edinburgh's Innerleithen Golf Club in the late nineteenth century.

If you have no tangible leads on organisations to which your ancestors might have belonged, it is worthwhile making an educated guess as to what they might have been. For a middle- or upper-class ancestor, think about school and university alumni associations, independent libraries, clubs that catered to scientific or literary aspirations and gentlemen's clubs. These men might have been trustees on the boards of local churches, charities or other religious organisations or might have sat on the committees of local businesses, schools or hospitals. For middle- or upper-class women, the associations will be harder to trace since females were barred from many men's clubs. There were, however, some female-only clubs – particularly towards the end of the nineteenth-century and by the 1920s and 1930s, as we have said, many sports clubs welcomed members of both sexes.

The social circles of a male working-class ancestor might have included public places such as music halls, pubs, athletic teams, amateur dramatics groups and even the open street. Some of this activity, of course, will be untraceable in the records but not so that of some of the working men's clubs, religious groups, friendly societies (see Chapter 6), sporting clubs and political clubs (the Irish Club, the Labour Club, for example) to which your ancestor might have belonged. Look in a trade directory or for more recent times, a telephone directory local to the area where your ancestor lived. The family history site www.ancestry.co.uk has a large number of online telephone directories. You will be presented with a list of local institutions and it will then be a matter of exercising some common sense to deduce the club(s) to which your ancestor is likely to have belonged. A grandfather who worked as an engine cleaner is likely to have belonged to the local Railwayman's Club, for example, whilst a great-uncle injured in the trenches may have joined the local branch of the Royal British Legion.

As a member of some or all of these in his local area (the clubs themselves very often had overlapping memberships), your working-class ancestor might well have left all sorts of evidence of himself in the records. If you are looking to find out more about your working-class great aunts or great-grandmothers in club records, you will probably be disappointed. In most clubs women could not be admitted as full members and therefore, though they might well have attended meetings or events at the club, their names will probably not be recorded anywhere. However, bear in mind that women were always active in working men's clubs running raffles and bingo and generally raising funds and these activities might well be mentioned in local newspaper reports.

Once you have an idea about an ancestor's club membership, you should check at an online bookstore to see if any relevant books have been published. These might be general books about the history of working men's clubs, for example, or more specific books about a particular local cricket or football team. Next ascertain whether the club in question (or a later version of it) still exists. If it does, it will almost certainly have a website, so try tapping its name into a search engine such as Google. Exercise care and attention when looking for your ancestor's club. In some cases, the club may have changed its name and its physical location, amalgamated with another club or closed down altogether. The Manchester Geological Society, for example, became the Manchester Mining and Geological Society and moved to Wigan, though its archives are now back in Manchester.

Many clubs today have websites with helpful potted histories of their several transformations. Some have their own historians, or people who have special access to the club records who might be able to help you with a specific request about your ancestor's membership.

If the club has kept its records on site, then, having ascertained by telephone or email exactly what kind of information these records include, you should arrange to pay it a visit. Alternatively, the records of old clubs might have been deposited in Local or County Record Offices. Find out their location by typing in the name of the club at the website of the National Archives, www.nationalarchives.org.

You should also consider taking out membership of the British Newspaper Archive (www.britishnewspaperarchive.co.uk). To start with, local newspapers will be useful in describing the kind of activities that went on in your ancestor's locality. More specifically, however, they might have references to the club in which you are interested. Newspapers reported the highlights of the club year: annual dinners, excursions, fundraising events, competitions and prizes, as well as the inauguration and winding down of clubs, legal disputes over shares in clubs and the like. Newspapers after 1900 might have relevant photographs of club buildings and members. And, if it is a sporting club, there might even be the results of matches with brief resumes of good performances!

Issue 1: What can private records tell me about my ancestor's social interactions?

Personal records such as letters, diaries and notebooks are the closest we will come to knowing anything about the social circles in which our ancestors mixed and the depths of their extra-familial relationships. Here are a couple of other examples of private sources which might just yield exceptional results.

Postcards

Postcards are often too quickly discarded by family historians. In fact, seen in their true historical context, they might tell us quite a lot about the friends (and of course relations) between whom they were sent. Postcards were first introduced in Britain in 1870 by the Post Office, but at this point were totally blank and bore a pre-printed stamp. From 1894, commercially-produced picture postcards were available and adhesive stamps could be bought and added to the cards before sending. The front of the card bore the address of the recipient and the back a picture and a message. Often the picture on these cards dominated and there was little room to write anything.

In 1902, the true age of the British picture postcard began. Now, the front of the card was dominated by a picture whilst the back, divided in two for the purpose, had space both for the address and a message. In the Edwardian period and during the First World War, the postcard was the standard way of transmitting short messages. As early as 1904, *The Sunderland Daily Echo and Shipping Gazette* reported that in one year 88 million postcards had been produced in Britain (1 June 1904). By 13 September 1905, *The Derby Daily Telegraph* was reporting that the 'picture postcard craze' had necessitated 'a large increase in the postal staff at Blackpool during the season. The authorities report a weekly average of 21,500 cards for the past four months. Three hundred thousand were sent in the busiest month – August.'

The quality of the relationship between the sender and the recipient of your postcard needs to be gauged against a number of factors. Postcards were a cheap means of communication, within the budget of most people (until 1918, a stamp for a postcard cost only ½d and although this went up to as high as 1½d in the early 1920s, by 1922 it was back down again to 1d). Costing less and requiring lower levels of literacy than letters, postcards were popular amongst people at all levels of society.

Next, bear in mind the fact that a postcard will have conveyed a high degree of physical intimacy with the sender, something difficult for us now to understand in our modern world of electronic communication. The stamp will have been licked by the sender, and the card handled by him or her as well as by the recipient. Indeed, so well understood was this physicality of written communication that people suffering from some diseases were sometimes advised not to send letters or postcards until they had recovered! Remember too that a vast array of possible views, scenes or themes were offered as pictures on postcards in the early years of the twentieth century and they will have been chosen very much with the recipient in mind. When looking at old postcards, consider the fact that the card itself (with its image and pre-printed verse or message on occasions) often became the *reason* for the communication, not merely the *vehicle* for it. Thus, postcards might tell us something about a recipient's hobbies, interests, sense of humour, artistic aspirations or the like.

Since post might be delivered up to seven times a day in large cities, postcards actually offered the possibility of a sort of a conversation in an age before the widespread use of telephones (something which didn't happen until the 1930s). It was possible, for example, to send a postcard to arrange a meeting for the next day and to be sure that it would reach its destination! The messages on postcards themselves are very often witty and unconventional, space was short, and stamps had to be paid for. Look out then for cleverness and verbal concision. Since postcards were open to view, messages were sometimes written upside down, in code or in cryptic ways to confuse postmen and readers other than the recipient.

All in all, postcards amongst family papers deserve a little time and attention. Close examination might allow you to sense the quality of a friendship in a way that no other record can.

Autograph books
Another delightful and oft-overlooked way of establishing some of the circles in which your ancestor mixed might be through an autograph book. These were popular from the late nineteenth century onwards, became a craze in the Edwardian period, declined in popularity by the 1920s, but then resurfaced in the 1930s. At first, they were favourite possessions of young middle-class girls, but increasingly they were kept by young people of both genders and of all classes. Most were leather-bound and pocket-sized with tinted pages. They were usually filled with the signatures (and other contributions) of family and friends. The content of autograph books will nearly always tell you something about the interests and aspirations of your ancestor and about his or her general social milieu.

Some autograph books were confined to the signatures of the famous people with whom the owner had come into contact. By 1907, newspapers were reporting that such books were becoming 'a fearful nuisance to public men. Former Conservative Prime Minister Mr Arthur Balfour had been beset by crowds of people of all sorts and all kinds, each armed with an autograph book and a fountain pen' (*Gloucester Citizen*, 8 April 1907). Other autograph hunters posted their books to 'people in the public eye' in the rash hope that they would be signed and returned.

Such 'celebrity' autograph books, however, are of less use to the family historian that those more mundane volumes, kept over the course of a lifetime which might include sections with entries from individuals in the particular groups or societies with which the owner of the book was associated at various times. A book might, for example, include the names of school friends, work colleagues, members of the local football team or amateur dramatics society. A young nurse named Millicent Jackson collected the contributions of many of the soldiers (and staff) at the hospital where she worked between 1915 and 1918 in her autograph book now held in Derbyshire Record Office. She also kept newspaper cuttings regarding the deaths of certain soldiers inside the book. Similarly, an autograph book belonging to Mrs G. B. Stammer of Brighton, kept in Suffolk Record Office (Bury St Edmund's Branch), includes the signatures of many of the men of 'C' Company, 9th Battalion, The Suffolk Regiment (1915–18). Her descendants may know what her connection with this battalion actually was.

By the middle of the twentieth century some workplaces were even giving autograph books, complete with many signatures and messages, to members on their retirement. This was the case in 1947 when Mr W. H. Thomas, the manager of the Exeter Employment Exchange retired. *The North Devon Journal* of 23 October recorded that 'Mr Thomas was presented with a barometer and an autograph book containing the signatures of all his old colleagues at Exeter . . . Mr Thomas . . . spoke of the happy times he had had at Exeter, where he had made numerous friends.'

Your ancestors' friends and associates may have contributed to their autograph books in creative and personal ways, turning them upside down, for example, or writing in their corners, folding the pages, or cutting holes in them. The occasion of writing an autograph also gave an opportunity for a contributor to exercise other talents peculiar to himself – sketching and designing word puzzles (such as anagrams and acrostics) being the two most obvious. In their entirety, the entries in an autograph book will give a flavour of the kinds of worlds in which your ancestor was moving at a particular time, or at particular times, throughout the course of his or her life.

Consider the nature of any entries carefully. Although many verses such as 'Roses are red/Violets are blue . . .' turn up time and time again, others are rarer and may tell you something about the education of the writers, their religion, or national or cultural background. In addition, the choice of verse or ditty may tell you something about the relationship between the contributor and the owner of the book. 'Love all/Trust few/Learn to paddle your own canoe,' wrote one young man who later broke off his romantic relationship with the owner of one autograph book, for example.

A well-presented autograph book studied alongside other family history records, can read like a detective story itching to be solved. Nellie Clementina McCarthy (later known under her adoptive name of Ellen Clementina Higley), a teacher born in London in 1880 kept a fascinating autograph book of signatures, verses and sketches dated between 1897 and 1901 (see Image 48). Most of the entries appear to have been contributed by a group of young girls with a considerable degree of education; not only was their handwriting sophisticated and in ink, but they made confident use of quotations from Shakespeare, Sir Walter Scott, other literary figures and the Bible. Many of the entries in the autograph book were also in French or German. As a young woman, Ellen had studied as an external student of London University; she gained a Bachelor of Arts degree in 1905 and later took up a post as a lecturer in English at Simla University in India. But the inscription on the flyleaf of the autograph book was evidently from an earlier period in Ellen's life and showed that it was a gift to her made in Ipswich in February 1897. Many of the verses are dedicated to 'Nellie' – indicating that Ellen was using this shortened form of her name at the time. What the seventeen-year-old Ellen was doing in Ipswich at the turn of the century was initially a mystery.

A search for Ellen on the 1901 census at www.ancestry.co.uk revealed nothing under the adoptive surname of 'Higley', but a search under her original surname 'McCarthy' and under the Christian name 'Nellie' yielded a delightful surprise (see Image 49). A Nellie McCarthy (of the right age) appeared as a student at a school – St Mary's Roman Catholic Convent boarding school in Ipswich. Nellie must have been sent there by her adoptive parents to get an education. And, surprise, surprise, beside her in the census return are the names of many of those other young women whose signatures appear in the autograph book – they were her fellow students! As the census records places of birth, the mystery of the different languages was also solved – the girls came from all over the world: from Hong Kong, India, Germany and Algeria amongst other places.

Nellie Higley's autograph book provides an interesting historical record of the kind of ephemera (wordplay and acrostics, for instance) that young girls in Nellie's situation found amusing at that particular time. More interestingly for the genealogist, it recreates the immediate social world of its owner showing Nellie's relationships with her peers, and the general regard in which she was held. Some of the young women in the autograph book would become her lifelong friends.

Issue 2: What can the records of clubs and other groups tell me about my ancestor?

What follows are some highly selective details about a number of different kinds of association to which your ancestors might have belonged and a summary of the kinds of records you might expect to find about them. It is by no means comprehensive and you will have to look to your ancestor's own life to imagine the multiple ways in which he or she might have been connected to his or her community. It's worth warning that club and society records may disappoint in that you might not come across the actual names of the ancestors you seek. At the very least, however, they will very probably contain a list of rules and standards of membership for the time when your ancestor was a member. It's worth keeping an on-going list of the names of people who were also members of the groups to which your ancestors belonged. They could well turn up again in a different context at a different point in an ancestor's life. The surnames 'Thornley', 'Bamford' and 'Heywood' crop up frequently, for example in the minutes of committee meetings at a Methodist church in Stockport in the 1930s, and they are there again as the donators of flowers at the funeral of a chapel member, Mrs Elizabeth Symes, in 1940. Beyond this, browsing through old minute books can be a fascinating undertaking in itself, helping you to understand what issues were exercising the minds of club members (your ancestors among them) at various times.

One example of such a serendipitous search occurred when a family historian looked into the records of The Ancoats Wesleyan Methodist Chapel in the late Victorian and early Edwardian period, held in Manchester City Archives. Though she could not find her ancestors mentioned by name, she was able to immerse herself in the concerns of the chapelgoers at that time. The organist, it seemed, had been in trouble because he had not been attending the chapel regularly. After being contacted by the committee, he wrote a letter back to them saying that he 'desired to be relieved of his position as soon as was convenient'. The chapel was also in urgent need of repair with the trustees reporting their desire to 'beautify' the building by removing the pulpit, replacing it with a platform, moving the organ to the end of the building; and improving the lighting and ventilation of the building. After raising money from the congregation and a brief period of closure, the church re-opened, presumably with all its decoration complete, in late 1894.

The researcher came across further delights learning, for instance, that in 1895, new instruments were purchased for the Band and it was agreed that they would be asked to play in the intervals between 'Tea' and the Public Meeting. The provision of tea itself seemed to have been an ongoing and vexed issue. On 8 July 1907, the committee resolved 'that [they] buy 12 tea urns to use in the central hall . . . and also that a price be obtained for a masher at tea meetings'. The committee returned to the issue of tea in October of that year when they resolved that 'the question of the tea masher be left over for the present'. It was not until 19 February 1908 that the committee came to an agreement that 'a tea masher be obtained'. And that 'Messrs R. Grange and J. Potts [two of the church's trustees]' should 'see about same'! The minutes and other papers of clubs and associations with which your ancestor was involved can, like these, bring their social world vividly to light, even if their names are not actually mentioned.

Working Men's Clubs

Some working men's clubs were founded in the nineteenth century as part of the so-called 'rational recreation movement' started by middle-class philanthropists to draw the working classes away from pubs, music halls and gin palaces and towards self-improvement. In this way, early clubs were considered – in the same way as parks, libraries and museums – to be for the public good. It was envisaged that education and training would be offered in clubs at the end of the working day. A large number of clubs appeared in the industrial North of England and these often became the social and cultural centre of working-class communities.

In time, the high educational ideals of clubs were modified and they became primarily places of relaxation where a little sport and light entertainment could be had. But clubs always retained a number of other, more worthy functions. Some acted as informal employment exchanges and mutual aid institutions, for example. Others made it their business to raise funds for local causes. And it was very often in clubs that political allegiances took seed and grew.

By 1862, the Rev. Henry Solly, a Unitarian Minister, had recognised the need to link together the proliferation of working men's clubs that were springing up all over the country. The Working Men's Club and Institute Union (today known as the CIU) was founded in London. The numbers of clubs in this union rose dramatically in the late nineteenth and early twentieth centuries from seventy-two in 1868 to 520 in 1880, 1,041 in 1901 and 2,007 in 1920. By the 1970s, 4,000 clubs were affiliated to the CIU, a non-political body. Today there are still over 3,000 working men's clubs in the union. The CIU together with the Royal British Legion and the Association of Conservative Clubs are all part of the Confederation of Registered Club Associations (CORCA).

Working-class clubs arose in many different ways. Some began as trade societies or trade unions, others were associated with a particular type of employment (e.g. miners' welfare clubs). Some started as mutual improvement societies or working men's institutes where the aim was mainly educational. Other clubs – such as 'Liberal' or 'Gladstone' Clubs – were affiliated to political parties. Soldiers returning from the First World War also set up their own clubs –

institutions which eventually became part of the Royal British Legion. The majority of so-called 'Labour' clubs were built as the Labour Party grew in size in the 1920s. A variety of other sporting and special interest clubs (such as fishing and football clubs) also arose over the course of the nineteenth and early twentieth centuries.

Though some working-class clubs were patronised by the middle classes, others were founded and run by the working-class members themselves. In some cases, groups of working men bought land and established clubs using their own skills and labour. The clubs were non-profit making organisations and were run by the members through a committee elected annually. Club members would pay a small yearly subscription.

By the 1880s, a typical working-men's club in an industrial town might have had about 600 members, most of whom would be skilled tradesmen such as boiler-makers, shoemakers, mechanics, tailors or shopkeepers. The club's facilities usually included a large hall that could be used for debating with a stage at one end, another room for refreshments and then several smaller rooms including perhaps a billiard room, bagatelle room and a reading room. The latter would provide a selection of the daily newspapers which would be spread out on tables. It was cheaper to pay a membership fee and read these in the club than to buy the newspapers for oneself.

As an example, Dartford Working Men's Club in Kent still houses records of club meetings going back to 1886, the year the club was founded. The club has also kept the names, addresses, ages and – perhaps most interestingly – occupations of all its members. Likewise, the records of Darton Liberal Working Man's Club, Darton, Yorkshire (stored at Barnsley Archive and Local Studies Dept) include minutes, accounts, membership and administration papers, and correspondence from the period 1912–1983. And these two are not alone, up and down the country, clubs of all sorts may still hold the key to how our grandfathers and great-grandfathers whiled away their recreation time.

A Private Gentleman's Club
If your great-grandfather was a member of the elite (the aristocracy, upper or increasingly the middle classes) a judge, a doctor or an

industrialist, a lawyer, an admiral, or a man of private fortune, the chances are that he was a member of a private club.

The largest number of gentlemen's clubs were to be found from the seventeenth century onwards in London. Many were the territory of aristocrats, politicians and royalty and the establishment of a large number of these predated the nineteenth century. Membership traditionally relied on pedigree, although there were always opportunists of lower social ranking who tried to gain entry! Lists of the London clubs from 1850 onwards may be found in nineteenth-century almanacs such as *The British Almanac* and *Whitaker's Almanac* (annual publications containing a variety of factual information and available now in any sizeable public library). Club membership became more and more popular in the second half of the nineteenth century. In 1850, *The British Almanac* listed thirty-two gentlemen's clubs in London. By 1910, there were eighty-one. According to *Whitaker's Almanac*, London's gentlemen's clubs had 30,650 members in 1870. By 1910, this figure had risen to 129,434 – a fourfold increase in forty years.

It is a misconception to think that women were never part of the world of middle- and upper-class clubs. Although females were rarely, if ever, admitted as full members, wives did sometimes have access to limited areas of the building. From the 1870s, there were a very small number of clubs in London that catered exclusively for wealthy or middle-class women – particularly those with advanced views about the role of women in society. In the 1890s, these included The Pioneer Club, The Alexandra, The Green Park, The Empress and The County. By 1899, there were twenty-four women-only clubs in London, two in Edinburgh and Glasgow, and one each in Dublin, Bath, Leeds, Liverpool and Manchester.

If you know that your ancestor belonged to a London club, think carefully about the kind of membership to which that club catered. The oldest club in London – White's (est. 1693) – began as a chocolate house but became a Tory meeting place – it is rumoured that Prince William is now a member. The Army and Navy Club (est. 1837), on the other hand, was an establishment for military types; and The Oxford and Cambridge (est. 1830) was comprised of alumni from those two universities. There were also a plethora of clubs of other types including artistic, literary, theatrical, occupational and sporting clubs. The most famous London clubs included Boodle's (est. 1762) www.boodles.org/ a private gentleman's club; The Carlton (est. 1832) www.carltonclub.co.uk/, originally a haven for Conservative politicians; The Oriental (est. 1824) www.oriental club.org.uk – original members were drawn from members of the East India Company and those working in public service in India; and The Travellers (est. 1819) www.thetravellersclub.org.uk/ – described on its website as 'a place where gentlemen travelling abroad could meet and entertain distinguished visitors from overseas'.

Occasionally the records of a private club will prove a real treasure trove for a family historian. One such club is The Savile, in London, which was established in 1868. This club has always prided itself on electing members less on the grounds of 'what a candidate does, or what a candidate is' and more on the grounds of what kind of person he is – the emphasis being on geniality and fellowship. As with many clubs, the name and premises of the Savile has changed a number of times over the course of its history. At first, it was known as 'The New Club' and occupied rooms in the Medical Club in Spring Gardens just off Trafalgar Square. Later it moved to Savile Row and the name changed accordingly. From there, the club moved to Piccadilly and then in 1927 to its current residence in Brook Street. If your ancestor was a member of this distinguished club, he might have rubbed shoulders – at various different times – with writers including Robert Louis Stevenson, Thomas Hardy, H. G. Wells, and Rudyard Kipling, musicians such as William Walton and Edward Elgar, and scientists such as Lord Kelvin and Lord Rutherford.

Thanks to the efforts of its Honorary Librarian, the Savile Club has a very useful electronic database of past members. In addition to names, titles, honours and dates of birth, the approximate dates of election and cessation of membership are given. A helpful key also allows you to find out whether a member resigned, died, failed to take up their membership or allowed it to lapse. In common with the records of many gentlemen's clubs, those at the Savile also record the name of the 'proposer', that is, the person who put forward your ancestor's name when he first became a member – something which can be helpful if you are trying to formulate an idea of the network of patronage and favours within which your aspiring great-grandfather operated.

Fascinatingly, the Savile database allows you to go beyond a simple search for a relative. One of its most helpful features is that it can help you trace your ancestor's paternal line. Next to the names of many members is a serial number which cross-refers to the details about the membership of that member's father. Secondly, the database helpfully points users to other potential sources of information on a particular member. It is recorded, for example, if a member appears in *Who's Who*, or the *Dictionary of National Biography* and if they later became a member of the Garrick Club.

Other elite gentlemen's clubs also still retain their records on the premises. London's Carlton Club, for example, has copies of Member's Lists and Candidates' Books going back to 1834 (the originals were unfortunately destroyed by a German bomb in 1940). These give details of when a member was elected, how long he remained a member, who proposed and seconded him and his address at the time of membership. There are even more details on members since 1940.

A Provincial 'Special Interest' Club
In the Regency and Victorian periods, clubs for the educated middle classes flowered in the provincial cities of Liverpool, Birmingham, Newcastle and Manchester. Some men would belong to more than one club in an effort to expand their networks as far as possible. Such urban 'watering holes' provided aspiring businessmen and professionals with news and information as well as a web of business contacts. Many of these clubs were known as 'societies', reflecting the fact that their activities turned around some cultural, scientific or professional interest. In Manchester, for example, a scientifically-minded great-grandfather may have belonged to the Medical Society, the Chemical Club, the Geological Society, and the Natural History Society.

As an example, the records of Manchester's Union Club, which ran from 1825 to 1948, are in the Manchester Archives and Local Studies Repository. These include rules, minutes, financial papers, membership lists, catalogues and letter books from 1875 to 1948. Such records might reveal membership lists, complete with names, ages, addresses and even professions, evidence of subscriptions, minutes of meetings and even measures taken against unruly members.

Typically the style of provincial clubs for the middle classes aped those much older and more prestigious clubs frequented by the gentry and nobility in London. They offered luxurious premises, libraries and dining facilities; some even provided overnight accommodation. Some clubs had gaming rooms where whist and hazard were played (sometimes all night). For less well-off members who could not afford the cost of entertaining at home, a club with catering staff could be a very useful alternative venue for a social event.

The Mothers' Union

You may discover amongst your family papers and possessions membership cards, or badges (with an intertwined motif of the letters 'M' and 'U') denoting that your ancestor was a member of the Mothers' Union, an Anglican organisation set up in 1876 by Mary Sumner, wife of the rector of Old Alresford in the Diocese of Winchester as a means of 'defending the institution of marriage and promoting Christian life' in local communities. Female ancestors who lived abroad with husbands in positions associated with the running of Empire might have belonged to branches of the Mothers' Union that were rapidly established in overseas dioceses in the early years of the twentieth century.

By 1892, the Union had 60,000 members and by 1900, numbers countrywide had risen to 169,000. From 1893, annual general meetings were organised, and in 1896, the Mothers' Union General Council was formed with Mary Sumner as President. For more information, you can visit the Archive of the Mothers' Union (c. 1890–2000), Lambeth Palace Library, Lambeth Palace Road, London, SE1 7JU. (See: www.lambethpalacelibrary.org; and www.mundus.ac.uk/cats/12/1322.htm). This includes minutes, correspondence, accounts, pamphlets, architectural plans, photographs and slides of the movement (mostly from the 1890s onwards). Some documents concerning important individual members of the Union are also available to view here. For records relating to local branches of the Mothers' Union, which may include membership lists or the minutes of meetings to which your ancestor contributed, you will need to search for the locations of collections via the National Archives website: www.nationalarchives.org.

A Private Library

Before 1841 (because there were no rate-supported libraries and no university libraries outside Cambridge, Oxford, Dublin and Edinburgh), groups of enlightened individuals in various towns and cities sometimes came together to found their own libraries. Even after library provision for the general public improved, the well-to-do continued to prefer the exclusivity of these private reading rooms.

If your ancestor was a member of an independent library, it's possible that you will be able to find out more about his life from records still held by the institution. At a pinch, you may even be able to find out which books he read!

The Association of Independent Libraries (AIL), founded in 1989, aims to forge links between Britain's independent libraries and has its own website with a directory of all member libraries (www.independentlibraries.co.uk). Take a look to see if there is one in the city from which your ancestor came. Be careful – not all the members of today's AIL were originally independent libraries with subscribing members – but some were and their records may well be worth searching.

If your great-grandfather was an engineer or architect in the North-East, he may have been a member of the Newcastle Literary and Philosophical Society which had its own library facilities. If this is the case, you are lucky – the Society has very full records including lists of members from 1793 to 1888. There are also membership subscription ledgers from 1895 to 1948 and membership rolls from 1948 to the present day. Both the ledgers and the rolls give the addresses of members when they joined, resigned or were struck off. But beware – the records of some institutions can be disappointing from a family history point of view. The Bishopsgate Institute in London, for example, had no share-holding members and details of individual borrowing members no longer exist.

Manchester's middle classes have been members of the Portico Library (founded in 1806) for over 200 years. Here they have been able to read the books and newspapers, have a meal and cement professional friendships. Each 'proprietor' is a shareholder in the Library. Their names, the dates at which they joined the Library, and their share numbers are recorded in a large, leather-bound tome entitled 'Portico Library Members' Book' which is available to view at the desk by prior arrangement with the Librarian. A 'List of Proprietors' and a 'Share Transfer Book' provide further useful information (see Image 50).

From the records of the Portico, it is possible to find out quite a lot about your ancestor, the type of business he was in, for example, and the addresses where he lived and worked. These records could help you put your ancestor into his social context (you can make an educated guess about what his friends and business associates were like, for example), by listing together all those who were members of the Library at the same time.

From such details it is possible to chart the changing fortunes of your family over several generations from the records of an institution such as a private library. By way of example, the addresses given for the sons of the original Portico library members tended to be in the suburban rather than urban districts of Manchester and their occupations were often rather more elevated than those of their fathers.

Bibliography

Abbott, E., *History of Marriage* (Gerald Duckworth and Co. Ltd, 2011).

Allan, G., *Kinship and Friendship in Modern Britain* (Oxford University Press, 1996).

Aries, P., *Centuries of Childhood: A Social History of Family Life* (Random House, 1965).

Bailey, J., *Parenting in England, c. 1760-1830: Emotions, Self-identities and Generations* (Oxford, 2002).

Bailey, P., *Leisure and Class in Victorian England: Rational Recreation and the Contest for Control 1830-1885* (Methuen, 1987).

Banks, J. A., *Prosperity and Parenthood: A Study of Family Planning Among the Victorian Middle Classes* (Gregg Revivals, 1993).

Bartley, P., *The Changing Role of Women, 1815-1914* (Hodder and Stoughton, 1996).

Bates, D., *Breach of Promise to Marry: A History of How Jilted Brides Settled Scores* (Pen and Sword Books, 2014).

Benson. J., *The Working-Class in Britain, 1850-1939* (I. B. Tauris, 2003).

Bothelo L., and Thane, P., *Women and Ageing in British Society Since 1500* (Routledge, 2001).

Brooks, A., and Haworth, B., *Portico Library: A History* (Carnegie, 2000).

Broughton, T. L. and Rogers, H. (eds), *Gender and Fatherhood in the Nineteenth Century* (Palgrave Macmillan, 2007).

Buck, A., *Clothes and the Child: A Handbook of Children's Dress in England, 1500-1900* (Holmes and Meier, 1996).

Campbell, Lady C., *The Lady's Dressing Room*, translated from the French of Baronness Staffe (Cassell and Co., 1892).

Cassidy, T., *Birth: A History* (Chatto and Windus, 2007).

Chamberlain, G., *From Witchcraft to Wisdom: A History of Obstetrics and Gynaecology in the British Isles* (Royal College of Obstetricians and Gynaecologists, 2007).

Chase, K., *The Victorians and Old Age* (Oxford University Press, 2009).

Cherrington, Ruth, *Not Just Beer and Bingo! A Social History of Working Men's Clubs* (Authorhouse, 2012).

Christiansen, R. and Brophy, B., *The Complete Book of Aunts* (Faber and Faber, 2008).

Clark P., *British Clubs and Societies* (Clarendon, 2000).

Cohen, D., *Family Secrets: The Things We Tried to Hide* (Penguin, 2014).

Crompton, F., *Workhouse Children* (Sutton, 1997).

Davidoff, L., *Thicker than Water, Siblings and Their Relations, 1780-1920* (Oxford University Press, 2013).

Davidoff, L. and Hall, C., *Family Fortunes: Men and Women of the English Middle Classes* (Routledge, 2nd edition, 2002).

BIBLIOGRAPHY

Davidoff, L., Doolittle, M., Fink, J., and Holden, K., *The Family Story: Blood, Contact and Intimacy, 1830-1940* (Longmans, Green and Co., 1999).

Davies A., and Fielding, S. (eds), *Workers' Worlds: Cultures and Communities in Manchester and Salford, 1880-1939* (Manchester University Press, 1992).

Davis, M. L., *No-One But A Woman Knows: Stories of Motherhood Before the War* (1915) (Longman, 1998).

Davies, M. L., *Maternity: Letters from Working Women* (1915) (Little, Brown, 1978).

Davis, G., 'Stillbirth Registration and Perceptions of Infant Death 1900-1960: The Scottish Case in National Context', *Economic History Review* 62 (3) (August 2009), pp. 629–54.

Donnison, J., *Midwives and Medical Men: A History of Inter-Professional Rivalries and Women's Rights* (Heinemann Educational, 1977).

Englander, D., *Poverty and Poor Law Reform in Nineteenth-century Britain, 1834-1914: From Chadwick to Booth* (Routledge, 1998).

Fiennes, Sir R., *Living Dangerously: The Autobiography of Ranulph Fiennes* (Macmillan, 1994).

Flanders, J., *The Victorian House: Domestic Life from Childbirth to Deathbed* (Harper Perennial, 2003).

Fletcher, A., *Growing Up in England, The Experience of Childhood 1600-1914* (Yale University Press, 2008).

Finch, J., and Mason, J., *Passing On: Kinship and Inheritance in England* (Routledge, 2000).

Fisher, K., *Birth Control, Sex and Marriage in Britain, 1918-1960* (Oxford University Press, 2006).

Forster, M., *Elizabeth Barrett Browning* (Vintage, 1998).

Fowler, S., *Workhouse: The People, The Places, The Life Behind Doors* (The National Archive, 2007).

Gandy, M., *Family History Cultures and Faiths: How Your Ancestors Lived and Worshipped: Expert Advice to Speed Up Your Search* (The National Archives, 2007).

Garfield, J., *Cousins: A Unique and Powerful Bond* (BackinPrint.com, 2000).

Garrett E., et al, *Changing Family Size in England and Wales, 1891–1911* (Cambridge University Press, 2006).

Gerrard, A. J. D. (ed.), *Fathers: A Literary Anthology* (Patremoir Press, 2011).

Goody, J., *The Development of the Family and Marriage in Europe* (Cambridge University Press, 1983).

Gottlieb, R., *Great Expectations: The Sons and Daughters of Charles Dickens* (Farrar, Straus and Giroux, 2003).

Hadfield, L., Edwards, R., Lucey H., and Mauther, M., *Sibling Identity and Relationships: Sisters and Brothers* (Routledge, 2006).

Hanks, P., Hardcastle, K., and Hardcastle, F., *Oxford Dictionary of First Names* (Oxford University Press, 2nd ed., 2006).

Higginbotham, P., *Workhouse Encyclopedia* (The History Press, 2007).

Hendrick, H., *Children, Childhood and English Society, 1880-1990* (Cambridge University Press, 1997).

Heritage C., *Tracing Your Family Through Death Records* (Pen and Sword Books, 2013).

Holden, K., *The Shadow of Marriage: Singleness in England, 1914-60* (MUP, 2010).

Higgs, M., *Tracing Your Servant Ancestors* (Pen and Sword, 2012).

Hughes, K., *The Short Life and Long Times of Mrs Beeton* (Harper Perennial, 2006).

Humphries, J., *Childhood and Child Labour in the British Industrial Revolution* (Cambridge University Press, 2011).

Jackson, M., *Infanticide: Historical Perspectives On Child Murder and Concealment, 1550-2000* (Ashgate, 2002).

Jalland, P., *Death in the Victorian Family* (Oxford University Press, 1999).

Jerrold, C., *The Widowhood of Queen Victoria* (1916) (Kessinger, 2007).

Johnson, P., and Thane, P., *Old Age from Antiquity to Post-Modernity* (Routledge, 2014).

Johnson, M. L. et al., *The Cambridge Handbook of Age and Ageing* (Cambridge University Press, 2005).

Keating, J., *A Child for Keeps: The History of Adoption in England, 1918-45* (Palgrave Macmillan, 2008).

Kertzer, D. I., and Barbagli, M. (eds), *Family Life in the Long Nineteenth Century: 1789-1913* (Yale University Press, 2002).

Kilday, A., *A History of Infanticide in Britain, c. 1600 to the Present* (Palgrave Macmillan, 2013).

Kirkwood, T., *The End of Age* (Profile Books, 2001).

Kuper, A., *Incest and Influence: The Private Life of Bourgeois England* (Harvard University Press, 2009).

Lamb, M.E., and Smith, B. S., *Sibling Relationships: Their Nature and Significance Across the Lifespan* (Lawrence Erlbaum Associates, 1982).

Laver, J., *The Book of Public School Old Boys, University, Navy, Army, Air Force and Club Ties* (Seeley Service and Co. 1968).

Lansdell, A., *Wedding Fashions, 1860-1980* (Shire, 1986).

Legood, G., and Markham, Ian S., *The Godparents' Handbook: Roles and Responsibilities* (SPCK, 1997).

Lejeune, A., *The Gentlemen's Clubs of London* (Bracken Books, 1984).

Levin, I., and Sussman, Marvin B., *Stepfamilies: History, Research and Policy* (Routledge, 1997).

Levene, A., Williams, S., and Nutt, T., *Illegitimacy in Britain, 1700-1920* (Palgrave Schol, 2005).

Loudon, I., *Death in Childbirth: An International Study of Maternity Care and Maternal Mortality, 1800-1950* (Clarendon Press, 1993).

McLaren, A., *Birth Control in Nineteenth-Century England* (Croom Helm, 1978).

McLaughlin, E,. *Illegitimacy* (Guides for Family Historians) (FFHS, 1985).

Marland, H., *Dangerous Motherhood: Insanity and Childbirth in Victorian Britain* (Palgrave Schol, 2004).

Mintz, S., *A Prison of Expectations: The Family in Victorian Culture* (New York University Press, 1985).

Mitchison, R., *British Population Change since 1860* (Palgrave Macmillan, 1977).

Morgan, D. H. J., *Family Connections: An Introduction to Family Studies* (Polity Press, 1996).

BIBLIOGRAPHY

Murdoch, L., *Daily Life of Victorian Women* (Greenwood Press, 2013).

Nagler, L. F., *The Hidden Mother* (Mack, 2013).

Nelson, C., *Family Ties in Victorian England* (Praeger, 2007).

Newby, J., *Women's Lives: Researching Women's Social History, 1800-1939* (Pen and Sword Books, 2011).

Oppenheimer, M., *Forbidden Relatives: The American Myth of Cousin Marriage* (University of Illinois Press, 1996).

Osborne, F., *Lilla's Feast: A True Story of Love, War and A Passion for Food* (Black Swan, 2006).

Packard, J. M., *Victoria's Daughters* (St Martin's Griffin, 1999).

Paley, R., *My Ancestor Was a Bastard: A Family Historian's Guide to Sources for Illegitimacy in England and Wales* (Society of Genealogists, 2004).

Pols, R., *Dating Old Photographs* (FFHS Publications, 2nd ed., 1998).

Pols, R., *Dating Old Army Photographs* (The Family History Partnership, 2011).

Pols, R., *Dating Nineteenth-Century Photographs* (Federation of Family History Societies, 2005).

Pooley, S., 'Parenthood, child-rearing and fertility in England, 1850-1914', *History of the Family* 18(1) (March 2013), pp. 83–106.

Radclyffe, E. J. D., *Magic and Mind* (1932).

Radford, E. and M. A., *Encyclopedia of Superstitions (1949) (Kessinger, 2004)*.

Robinson, H. P., *The Studio and What to Do In It* (1891) (Kessinger, 2010).

Rossini, G., *A History of Adoption in England and Wales* (1850-1961) (Pen and Sword Books, 2014).

Ruggles, S., *Prolonged Connections: The Rise of the Extended Family in Nineteenth Century England and America* (University of Wisconsin Press, 1987).

Sampson, A. and S., *The Oxford Book of Ages* (Oxford Paperbacks, 1985).

Sanders, V., *The Tragi-Comedy of Victorian Fatherhood* (Cambridge University Press, 2009).

Sheetz-Nguyen, J., Victorian Women, *Unwed Mothers and the London Foundling Hospital* (Continuum, 2012).

Shipley, S., *Club Life and Socialism in Mid-Victorian London* (Journeyman Press, 1971).

Schweitzer, P. (ed.), *Dividends of Kinship: Meanings and Uses of Social Relatedness* (Routledge, 2000).

Shrimpton, J., *Tracing Your Ancestors Through Family Photographs: A Complete Guide for Family and Local Historians* (Pen and Sword Books, 2014).

Shrimpton, J., *How to Get the Most from Family Photographs* (Society of Genealogists Enterprises Ltd, 2011).

Solly, H., *Working Men's Social Clubs and Educational Institutes* (Kessinger, 2009).

Stewart E. A., *Exploring Twins: Towards a Social Analysis of Twinship* (Palgrave Macmillan, 2000).

Thane, P., *Old Age in English History: Past Experiences, Present Issues* (Oxford University Press, 2002).

Thane, P., *The Long History of Old Age* (Thames and Hudson, 2005).

Tomalin, C., *Charles Dickens: A Life* (Penguin, 2011).

Tremlett, G., *Clubmen: The History of the Working Men's Club and Institute Union* (Secker & Warburg, 1987).

Turner, W., *Pals: the 11th (Service) Battalion (Accrington), East Lancashire Regiment* (Pen and Sword Books, 1993).

Ward, M., *The Female Line: Researching Your Female Ancestors* (Countryside Books, 2003).

Wilkes, S., *The Children History Forgot* (Robert Hale, 2011).

Wilkes, S., *Tracing Your Ancestors' Childhood* (Pen and Sword Books, 2013).

Ziegler, Philip, and Seward, Desmond, *Brooks's: A Social History* (Constable, 1991).

Useful Websites

www.aboutbritain.com/articles/victorian-names.asp On Victorian naming practices.

www.ancestry.co.uk Commercial site for UK genealogical records.

www.bbc.co.uk/history/interactive/timelines For timelines relating to Kings and Queens, Prime Ministers and Politics.

www.bl.uk/timeline The British Library history timeline.

www:booth.lse.ac.uk/ The Charles Booth Online Archive.

www. brew.clients.ch/willslezayre.htm The will of Elizabeth Brew of Lezayre.

www.britishnewspaperarchive.co.uk The British Newspaper Archive.

http://www.canadiancrc.com/paternity_determination_blood_type.aspx On blood groups and paternity.

www.childsupportanalysis.co.uk/information_and_explanation/world/history_uk.htm A timeline about the history of child support in the UK and elsewhere.

http://www.cityoflondon.gov.uk/lma London Metropolitan Archives

www.cottontimes.co.uk/poorlawo.htm For more on the nineteenth-century workhouse.

www.en.wikipedia.org/wiki/Posthumous_birth Useful information on the definition and legal implications of posthumous births.

http://www.elenagreene.com/childbirth.html Useful history of obstetrics.

www.emblah13.wordpress.com/2014/06/08/victorians-in-the-family-way-photographs-of-pregnant-ladies/ Photographs of pregnant women in the Victorian era.

www.findmypast.co.uk Commercial site for UK genealogical records.

www.flickr.com/groups/thevictorianfather. A gallery of Victorian fathers and their children.

www.fashion-era.com/mourning_fashion.htm More on mourning fashions.

https://www.flickr.com/groups/1172425@N21/ Help with identifying old uniforms 1700–1945.

www.thewww.forensicmag.com/JJ14_Paternity On forensic methods for testing paternity.

www.thegenealogist.co.uk Commercial site for UK genealogical records.

www.hansard.millbanksystems.com/search/consanguinous?speaker=sir-john-lubbock&year=1870 The Hansard transcription of the full Parliamentary debate on cousin marriage in 1870.

http://www.theguardian.com/artanddesign/gallery/2013/dec/02/hidden-mothers-victorian-photography-in-pictures Hidden mothers in Victorian photographs.

www.historicaldirectories.org Trade directories online.

www.historyandpolicy.org/papers/policy-paper-107.html On the changing shape of families in history.

BIBLIOGRAPHY

www.historyofwomen.org/timeline/html A timeline of legal and other changes affecting women in history.

www.historyorb.com Find out what was going on in the world, the country and the locality at the same time as key events in your ancestor's life.

http://www.djo.org.uk/household-words.html Charles Dickens's *Household Words* journal online.

http://www.independentlibraries.co.uk/ For Britain's independent libraries.

www.justice.gov.uk/courts/probate/copies-of grants –wills Order copies of your ancestor's will.

www.lambethpalacelibrary.org Lambeth Palace Library which includes the records of the Mother's Union.

www.nameberry.com A multifaceted site on the history of naming and the popularity of certain names.

www.nationalarchives.org The National Archives.

www.paulsadowski.org/BirthDay.asp) Find out the likely date upon which your ancestor was conceived.

www.pinterest.com/maklinens/vintage-1920-1940-children-clothing/ Baby clothing from the 1920s to the 1940s.

www.queenvictoriasjournals.org Queen Victoria's Journals online.

www.savileclub.co.uk/ The Savile Club, Mayfair.

www.sciencemuseum.org.uk/broughttolife/themes/diseases.aspx On diseases and epidemics in the UK.

www.theguardian.com/artanddesign/2013/dec/02/hidden-mothers-victorian-photography Hidden mothers in Victorian photographs.

www.theportico.org.uk The Portico Library, Manchester.

www.victoriandotage.wordpress.om On ageing and mental illness during the Victorian period.

www.visionofbritain.org.uk/ Maps, statistical trends and historical descriptions of parts of Britain. Includes reports on the nineteenth-century censuses.

www.warwidows.org.uk/ War Widows Association of Great Britain.

http://en.wikipedia.org/wiki/History_of_labour_law_in_the_United_Kingdom History of Labour Law in the UK.

www.wmciu.org.uk/index.htm The Working Men's Clubs and Institute Union.

ww.workhouses.org.uk/ On the socio-economic and architectural aspects of workhouses.

Index

INDEX